Katie Judkins

To Tyler ——
Let your light Shine!
89
Chad Lewis

"*Surround Yourself with Greatness* is a must read for everyone, but especially for young people—boys or girls—who have a desire to be successful in any chosen endeavor. It's also never too late for us 'old folks' to be motivated and continue to surround ourselves with people who will enhance our lives—people like Chad Lewis. It was my great privilege to coach Chad in college and I was inspired by him even then. Enjoy the book—it has something for everyone and all who read it will be uplifted."

—LAVELL EDWARDS, former Head Coach,
Brigham Young University

"*Surround Yourself with Greatness* reveals the passion of a true champion. In his book, Chad Lewis shares the knowledge and wisdom he gained through exceptional experiences as a husband, father, son, brother, friend, missionary, and NFL star. Chad's friendly narrative style made me feel like I was sitting next to him listening to an old friend recount wonderful life lessons."

—TOM HOLMOE, Athletic Director,
Brigham Young University

"The perfect medicine for our current world condition. It's a message of gratitude in the midst of great difficulty. Our families would be closer and our days brighter if we practice this message."

—GOVERNOR GARY HERBERT,
State of Utah

"*Surround Yourself with Greatness* is a feast of compelling stories, skillfully told. I genuinely enjoyed the book and felt inspired by the power of its message."

—MICHAEL O. LEAVITT, former US Secretary
of Health and Human Services

"I absolutely loved this book! It is both insightful and inspiring. Chad Lewis is simply remarkable—a courageous man in spirit as well as in practice. *Surround Yourself with Greatness* is his story, his inspiration for leading a life of honor and integrity, guided by a tremendous faith in humanity. Over and again, Chad reaches for light in the darkness and finds those coaches, neighbors, teammates, and mentors who inspired greatness in him. As Chad powerfully proves, surround yourself with greatness and reap the rewards of a life well lived."

—STEPHEN M. R. COVEY, author of the
New York Times bestseller *The Speed of Trust*

"If the going ever gets really tough, I want Chad Lewis in my camp. He is a marvelous American who loves God, who loves his wife and children, who loves his parents, neighbors, and teammates, and who loves football like I do. There is profound power in the wisdom of 'surrounding yourself with greatness'—great people, great books, great music, great art, and great deeds. This book is filled with lessons of love, gratitude, patriotism, and teamwork."

—HARVEY GARDNER,
founder of Page Steel

"Much more than Football 101, this book is a post-graduate course that every present and future football player and coach should read, study, and think about until they have incorporated these lessons into their own psyche. The author highlights many tender moments in a very tough business. It is the best insight into pro-football insider life and details I have ever read. The author is the kind of sports hero the youth of today need. Every parent should make sure their teenagers read this book."

—ROBERT E. WELLS, educator

"As I have read Chad's book about his experiences with so many successful and great people that he has become friends with, I am reminded about what someone has said about greatness. If you want to become great, you forget about greatness and you associate with great people—it rubs off. And it's what one does for others, especially for those who have no other way than for someone to give them that little extra lift. It is evident in Chad's book that he has associated with so many great people, and in my eyes, that is what makes him great also."

—V. JAY WADMAN, President,
American Indian Services

"Packed with Chad's real-life experiences, *Surround Yourself with Greatness* is a powerful message for all of us! Chad has practiced this principle his entire life, immersing himself in goodness, hard work, and positive choices. As good an athlete and competitor as Chad is, he's an even better husband, father, brother, son, and friend! I love this book and plan to give it to my family and friends to read!"

—MATTHEW J. HAWKINS, COO at SirsiDynix
Coporation, Harvard Business School graduate,
high school rival, and lifelong friend

"When fifteen-year-old, skinny, freckled-faced Chad Lewis told me he was going out for football, I said to myself, 'Chad, you will get trampled to death!' His tenacity and positive attitude then and all throughout his career resonates loud and clear in *Surround Yourself with Greatness.* Chad chose for himself paths of greatness and makes the reader and all those around him want to do the same!"

—PHYLLIS BESTOR, Chad's high school
English teacher, mentor, and dear friend

"If everyone would pause long enough to see the good in the world around them, they would be astonished at the power that surrounds them if they would but embrace it. Chad Lewis invites us to see that light around us and gives us a unique glimpse into a human heart that has been tuned to the Infinite and his fellow men. No one can read this book and not become a better person because of it."

—ROBERT C. GAY, CEO and Cofounder,
HuntsmanGay Global Capital

"While in his young years Chad Lewis realized the importance of surrounding ourselves with good people, good causes, good music and good opportunities for developing greatness and leadership. With this in mind, this book is a must read for any young people who want to learn early in life the secret of success and happiness. It will unlock their potential to accomplish many great things in life. In fact, it's a treasure that will open the door of vision and opportunity for any reader, both young and old."

—DALE T. TINGEY, Director of
American Indian Services

SURROUND YOURSELF
WITH GREATNESS

SURROUND YOURSELF WITH GREATNESS

CHAD LEWIS

FOREWORD BY
STEVE YOUNG

SHADOW
MOUNTAIN

All photographs are used courtesy of the author except where otherwise noted.

Visit us at ShadowMountain.com

Library of Congress Cataloging-in-Publication Data

Lewis, Chad, 1971–
   Surround yourself with greatness / Chad Lewis.
     p. cm.
   Includes bibliographical references and index.
   ISBN 978-1-60641-195-7 (hardbound : alk. paper)
   1. Lewis, Chad, 1971–   2. Football players—United States—Biography.
3. Mormon athletes—United States—Biography.   4. Self-realization—Religious aspects—Church of Jesus Christ of Latter-day Saints.   I. Title.
   GV939.L48L49 2009
   796.332092—dc22
   [B]   2009030279

Printed in the United States of America
Quebecor World Book Services, Fairfield, PA

10   9   8   7   6   5   4   3

To Michele, the love of my life,
and to our seven children,
Emily, Sarah, Jacob, Jefferson,
Maxwell, Tanner, and Todd

CONTENTS

CONTENTS

FOREWORD

Everyone knows that I followed a legend playing for the 49ers. Joe Montana made the game look easy because he saw the field and knew how to get the ball to the right guys. It was a similar situation at BYU when I followed the great career of Jim McMahon. What people don't always know was how difficult it was to replace those guys at the same level where they left off. The most important football lesson I needed to learn as a quarterback was how to see the game even when I couldn't see my guys. I had to trust my instincts, the hours of practice and preparation, my coaches, my teammates, and my timing, and throw the ball into precise windows that may or may not have been open at the time I needed to throw it.

In Chad Lewis's book, *Surround Yourself with Greatness,* it is obvious that Chad learned this vital lesson at an early stage of his life. His love for his family and his faith in God have allowed him to see what life is all about and what can help all of us find more happiness and joy out of life.

I have known Chad for many years. I often refer to him as one of the best guys you will ever meet because his focus is always on those around him. Whether it is helping out with my charity golf tournaments or skiing with the disabled as a part of the Wasatch Adaptive Sports program at Snowbird or speaking to companies and youth groups, Chad is comfortable around all types of people. He is not afraid to reach into their souls or kneel on the snow and help them smile.

Life is similar to football with the unique bounces that come our way. The shape of the ball and the surprise of life necessitate our learning to cope with challenges. Chad learned that lesson the hard way during his family's greatest challenge. The concept of consciously surrounding ourselves with greatness is a simple way for us to reach our greatest potential without getting sidetracked or lost in the trials of life. I learned as a quarterback that excuses don't cut it. This book will help you see through the clutter to the things that really matter so you can discover joy and happiness and not just come up with excuses. Joy is possible in the middle of heartache. Success can be attained even when everything might seem against you.

People have asked me many times how I have kept my faith while working in a profession that has many of the trappings that could bring me down. Chad's message paints the picture of what helped me find success. I was surrounded by a wonderful family, great and supportive friends, and my own inner desire to choose the right. I have found this to be the essence of confidence. My best successes have come when I have had a healthy mix of giving my best effort and striving to adhere to what I know to be right.

I enjoyed the great chemistry I had with my tight end Brent Jones. Chad Lewis and Donovan McNabb had a similar bond. I know how fun it is to play football when that kind of interplay is working. As a former quarterback, I take pride in knowing how much Chad thinks of Donovan. That is why I would have loved to have Chad on my team.

I know Chad's wife, Michele, and I know that Chad would

not be who he is without her. I refer to her as a pioneer woman because she embodies the great qualities Chad had on his mind when he wrote this book. She is the greatness in his life.

I am proud that Chad calls me his friend.

—STEVE YOUNG
Hall of Fame quarterback,
San Francisco 49ers,
ESPN Analyst

PREFACE

Human beings are very similar no matter where we come from or what we look like—we all want to be happy. And though life provides many opportunities to pursue happiness, it can also be brutal and tough.

I have experienced some of the pain life has to offer, and I have also enjoyed much of the happiness that is available. As I look back over the events of my life, I have discovered an important truth: our happiness depends in large part on what we learn from the people with whom we associate and how we respond to the situations in which we put ourselves.

I've also discovered that happiness is not the byproduct of making mistakes. I have made more mistakes than I care to admit. Mistakes are painful. They hurt us and they hurt other people. The pain and the guilt caused by a mistake can last forever if we don't correct it, apologize, or seek forgiveness.

I have found that happiness results when we show kindness to others, make good choices, work our hardest, and use the gifts that we have all been given to make this world a better place.

But the fact is there are very few truly "self-made" men in the world. We are, from birth, constantly surrounded by people and situations that influence our choices and the trajectory of our lives. In the beginning and through our formative years we are almost totally dependent on others. Parents, family members, school teachers, religious leaders, coaches, friends, and even strangers all exert an influence on us—for good or bad. And after we become so-called grown-ups, we are still influenced by other people.

I have been fortunate to have associated with some great people—all of whom have contributed to my happiness and whatever success I have enjoyed. These people have helped shape and mold me, and reflecting on their influence has taught me a simple but great principle. *It is the importance of surrounding ourselves with greatness.*

The stories included in this book illustrate this truth.

From my dad's miraculous recovery from a devastating illness, the lessons learned from serving the Chinese people of Taiwan for two years as a missionary for my church, the experience of playing football at BYU, and my nine-year career in the NFL come the powerful stories that illustrate the critical need to surround ourselves with greatness. The people I have met along the way are living examples of this principle.

Though I name names, this book is not an exposé. Instead of sensational stories depicting failure and destruction, you'll read about strong people whose friendship, character, and goodness have had a profound impact on me and helped shape my life.

Though it may be in a different arena, you can also enjoy success and happiness. The key is: Surround Yourself with Greatness.

INTRODUCTION

With less than a minute on the clock, and time ticking down, and light rain continuing to fall as it had the whole game, the Eagles were driving on the Cowboys and preparing to score the go-ahead and game-winning touchdown against our most bitter rivals. This was not just any game. This was a chance to pay the Cowboys back for our week-three, Monday night, last-second loss in Dallas. Now, we were on the eight-yard line, and the frenzied Eagles' crowd was going bananas.

The line between winning and losing in the NFL is razor thin. You learn how true the adage from the wise farmer is: "Never count your chickens until they are hatched." But in this case, the Eagles' egg was rocking back and forth, cracks were starting to appear, and the bird was as close as could be to popping out of the shell.

Veterans Stadium was a powder keg of emotional energy. I was just as excited as the fans watching our team drive down to the eight. During this particular game, I had not played in a single offensive play. Up until this point of the season, I had mostly been used only in red-zone situations, plays inside the twenty yards extending from the opponent's goal line. Now we were in the heart of the red zone.

Suddenly, Ted Williams, our running-back coach, turned and yelled for me to go into the game.

My heart skipped a couple of beats when he called my number. We had already lived through the effects of a disastrous, last-second defeat to these same hated Cowboys. I did not want to make a mistake out there and lose it for our team.

When I got into the huddle, Rodney Pete, our quarterback, looked across right at me when he called the play. It was: "West Right F Left, 322 Scat Y Stick-Nod!" It was a perfect play for a tight end. It required a double move, which was the best call on a slick field.

When the ball was snapped, I was to run straight forward for five yards and then break to my right for about three steps toward the sideline, just long enough to entice the strong safety to bite on my route and hopefully come down hard from the secondary. After three hard steps toward the sideline, I was to turn back for the middle of the end zone on an angle toward the goalpost and if all went according to plan, Rodney would lay the ball between the 8 and 9 on my jersey, and we would win the game. Simple.

The ball was snapped, I got a clean release off the line of scrimmage, and made my first break toward the sideline. When I broke back toward the middle of the field, the strong safety slipped on the wet turf, and I ran free and clear into the end zone. I was wide open . . .

CHAPTER 1

THE BOMBSHELL

It was two o'clock in the morning, and I was sitting next to a technician witnessing a real nightmare. I could see my dad through the glass wall as he lay in an MRI (Magnetic Resonance Imaging) machine suffering from a giant headache. To say he was in severe pain would be a gross understatement. I thought he was dying. He couldn't move his left side. That included the left side of his face. His speech was slurred, and I could barely understand what he was saying.

For the MRI machine to give a clear reading of the inside of a body, the patient must lie completely still. But Dad could not lie still. He was suffering and in agony. There was a microphone in the machine that transmitted the sounds he was making into the monitor room where I was sitting with the technician. His moaning did not stop, and he kept saying over and over, "Severe pain." I was helpless and scared. I did not want to lose my dad. He was only forty-seven years old; I was only eighteen. My mom stood next to me as we watched and listened to him struggling to survive.

I had only seen my dad in that kind of pain once before. It

had happened while we were on a winter outing with the Boy Scouts up Spanish Fork Canyon. I was thirteen, and Dad was the Scoutmaster of our troop.

The troop had been divided into two groups. One group was snowmobiling, and the other was tubing. Both activities were a lot of fun. Flying down the mountain on the pumped up tube from a car tire is just about as fun (and dangerous) as one could imagine. We had a great hill. It was steep enough to get going fast and had a jump at the bottom that was just big enough to get some adrenaline pumping.

I was riding a snowmobile when someone raced up to my group and said that my dad had been hurt on the tubing run. They said he had gone off the jump and landed on a rock that was just under the snow. Now he was on the ground and not moving.

A jolt of fear ran through me. To me, Dad was Superman. He ran five miles every morning before work. He was obsessed with eating healthy food and avoiding sugars and fats in his diet. He was never sick, and he never showed any pain. In my mind, he was as tough as they came.

When I got to the tubing hill, Dad was lying on the snow surrounded by the Scouts and other leaders. I glanced up to the tubing hill and saw where he had come down the mountain and the dark rock on which he had landed. Just imagining his weight coming down on that hard surface made my own body ache.

As I got closer, I was shocked to see his usually happy face racked with pain. When I asked him if he was going to be all right, he didn't answer but only continued to groan.

The leaders decided to load him into the van and head for the hospital, ten miles away in Provo. But where would we put him? He was in too much pain to sit in one of the seats. He would need to lie down. We took all of the gear out of the back of the van and tried to make a place for him to put his 6'5" 210 pound frame.

Once we got it cleared out, we put down some blankets and coats so that he could have some padding.

The men got a blanket under him and with many helping hands were able to lift him and slowly carry him through the deep snow to the van. As they gently laid him in the back he was still groaning in unrelenting misery.

Then we headed down the canyon. During the drive, Dad's pain finally started to subside, and when I asked him if he was going to be okay he said that he thought he would. He even decided not to go to the hospital but to go straight home instead.

Dad was a doctor, a family practitioner, who had delivered nearly two thousand babies in the Orem, Utah, area, and he did not want to lie in the hospital as a patient when he could take care of himself at home. So we drove home and helped him out of the van.

Over the course of a week, he recovered to full strength. But he developed a massive hematoma on his hip and back, which turned into a wicked-looking black and purple bruise that grew bigger each day for a few days before it finally started to clear up.

That accident happened five years before we were sitting in the hospital MRI room, watching him go through another painful event, this time of cataclysmic proportions.

To find out what was wrong with his head and discover why he was having such pain, the MRI took dozens of pictures of his brain. It was a huge machine with a tubelike opening for the patient's body. While he was lying in the bowels of the machine, Dad's face was only three or four inches away from the top of the tube. To him, this was more a coffin than anything else.

Trying to help him lie still in his claustrophobic cave, I used the microphone on my end of the MRI machine to speak to him. I kept telling him that he was doing great, to hang in there, and that it was almost over. His response was always a moan about being in pain. Time halted to a standstill. The agonizingly long forty minutes he would be in the MRI gave me time to reflect back.

Just a few weeks before Dad's unexplained headache, I had completed a class in human anatomy at college. We had memorized every bone and each part of the body. We also had the opportunity to study a cadaver. I was fully engaged in that class. I worked and studied very hard to receive an A in that class. I loved it.

That recent education gave me a little background, and I watched with interest as the images of Dad's brain were coming onto the screen in front of us.

I was puzzled by one of the images of the right side of his brain. It was different than all the others. Instead of showing elaborate detail of the inner structure of my dad's living brain, the image appeared only as an enormous white spot. It certainly did not look right.

I asked the technician what that spot was in the middle of my dad's brain. He pointed to a chart on his desk. The chart indicated two possibilities: One was simply fluid, most likely brain fluid. The other possibility was blood. He told me that it was such a large spot that the likelihood of it being blood and my dad still being alive was very small. If it were blood, there was no way he would survive it.

Just then a group of doctors came into the room. As they stood looking at the images of Dad's brain, Dr. Nielsen said, "That is blood."

Imagine how my mom and I felt. We looked at each other with panic. This wasn't just bad news; this was a death sentence. A spot of blood that big meant everything bad. It meant a stroke, hemorrhaging, paralysis, and death.

I listened as the doctors discussed what might be done. I heard their words. I heard the stress in their voices. I felt the intensity of the moment more than they would ever realize.

This was my dad they were talking about. This was his life.

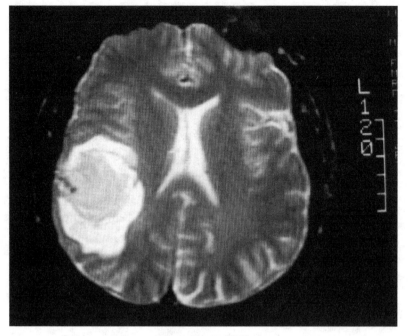

Roger Lewis's MRI

This was my mom's husband. This was *our* life, *our* hope, and *our* greatest friend who was in dire straits.

They were talking about the possibility of surgery. They also discussed doing nothing and just watching him through the night and hoping that he made it. Some thought it might be too late to have surgery.

Right in the middle of their assessment and their conversation, I blurted out, "You *have* to do something! That is my dad. You *have* to try. You can't let him just die. You *have* to do something!"

The doctors looked at me. They were probably wondering what I was even doing in there. The neurosurgeon was Dr. Carl Nielson. The internist was Dr. Lyman Moody, a family friend who had known my dad for many years.

After hearing my emotional outburst, they calmly went back

to their discussion. Mom and I were feeling more and more helpless with each passing minute. What could we do? What could we
say? Could we make a difference? I know that I was praying in my
heart that *something* would happen to save my dad's life.

Dr. Nielson was saying that they might be able to go in right
then and find the source of the bleeding. I wasn't saying anything
to them, but I was nodding my head. I was all about that. Surgery!
That sounded great. Doing nothing, that sounded deadly.

Finally, they decided to get Dad out of the MRI and take him
into X-ray for an angiogram. I did not know what that was, but
was able to figure it out pretty quick by listening to them. An
angiogram meant injecting dye into his artery or vein. This would
be followed by taking an X-ray to locate the exact area of Dad's
hemorrhaging before performing brain surgery.

Having made their decision, the doctors loaded Dad on a gurney. His pain was getting worse. The pressure in his head was literally killing him. He did not have much longer before he would
be gone.

As they began rolling him towards X-ray, Dr. Moody told my
dad the prognosis and the plan of action. Since they were both
doctors and very familiar with each other, Dr. Moody spoke with
total frankness.

He said, "Roger, we have some bad news for you. You have an
aneurysm on the right side of your brain."

I wondered if Dad would be able to communicate with Dr.
Moody. But he left no doubt that he could still think and talk.
After Dr. Moody had informed him, Dad's response was, "Oh,
hell!"

I was walking next to the gurney, looking at my dad. I knew
immediately by his facial expression that he knew what he was up
against. I wanted to reach down and fix his brain. I wanted to take
his pain away. I wanted to pull an ejection handle and blast all of
us away from the unfolding catastrophe.

As soon as we got in the hallway heading for X-ray, I ran to the phone and called my brothers Jason and Todd. I told them that Dad most likely would not make it through the night and to come down to the hospital at once. I told them to call our other brothers, Dave and Mike. I never thought I would be saying what I was saying. Telling my brothers that our Dad would likely pass away that night was so foreign and brutal. I did not want to admit that it was true, but I wanted them to race to the hospital and see him in case it was for the last time. My two brothers could be to the hospital in five minutes if they flew. My mom called Dave, who was in California, to let him know of the situation. He had just gotten married and had moved out of the house two weeks before.

As I hung up the phone, we quickly made our way into X-ray. The room was alive with doctors and nurses in green hospital garb who were a blur of activity surrounding my declining dad. Mom and I stood by in shock as we tried to process the frantic scene. Dad's condition was obviously getting worse. His only response to the whirl of color and life that surrounded him was the same continued painful moaning that proved he was still alive.

There was no painkiller given to him because he was obtunded, meaning he was half-awake but not totally out. He was conscious enough to continue begging for morphine, but none was given. It would have been medically irresponsible to give morphine to a person who was already only half-conscious. Morphine could shut off his breathing. Instead, he was dying from the pain.

Somehow, though the room was buzzing with frenetic activity, I noticed music playing. It was weird to have this sweet music juxtaposed against the chaos. The song was "Imagine" by John Lennon. Before that night I had liked the tune. However, the first line of that song says, "Imagine there's no heaven, it's easy if you try." When I heard that cynical first line, I wanted to turn the music off. Any peace that song might have offered through its beautiful melody was crushed by the horrible lyrics.

My dad was on the verge of stepping out of this world and into heaven. I believed in heaven with all my heart. I knew if he did pass away, he would step through the veil that stands between earth and heaven and would meet that God who gave him life. I was angry at that song. I vowed never to listen to it again. It disavowed what I believed.

The longer I stood on the sidelines of this fight for life, the more I felt drawn into the battle. I could not stand there any longer, merely watching others do their jobs while I did nothing. I moved to the table he was lying on and grabbed his right hand with my right hand. I was crying then as I looked into his face. I told him how much I loved him. I told him that everything was going to work out right.

Jason and Todd had made the short trip from our house to the hospital. They found their way to X-ray and were now standing in the middle of this struggle for Dad's life. Jason was twenty-one years old and had only recently returned home after serving two years on a church mission to Buenos Aires, Argentina. Tall and slim, at 6'4" 200 pounds, with thick jet-black hair, his skin was always dark tan and he looked like a fashion model. It was obvious from the look on his face that he knew how serious this situation had become.

He was standing with Todd, who was shorter and younger than Jason. Todd was only sixteen and had thick red hair and freckles all over his face. He stood 6' and weighed 170 pounds. He had tears in his eyes and an expression of fear on his face.

They stood next to our mom and our neighbor Larry Heaps. Larry had come down to the hospital at the same time that my Mom and I had. He came to offer support and to help us in any way possible. I was so grateful that he was there. He had been one of the guys whom I idolized growing up because he played football for BYU as a wide receiver. He was a big man at 6'4" 230 pounds. He was now forty-two years old but looked as though he could still play college football. I loved him for many reasons. He was a great man who took time to be with his kids, and one of his sons, named Jason, was one of my good friends. Jason was a year younger than I, but we always played with each other as kids. Larry would often play catch with us in the backyard and run us through football drills he'd learned at BYU.

Larry had also been one of my Scout leaders. He lived two houses away and we had been neighbors for fifteen years. There was another layer to our friendship. As a part of his membership in The Church of Jesus Christ of Latter-day Saints, Larry had accepted the assignment to be our family's home teacher. A home teacher is someone who holds the priesthood and is responsible to look after the families he is assigned. He visits them in their homes at least once a month, inquires about their temporal and spiritual needs, and teaches a gospel lesson. With that kind of relationship, the home teacher also becomes a close ally when problems and emergencies arise. We considered Larry a close friend of the family.

The doctors were prepping Dad's body for the angiogram. They inserted a catheter into his femoral artery and began feeding a small tube up to the carotid artery. The purpose of the tube was to inject some dye, or contrast material, into the artery that fed directly to his brain. By taking an X-ray immediately after the dye was distributed to the desired area, the image would show how blood was flowing through the arteries. Since the MRI had already showed a massive clot on the right side of my Dad's brain, this arteriogram would give further detail on the exact whereabouts of the blockage, aneurysm, and location of hemorrhaging. This was the last piece of information that the neurosurgeon would need before he started brain surgery.

The radiologist, Dr. Rod Peterson, knew my dad very well because they had gone to medical school together at the University of Utah. He told my father he was going to pump some dye into his brain and that he might feel some warmth or heat. As soon as this dye was introduced into the catheter, Dad groaned loudly in great distress. He told me later that it felt as though his head was being pumped full of burning hot lava and that his brain was melting.

Dad was having a terrible time lying still for the X-rays. He tried to speak. He kept pointing to his head and complaining, "Severe pain."

After several minutes the tempo and urgency in the room picked up dramatically when Dr. Nielson announced that Dad was experiencing the classic symptoms of Cushing's triad. I later learned that meant an increase in systolic blood pressure, brady-cardia (a dramatic slowing of the heart), and irregular respiration. All this was being caused by the hemorrhaging. The bleeding was pushing his brain down on the brain stem, and it was literally killing him. I could tell just by looking at his colorless face that he was close to dying.

Dr. Nielson is not a weak person and he took charge. He was a Navy man and embodied strength in the way he walked and talked. He was battle tested, and he was all business. He ordered that Dad be lifted off the X-ray table and placed on the gurney. It was go time, and he wanted to leave for surgery now. Not in fif-teen seconds, right now!

Because Dad was so big and tall, the nurses were struggling to move him over. Dr. Nielson barked out, "There is no time to be timid. Get him onto that gurney and let's go!"

Without thinking, I acted. The gurney was between me and my dad on the X-ray table. I leaned on the gurney, put my arms under him, and lifted with all the might and adrenaline that I had and pulled him onto the gurney.

As they started to wheel Dad out of the X-ray room, Dr. Nielson followed, walking backwards, talking to us. The last thing he said before running down the hallway after Dad was, "I can't make any promises. All I can say is it doesn't look good."

With that, he was gone.

The five of us—I, Mom, my brothers Jason and Todd, and Larry Heaps—stood there in total shock. Everything that had just happened had gone by in a blink. The reality of it was horrible. We might not ever see him again. That possibility cut deeper than I could have imagined. My heart was ripped open. I was scared and I was exposed. I had never been through anything that tough before.

Just then my brother Mike came sprinting toward us. He filled up the whole hall with his huge frame. He was playing football at the University of Utah as a defensive end and was a giant of a man at 6'6" and 270 pounds. With his full head of bright red hair and a face full of freckles, his smile could light up a room. But there was no smile on his face now. His face was full of determination. If you have seen Mike play football even one time, then you know the look. Breathing hard, he asked, "Where is he?"

I told him that he had just missed him, that he was only a few seconds away in the direction of the operating room. We ran in that direction to see if we could catch him before they started surgery, but it was too late. Mike was only seconds away from seeing him, possibly for the last time.

Todd sat down on a bench in the hallway and began to cry. Was that the last time he would ever see Dad again? Larry sat down next to Todd and put his arm around him, trying to assure him everything would be okay.

Years later, Todd said that at that moment he felt the warmth of the Holy Ghost stronger than at any other time in his life. This assurance of comfort and peace washed over him, and he had the feeling that everything would be all right and that our dad would be fine. That feeling was completely opposite from the reality that was happening.

We looked for an empty room where we could offer a prayer for my dad. We found one and all knelt down and my mom asked Larry to offer a prayer for our family. It was comforting to put all of our petitions and our faith in the Lord. I was so grateful that Larry was there with us and that we still had our faith that we could rely on in such a terrible time.

Things did not look good, just as Dr. Nielson had said. In fact, the situation was a whole lot worse than we could even imagine, as Dr. Nielson would later explain to us.

Dr. Nielson was trained at Parkland Memorial Hospital in Dallas, Texas, where he saw a tremendous amount of trauma. He said he had seen a lot of people with similar cerebral hemorrhages and not even one percent of them had survived surgery. They didn't even take most of them to surgery. He explained that such hemorrhages create enormous pressure in the cerebrum and the resulting edema, or swelling, pushes down on the brain stem and kills the person. He didn't think our dad would have survived another few minutes without immediate surgery.

Dr. Nielson said he was not even sure why he decided to operate, since Dad's condition was so dire. Most neurosurgeons wouldn't have. In his opinion, the surgery puts the family through a whole lot of misery for nothing. Not only would the person die, but the family would have to suffer through the agony of waiting for the surgery to be done, only to be told it wasn't successful.

The surgery is hideous to imagine. It involves quickly shaving the head, using a scalpel to cut through the scalp and peel it back, drilling holes in the skull, and then using a jiggly to remove a large piece of the skull.

This was to gain access to the clot and remove it. If Dad were to have any chance, all this had to be done quickly. Speed was the name of the game.

The challenge was not only in removing the clot but preventing additional bleeding. Hemorrhaging is the enemy to a neurosurgeon and his patient. There would be blood from the damaged vessel and blood from all the severed vessels around it.

There was an additional problem. Dad had been on aspirin (an anticoagulant), something that should have made successful surgery impossible. In fact, Dr. Nielson said that if he had known Dad was being treated with aspirin he would not have performed surgery. The bleeding should have been uncontrollable.

Dr. Nielson later told us he exposed the blood clot and went for it as fast as he could. He just sucked down through the brain and buzzed bleeders as he went. He put in a big sucker, the kind one uses in abdominal hemorrhages. A huge amount of blood popped out, and then the wall of blood started flowing. He cross-clamped arteries and permanently clamped off the right middle cerebral artery and three others.

He put in coagulating materials, lined the walls, and filled the area full of cotton balls, probably as big as a baseball. Then he continued to irrigate with saline, sucked that out, and then rinsed the blood out, hoping to stem the bleeding. Removing the blood clot took him about two minutes, maybe less. All the rest of the time was taken up trying to staunch the bleeding.

While this was going on in the operating room, our family was in the waiting room trying to deal with this tragedy. We were confronting for the first time the real likelihood that we would never see our father again.

But we never lost the breath of *hope*. We had something to hang on to. That something transpired in the few minutes before my dad was brought to the hospital. It came in the form of a priesthood blessing given to him by my brother Jason.

Earlier that evening, Dad had complained of a headache. Over several hours, the pain intensified. By six o'clock he was nauseous as well. It got to the point where his speech began to slur. Even though Dad assured our mom that there was nothing serious going on, she worried about it enough to call Dr. Moody. He did not like the sound of things.

Mom told Dr. Moody that each time my dad infused the IV medicine he was taking at home to treat an infection of the lining of his heart, his headache would get worse. Our parents thought this was a reaction to the antibiotic, and between them and Dr. Moody, they decided he should stop taking the medicine for the night. Dr. Moody told Mom that if things got worse in any way, to take Dad directly to the hospital.

Things did get worse. A lot worse.

While Dad was in the bathroom washing his hands, he noticed that the hot water was almost burning his right hand, but he couldn't feel it on his left hand. Recognizing he had a problem, he stumbled out of the bathroom and toward the bed. As he tried to walk, he experienced heavy hemi paresis (partial paralysis) of his entire left side.

In a panic, he called for my mom, but with his speech slurred and muffled, he was not able to yell loud enough for her to hear.

Jason and Todd were both downstairs at the time watching TV. Jason heard some strange sounds that he couldn't make out at first. The sounds persisted until he went upstairs to investigate. He heard Dad calling out, "Dear, dear!" His calls were more of a moan since his tongue was only half working.

Mom immediately called for the paramedics to come.

With the ambulance on the way, Mom called Dr. Moody to inform him that they would be heading directly to the hospital. She also asked Jason to get our neighbor and home teacher, Larry Heaps, and to give Dad a blessing.

Larry came over immediately, and he and Jason gave Dad a priesthood blessing.

While administering the blessing, Jason felt inspired to bless Dad that he would return to health and that everything would be okay. He told him that his time on this earth was not over and said that his mission was not complete. Jason said that it was a simple blessing, but that the feeling that our father would be okay was unmistakable.

After the blessing was given, the paramedics showed up, got my dad on a stretcher, and loaded him into the ambulance for the emergency run to the hospital. The ambulance pulled away from our home, and I drove up thirty seconds later. I was greeted by Larry Heaps in our driveway. I jumped out of my car and said to him, "What's up, Larry?" I thought it was a little strange that he was greeting me at a late hour, but I was happy and excited to see him.

As soon as I looked into his face, and before he even said a word, I knew that something was wrong. He said that my dad had just barely left in an ambulance and that he was having what my parents thought was a reaction to some antibiotics. Larry also said that he would be heading down to the hospital with my mom.

Whoa! That was a shocker to me. I had been with my parents earlier in the day, and we had watched a video together. Dad had a slight headache at the time, but I did not think anything of it until Larry started to explain what had been happening. He did not have very many details, but what he did have got my heart racing.

While we were talking, Mom came out of the house, and we jumped into the car and took off for the hospital. I drove like Mario Andretti, and we made the trip in about three or four minutes. Jason and Todd stayed at home because Mom promised to call them as soon as we had more information.

As a doctor running a family practice in Orem, my dad learned how to screen patients' needs by asking them to rate their pain on a scale of 1 to 10. It became a proverb in our home that a sore throat was not a 10. It could be a 5 or a 6, but it certainly was not a 10. When a patient would calmly tell Dad that they were dealing with pain that was a 9 or a 10, he would use that as a good time to clarify his pain scale. He would physically get down on the floor and roll around in mock agony, demonstrating what a 9 or a 10 actually looked and sounded like.

When he did it in our home, we would all laugh. Then we knew that our pain was really about a 2 or 3. We loved his story of the pain scale and knew that he had a very high tolerance for pain and showed it through a whole lifetime of dealing with small issues without getting bothered by them.

So when he complained of severe pain at the hospital, I knew that we were in for a long night. The only other thing that he mumbled to Mom and me and the doctors who were attending him was, "Morphine." He would later tell us his pain that night was 11 on a scale of 10.

As Lewis boys growing up in his home and being very familiar with his pain scale, that was a cataclysmic upheaval of deadly proportion.

Dr. Moody made the call for my dad to get the MRI. That takes us back to the beginning of this story, my sitting next to the MRI technician learning of this bombshell, which was a stroke. It also brings us back to the waiting room and the *hope* from the priesthood blessing that carried us through that night.

Once he was taken in for surgery, the minutes crawled by. Over and over we took turns asking Jason to describe again what he had felt while blessing Dad. What were the feelings that had come to his mind and heart? We wanted to be assured. In a way that could only be described as divine, we were given hope. It was a peaceful feeling. It didn't make the time pass any faster, but we felt a measure of hope that buoyed us up and gave us a reason to believe that our dad would make it through the night.

At the exact same time, hundreds of miles away in California, Dave and his new bride, Jonna, were pondering the phone call that they had gotten from Mom. They were awakened at two in the morning and told that Dad was going in for emergency brain surgery and that he might not make it through the night. If he did make it, he would probably never be able to walk again. Dave recalled his reaction by saying, "My wife and I knelt down and prayed. It was interesting because a feeling of peace came over us. We were even able to go back to sleep, and when we woke up the next morning, we learned that Dad was still alive." Dave and Jonna left that morning to drive to Provo to be with Dad and the rest of us through the crisis.

CHAPTER 2

THE ROAD TO THE HOSPITAL

To appreciate the scope of the miracle of my father's recovery, you need to know the severity of his illness.

None of us saw my dad's stroke coming. He was, in fact, a health nut. He ate healthy foods and even made his own bread. That bread was about as dense and solid as a cinder block and tasted not much better. His recipe included just about anything and everything that looked or even sounded healthy.

Along with being obsessed with eating healthy, Dad also ran. He did it more for the health benefit than enjoyment. But if you asked him, he would say that he did it out of love. That is, he loved his family and wanted to be around long enough to see us grow up with our own families. So run he did.

He ran the Boston Marathon in 1979. He was not just a casual runner. His time in the Boston was three hours and six minutes. That qualifies as heroic in my book. His running companions for that race were good friends Rex Lee and Lyman Moody.

Rex was the solicitor general for the United States from 1981 to 1985 and later served as president of Brigham Young University for six years. He carried himself with such class and was a favorite of all the students. I loved it when he would come into the locker room before or after a game. It was obvious that he cared about all of the players because he would take time to visit with us for more than just a token handshake. On more than one occasion he and I talked about the time when he ran the Boston Marathon with my dad. Rex died of cancer in March of 1996 while I was preparing to play my senior year at BYU.

I will never forget visiting him in the hospital the week that he passed away. My wife and I and my brother Dave stopped in to see him. There was a sign in front of his door that said only immediate family members were allowed in. The nurse who was attending the room said that we would not be able to see him. But hearing our petition from his bed, Rex asked who it was that wanted to see him. When the nurse told him that it was Chad and Michele Lewis, he said, "Let them in. They are family!"

He was so gracious and kind to us. Michele and I played for our teams in the BYU athletic department while he was president. He was always at our games and loved getting to know the student athletes. We both grew to love him very much.

He was very ill, but when we asked him how he was doing, all he wanted to do was talk about us. He asked us about our lives, the upcoming football season, and spring practice that would soon be starting.

His feet were sticking out from under the sheet, and we noticed he had only four toes on one of his feet. My brother Dave asked him why that was. He responded with a twinkle in his eye that his toe had been bugging him so he'd had it cut off.

Even though he was in the last week of his life, you wouldn't have known it by his attitude. He was positive, upbeat, and optimistic. I don't think he had a resentful bone in his body. I always thought it was awesome that my dad ran the Boston with him, and I always will.

Lyman Moody is a doctor of internal medicine at Utah Valley

Regional Medical Center, where my dad worked and delivered babies. He was also Dad's Saturday morning running partner. Saturdays were the days they would do their longer runs, in preparation for their marathons. They would run and talk about a number of things since they would usually be out there for a couple of hours.

Lyman was always considered a family friend. We didn't do many things together, but whenever his name was mentioned, it was with the greatest respect. He was a kind person in every way. He spoke with a wonderful vocabulary and a high level of education and wisdom. His body was short and lightweight, which was perfectly suited to running marathons. My dad would refer to Lyman as genetically disposed to run, whereas he was genetically disposed to play basketball, but never did. Dad was tall and athletic but saved all of his coordination for the doctor's office and hiking in the mountains. He could not play basketball very well and so he never did. He did play football in high school for the Cedar City Redmen, but he didn't like it all that much. He thought it more than strange that all of his sons played football and that we played pretty well. His sport was the track and more particularly the discus. He placed second in state his senior year at the state high school track meet held at BYU.

Along with running the Boston Marathon, Dad also ran the Deseret News Marathon in Salt Lake City twice. To condition himself, he ran five miles every morning with a group of neighbors and friends that included Jim MacArthur and Buck Rose.

Dr. Lyman Moody is a wonderful man and physician. With great attention to detail, he provided loving care to my dad and my family and many others. You can see that my dad also believed in surrounding himself with great people.

In January of 1990, Dad had an infected tooth that required a root canal, which was performed by our dentist and family friend Louis Erickson. Before doing the dental work, Lou asked my dad

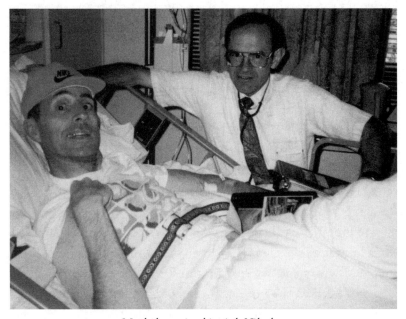

My dad wearing his pink Nike hat,
visiting with his good friend Dr. Lyman Moody.

if he had any preexisting heart condition, such as a heart murmur or heart disease, that required him to take penicillin against infection. Dad said that he didn't need any of that sissy stuff and that he was way too healthy to need anything to protect his heart.

He later quipped that this infected tooth was an atomic bomb that could ruin your whole afternoon.

The first real sign of trouble began in March. Mom and Dad went to St. George, Utah, to attend a convention. They had a wonderful time. St. George is such a beautiful place to visit, especially in the early spring, when northern Utah is still pretty cold. Though they enjoyed the beautiful weather and the fine conference, Dad developed a raspy cough, which made it difficult for him to talk.

After their return from St. George, the cough persisted. Over the next few weeks, he also began having bothersome night sweats.

He would wake up in the middle of the night soaked with perspiration and was having to change his wet pajamas up to three times a night.

His morning running routine began to change as well. He didn't have the energy to run his customary five miles, so he shortened his mileage. Then he cut back to a walk, but that winded him so that he had to give that up as well.

He also developed a lower-back ache. The pain continued to get worse, going from a dull ache to sharp pains that became severe. He was not having any success on his own figuring out what was happening to his body.

He eventually called his friend Lyman Moody and described what he was experiencing. Lyman was going on vacation for a couple of weeks and referred him to Dr. Lynn Bateman. For the next two weeks, Dad and Dr. Bateman discussed all of the symptoms and concluded that there was an infection. They started treating it with Voltarin, a powerful anti-inflammatory, and an antibiotic called Cipro. Dad also had an irritating case of chronic heartburn that he treated with Carafate. Everything was going wrong with his body—even the color of his face was beginning to appear sickly. I wondered if he had cancer or something drastic like that. He had never been sick, and seeing him this way was alarming to me and the rest of his family.

Dr. Bateman did a battery of tests. He performed a CT scan to see if Dad had lymphoma. They took several X-rays. These tests were negative.

When Dr. Moody returned from his vacation, Dad paid him a visit on June 8. While listening to my dad's chest, Dr. Moody asked him, "How long have you had this murmur?"

"I don't have a murmur," Dad said.

Lyman handed the stethoscope to him and said, "Here, you listen."

He put the stethoscope earpiece into my dad's ear, and sure

enough, he had a heart murmur that he'd never detected before. It was a systolic ejection murmur that couldn't be missed. It was so pronounced he didn't even need a stethoscope to hear it. In medical terms, it was "a three over a six," a severe measurement.

Lyman said, "New murmur, history of night sweats, most likely diagnosis: subacute bacterial endocarditis." That meant an infection of the inside of his heart. In my dad's case, it was an infection of the mitral valve.

Dr. Moody wanted to put Dad in the hospital, but true to form, Dad said, "Not today." He was a little too tough and a little too stubborn to think he needed to stay in the hospital. What they say about doctors being the worst patients held true with my stubborn father.

Dr. Moody told him that if he wasn't going to check into the hospital, he should at least get the blood cultures immediately to find out about the infection. Six blood cultures were taken, and they all started showing up positive for strep veridans. Usually if a person is taking antibiotics, there would be enough residual antibacterial activity in the blood to suppress the bacterial cultures from growing. But the infection was severe enough that all six cultures indicated the same thing. My dad had a massive infection in his body. Now they finally knew what the problem was and they could attack it with IV antibiotics. The medicines they prescribed were penicillin and gentamycin.

Dr. Moody treated Dad with IV antibiotics for six weeks. There was a pic line, or a small tube, that went from my dad's arm to his heart. He was able to treat himself at home and take the medicine three times a day. He loaded the refrigerator in our basement full of this IV medicine and began taking twenty-four million units of penicillin a day. Dr. Moody also said the history of endocarditis followed a typical track—a tall guy with some of what doctors would call the findings of Marfan's syndrome.

It is the syndrome that Abraham Lincoln had. Such people are tall and have valve leaflets that tend to prolapse and leak a little. With that leakage they are subject to getting infections on the heart valves. Those infections often develop following dental work, where small bacterial organisms flake off and go from the mouth and into the bloodstream. They attach themselves to a heart valve and grow. Then those bacteria will shower off the heart valve and travel all over the body. They go to hundreds of places, but the antibodies in the blood generally take care of them. But with my dad, there were two places where there was not a real good blood supply and the infections were not taken care of. One was in the brain and the other in the abscess in his spine. The infection in the brain was called a mycotic aneurysm. It's not due to a fungal, or mycotic, infection but to a bacterial infection.

No one was aware of the aneurysm at that point. It was a ticking time bomb that was still getting ready to explode.

My brother Dave was getting married on June 15 in Los Angeles. To be there, Dad had to check himself out of the hospital, get a ride to the airport, and get on the plane carrying his bag full of medicine and with an IV hanging out of his arm. As soon as he landed he was to give himself another dose of medicine. He was very attentive to giving himself the medicine on time, and he successfully accomplished those tasks.

When Dad spoke at the wedding dinner he was funny and full of life, but the color of his skin was still not right. The wedding photos show how pale he looked at the time. Also, on the day of the wedding, he had to crawl to the bathroom because the pain in his back had become debilitating. It was a wonder he was able to make it through the wedding and the reception without incident. Little did we know that the infection was growing in his brain.

After returning to Utah, the treatment continued. There was an abnormality on June 24. Dad thought he was having an allergic reaction to the medicine. He also had some bad headaches and nausea, and he called Dr. Moody again. My dad was adamant that it was because of the medicine, even though Dr. Moody didn't agree. They decided to change the medicine to Ancef.

When the headaches continued, Dad thought he was having allergic reactions to the Ancef as well. Dr. Moody told him, "We've got to keep the antibiotics going. We cannot stop them now because you are short of the six weeks of therapy required to get rid of the bacteria that have settled on the heart valves."

The headaches and the countdown continued.

The first part of this miraculous story was just that—a miracle. The fact that Dad lived through the surgery was a miracle. The competence of the doctors and nurses who helped save his life was a miracle. The fact that Dr. Nielson was able to work fast enough to remove the clot with not a minute to spare was a miracle. The peace and hope that we felt from the blessing that Jason and Larry had given my dad were also a miracle.

Dr. Nielson finished the surgery. He was able to get the bleeding to stop. But he thought there had been irreparable damage done to all the cortical pathways of my dad's brain. He thought it was a miracle that my dad lived, but he had very low expectations that he would wake up, and in fact expected him to be in a coma for weeks or even months. He said he would be surprised if Dad were able to open his eyes and move around in a year. He felt certain our father was in for a long recovery.

At 8:00 A.M. following the surgery, Dr. Nielson came to the waiting room where all of us had endured a very, very long, sleepless night. He first announced that Dad had survived the night and had made it out of brain surgery. He was in recovery and would be moved to the intensive care unit (ICU) in the next half hour. He also said that his vital signs were good but that he had lost a lot of blood from the aneurysm. His intellect would probably not be impaired and his speech should be okay after a while, but the next twenty-four hours would be critical. Then he gave us the news we all dreaded. Mom's husband and our dad would probably have permanent paralysis on the left side of his body, and we should prepare to take an invalid home.

Mom took in the information like a champion. Her visible strength deepened our resolve. She continues to exhibit pioneer-like strength to this day. Four of the five Lewis boys were there to hear the news. Knowing our dad, we told Dr. Nielson that our father was going to walk out of the hospital.

That made Dr. Nielson angry.

He said, "You boys have no idea what I did to save your Dad's life. I put four metal clamps in the artery system of his brain. Not in the branches, but in the trunk of the artery network. Your Dad will never walk again. You need to prepare your house for a wheelchair."

We certainly meant no disrespect to Dr. Nielson and his heroic lifesaving work. What he had done made us want to hug him. But we repeated that our dad's hospital stay would end with his walking out of the place. After that, Dr. Nielson focused on our mom for the rest of the conversation. He avoided looking at the four of us boys.

CHAPTER 3

ALIVE

He was alive. Who cared about the rest of the information at that time? We were thrilled with the news. We were a little scared about the uncertainty that lay ahead, but our prayers were indeed answered. Our dad was *alive.*

We hugged each other at the news. It couldn't have been better. The feeling of hope and peace that we had enjoyed through the night confirmed that the priesthood blessing had been partially granted. Because of that, we also believed the rest of the blessing would be realized—that he would return to health.

The ICU was on the second floor and we went up there as soon as our father was out of recovery. As soon as we were allowed into his room, the four of us boys went in to see him.

When we walked into his room we called to him and let him know that we were there and that we loved him. We looked at his black hair that had been shaved off on one side. He had two drainage tubes coming out of his head. He had an IV hooked up to his arm. It seemed like he was hooked up with more wires and tubes than was possible. We asked if he was all right. When we did that, he stuck his right hand up into the air above his body and started snapping his thumb with the rest of his fingers. It was the same movement as if he were moving a Muppet's mouth open and closed.

We weren't sure what he wanted for a minute. Then we realized that he wanted to grab someone's hand. I stuck out my hand and grabbed his, and when I did that he squeezed my hand with the strength of Samson. He held onto my hand for a few long seconds, squeezing it with gusto the whole time. As soon as he finished squeezing my hand, his arm dropped down on his body and he was entirely out of it. The nurse who was there suggested that we come back and visit him later when he was awake.

We all patted his body and told him that we loved him. It was a touching reunion. It was like beautiful sunshine after a night of storm. My brothers kept asking me how hard he had squeezed my hand. And I would grab their hands and squeeze them as hard as my dad had mine. His strength was amazing. We decided that it was his way of letting us know that he was a fighter, that he would be okay, and that he loved us. Never will a firm handshake mean more to me than that one did on that sunny morning.

Out in the hall we were met by our bishop, Jim MacArthur, who for years had been one of my dad's early morning running companions. He was joined by Dick Beeson, who was a neighbor and counselor to Jim in the bishopric. Dick was also the Orem City librarian and a great family friend. Another neighbor and close friend, Greta Bandley, was also there. Greta's son Shawn was one of my best friends and was then serving as a missionary in the England London Mission. We hugged all of them, grateful to be surrounded by good people in such a stressful time.

The next time we got to see Dad was later in the day. He was awake but his face was paralyzed on the left side, and he couldn't move his left arm. We told him that we loved him, and he cried and said that he loved us too. His eyes had a little touch of being disoriented as he looked around. We all wondered if there was any brain damage that was going to affect his personality, or his memory, or everything about him. We were definitely ready to deal with it, whatever it was. We were just so happy that we were speaking with him.

Dad had read many books on life after death and many of the authors described a similar experience of entering a tunnel and "moving toward a light." Mike asked him if he had seen any light or had any vision during surgery, and he jokingly said that he wasn't that lucky. He had not seen the light, and he had not seen the tunnel, and that disappointed him. He said that all he got was surgery. He thought the amount of pain that he went through warranted his seeing something.

As we were talking with him, I looked on the wall at the calendar that hung there. It was Monday, July 2, 1990, the day Dad's life was spared, our prayers were answered, and the Lord's mercy was bestowed on his behalf.

While I was driving home from the hospital, a beautiful song came on the radio. It was Bette Midler's recording of "Wind Beneath My Wings." The words touched me, and I became so emotional I pulled the car to the side of the road and just cried. I was drained from the ordeal we had all gone through and was so grateful to the Lord for sparing my father. I could not comprehend the goodness of God in watching over us. I cried each time that I heard that song for the next ten years.

The next day our family, joined by my brother Dave and his wife, Jonna, who were home from their honeymoon, gathered again in the ICU. We were asking Dad about the condition of his left side. He was totally numb on that side of his body, and he could feel neither a sharp pinch nor a poke.

He did something that caught all of us off guard. He asked us to sit him up in bed so that his legs could hang over the edge. We were stunned. He still had two drainage tubes inserted into his head and was hooked up to several IVs as well. We asked him if it would be safe for us to lift him up. He said in his new mumbled way of speaking, "Oh, yeah. Oh, yeah!"

Since he was a doctor, and doctor knows best, we did what he asked. It took some real teamwork to get him into position. His tall frame was difficult and awkward to move. His left side was deadweight and felt like a big sack of rocks. When we finally got him into a sitting position with his legs hanging over the side, he exhaled in a way that we could tell made him feel good. It was the first time since his headaches and stroke that he felt somewhat comfortable.

We had to hold him steady because he did not have the strength or the balance to hold himself up, but he enjoyed sitting there for a minute or two. Then he completely surprised us again by saying, "Okay, now stand me up!"

Could we do that? We asked him if he was serious. He again said, "Oh, yeah."

So even though it didn't seem right with all of the tubes and wires hooked up to his body, we stood him up. We took it as a sign that he was not content to sit in that bed. It was a message that he wanted to get out of that hospital and walk. We were pumped. It was a great feeling.

That feeling of exhilaration was shattered when the ICU nurse walked by the room and saw what was happening. She almost shrieked and then ran into the room, ordering us to lay him back down on the bed. She was as serious as a heart attack and was letting us have it. She asked us if we knew what the tubes were that were coming out of his head. Before we could answer, she told us that they were there to relieve the pressure that would build up in his brain. She told us that we could have killed him by standing him up like that and changing the pressure in his head.

We had no idea that it could have killed him! We had asked him if it was okay and he had said yes. He was the doctor, not us. Then the nurse ordered us to get out of the room and out of the

ICU. We thought it was one thing to have just about killed our dad, but it was another thing entirely to go so far as to be kicked out of his room. So we told the nurse we were sorry for standing him up and promised we wouldn't do it again. But we also told her that we would not be leaving the room. We were going to stay right there with him as long as he was awake.

Incredibly, she acquiesced and let us stay. We were still somewhat in shock that Dad would have asked us to stand him up when it could have thrown a blood clot and killed him. We asked him why he asked us to do that if it could have been so serious and even fatal. He just mumbled that it was all right. And to our utter amazement, as soon as he could see that his nurse was out of sight, he said, "Okay, let's do it again!"

There was just too much tension in the room, and we all cracked up laughing. He was not laughing, though. He was serious. He thought the nurses were being way too cautious, and he wanted to do it again. We refused to do it, but we were totally fired up that he had that kind of determination. We didn't know if his judgment had been compromised from brain surgery, but we were very excited about his will to walk and his will to live. He was tough and he had the fight in him to get better.

Something else happened that lifted our spirits. When we got home from the hospital that morning, there was a brand-new refrigerator in our kitchen. Our old refrigerator had been on the fritz for the past couple of weeks. We had tried a couple of things to keep it going, but now it was gone. The members of our ward had caught wind that it was dead. Without any fanfare, they had purchased a new one. Our mom cried when we walked into our kitchen and there was a brand-new refrigerator all plugged in and even stocked with food.

Not only did we have a whole bunch of food in the kitchen, but we also had a gigantic gallon-size container of mayonnaise, a year's supply. Mike was home the day after my Dad's stroke when a neighbor, Suzy Dastrup, called and asked how she could help. Mike was making a sandwich at the time and was fishing without success for the last couple of white lines of mayonnaise in the jar. In the middle of his attempts, she called. Without really thinking how it would sound, he said, "We could use some mayonnaise." He was being funny and frustratingly serious at the same time. But, along with a wonderful new refrigerator, we saw this huge jar of mayonnaise with a little note from Suzy. It was a simple and inexpensive gesture that was a symbol of our being surrounded by considerate and loving greatness. Mom wasn't the only person to shed tears of gratitude over those kind acts of Christian charity.

CHAPTER 4

BLESSINGS BOOK

We spent the Fourth of July with Dad in his ICU room. One of the nurses told us that when she went into his room that morning, she had wished him a happy Fourth, and he had responded immediately by singing "Yankee Doodle Dandy." Here are the words:

> *I'm a Yankee Doodle Dandy,*
> *A Yankee Doodle, do or die;*
> *A real live nephew of my Uncle Sam's,*
> *Born on the Fourth of July.*
> *I've got a Yankee Doodle sweetheart,*
> *She's my Yankee Doodle joy.*
> *Yankee Doodle came to London, just to*
> *   ride the ponies;*
> *I am the Yankee Doodle Boy.*[1]

It was a great sign that he could remember and recall lyrics to songs from his youth. His brain was working. When the nurses mentioned that he was too long for the hospital bed, he sang another song. This time it was "Grandfather's Clock." The first part of it goes like this:

> *My grandfather's clock*
> *Was too large for the shelf,*
> *So it stood ninety years on the floor;*
> *It was taller by half*
> *Than the old man himself,*
> *Though it weighed not a pennyweight more.*
> *It was bought on the morn*
> *Of the day he was born,*
> *And was always his treasure and pride;*
> *But it stopped short,*
> *Never to go again,*
> *When the old man died.*
>
> *Ninety years without slumbering*
> *Tick, tock, tick, tock,*
> *His life's seconds numbering,*
> *Tick, tock, tick, tock,*
> *It stopped short*
> *Never to go again,*
> *When the old man died.*[2]

Dad's ability to remember poems and songs became a big part of his personal rehab. It gave him a way to connect in a non-threatening way during visits with family and friends. It had the effect of disarming people of their apprehension about his condition. He brought a smile to their faces before they had time to worry about staring at his half head of hair or consoling him about his tragic state.

That night, after Dad fell asleep, our family went to a hill in Orem overlooking the valley and watched the fireworks at the BYU "Stadium of Fire." It was a strangely joyful and somber night. We were still full of joy that Dad was alive and had been saved by a miraculous surgery. But the full weight and reality of his long-term situation was also settling on each of us. It was heavy. It was a major life change. We were slowly adapting to the role we would all play in dealing with his health issues and lack of mobility.

On July 5, after three and a half days in the ICU, Dad was moved to a regular room. That night, Todd and I went down to the hospital after midnight because Dad was having nightmares. After waking from a dream, he would kick the wall until the nurses entered his room. Todd and I stayed with him for a good portion of that night. We just talked and hung out until he could fall asleep again. When Dr. Nielson stopped by for a visit, he mentioned that because of the brain's swelling, Dad was experiencing emotional bombardment intoxication and that it could last up to a year.

One night Dad thought he was surrounded in foam padding and he needed us to save him from the nurses. He also tried to convince the nurses that he needed money to buy bowling balls. He started to feel as though our mom was in cahoots with the nurses in limiting the number of visitors he could have. He wanted to see everyone and thought the nurses were severely limiting his interaction with others.

On July 6, two major events happened. The first was another surgery. Dad was having so much pain in his lower back that his doctor thought it necessary to have a procedure done on his bulging disc, which had been caused by the endocarditis infection. I wondered if he was strong enough to handle another surgery. From my perspective, it was a surgery. From the doctor's perspective, it was a procedure. I was very glad that the doctors were working from their perspective and not mine.

Dad was wheeled from his room and back downstairs to the operating room. I was thinking they were going to put him under but they only gave him a sedative, or muscle relaxant. Wondering if he had the strength to tolerate the ordeal, Mom, Todd, and I were watching the procedure from behind a window in the room. They basically stuck a small hose into his back and sucked out loose material, disc fragments, and fluid. Dad handled the procedure very well and was proving to be one tough customer.

Later that afternoon the second major event happened. Mom bought a journal. It was a small, eight-by-five-inch journal with a picture of a teddy bear and a bird on the front. Right in the middle of these tender and anxious times, not knowing what the future would bring, she called this journal our "Blessings Book." She wanted us to focus on what we had instead of what we didn't have. She wanted us to recognize the Lord's hand in our lives. She also wanted us to focus on things that would be good and great.

This is the first entry we made in the Blessings Book:

> We are so thankful for:
> Dave and Jonna
> Mike
> Jason
> Chad
> Todd
> Many friends and family
> Many neighbors
> Prayers
> Fasting for us
> Good hospital
> Good neighbors
> Caring hospital personnel
> Jan's job at Northwestern Mutual Life
> Educators Mutual Life Insurance Company

This practice of writing down all of our blessings continued day after day for as long as Dad remained in the hospital.

For as long as I could remember, our family had always had prayer at night before we went to bed. Each night one of us would offer the prayer. We would kneel on the floor, fold our arms, and close our eyes. The prayer would be a heartfelt and sincere expression of gratitude to our Father in Heaven for the blessings He had given us that day. We would also petition the Lord for the blessings and favors that we stood in need of. We always closed in the name of Jesus Christ.

After we finished praying, we would all stand up and give a hug to my mom and dad and tell them that we loved them. Mom decided that we would continue to have our family prayer each night at the hospital. If we could make it, we were there. If we couldn't be there, the invitation was always open. It was a great way for us to stay close as a family and to continue to show our gratitude to God as well as plead for His kindness in blessing each one of us, especially our father.

The days started going by a little faster. Getting through the first week was like climbing Mount Everest. We did it with the help of many friends and a great team of doctors and nurses at the Utah Valley Regional Medical Center. The people who worked there were incredible. They were like angels.

My dad's skin color started looking a lot better. His eyes were more alert and his speech was not as slurred. He even started smiling at the end of that first week. It felt as though good improvements were coming on top of good improvements. Good things were happening.

By the time we got to the next Sunday, exactly one week since his stroke, we had made a family visiting schedule so that we could take turns being with him and so that he could have someone from the family with him all day.

One of the great humbling and learning experiences I had was helping him use the restroom when a nurse was not available. It was weird at first to grab the plastic urinal bottle and help him do something that he could not do for himself. I quickly learned that there was no shame in serving him in that way. The only shame would have been if I had been unwilling to help him relieve himself because I thought I was too cool to do something like that.

While I was serving Dad, it started to dawn on me just how much my parents had served me throughout my life. From changing my diapers as a baby to preparing all of my meals, they had served me with love and kindness for 18½ years. I started to ask myself how I could have ever complained about anything before. How could I have grumbled about *any* meal that was ever prepared for me? How could I have ever treated them with *any* rudeness? My love for my parents was growing more now than at any other time in my life. My gratitude was growing at the same rate as I realized I could have been so much better.

Dad's favorite piece of music was from Beethoven's Ninth Symphony, the "Ode to Joy." He asked me to bring it from home down to his room. He played that beautiful tune over and over on a tape recorder next to his bed. And each time he listened to it, he would weep.

He tried to hide his emotions. When he would start to cry, he would smile, but his half-paralyzed face was distorted into the mouth of a little child that wept. It wasn't a sad face, but the face of someone being touched by an angel or, in his case, moved by powerful music.

The familiar melody became as much a part of his hospital room as the equipment that was helping keep him alive. It was touching to watch him get so emotional as he listened to it. The tune started to settle over my soul in a similar way. I did not weep when I heard it, but I felt a powerful love for my dad and my family. I had plenty of opportunities to hear it, that's for sure, and I think I liked it more each time.

On July 9, Dad was moved from the fourth floor to the rehab

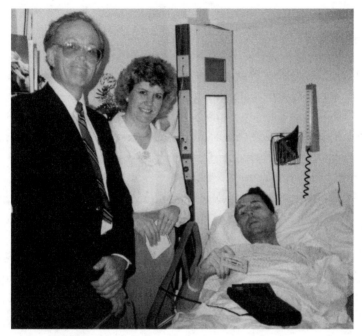

Dad's brother Bill and his wife, Diane, visit Dad in the hospital.
Dad is holding his tape of Beethoven's Ninth Symphony, the "Ode to Joy"!

center at the south end of the hospital. He was introduced to a whole team of therapists and specialists who were led by Ron Liston. These people were more than tremendous. They cared for my dad just as they would have treated their own parents, and they became family to us. I was completely amazed at the patience they showed while caring for him and working with him through each of his exercises. He was set up with speech therapists and occupational therapists, physical therapists, and every other kind of therapist you can imagine.

After the first full day of rehab, he and I had a nice conversation about what lay in store.

"Was rehab hard today?" I asked.

"Yeah, REAL hard, harder than calculus!" he said.

We were gearing up for the long haul. As a family, we knew it was going to be the hardest thing that we would ever accomplish together. And that was the best part of the whole ordeal; we were doing it *together*. We all felt more connected than ever before. We felt a great love for each other. We felt a stronger bond and a willingness to be more patient with each other and our dad.

There was a steady stream of friends and family at the hospital. It was inspiring to see so many relatives and friends of my parents stop to see him and offer their help and desire to serve. It reminded me of that joyful scene in the movie *It's a Wonderful Life* when all of George Bailey's friends poured into his living room to bail him out of financial ruin. The compassion, friendship, love, kindness, and charity extended to us sustained our family.

With his half head of hair, Dad looked like a punk rocker, but his condition was too delicate to worry about his hair up to that point. We were just happy that he was alive, that he was talking and communicating with us. His brother Bill and Bill's wife, Diane, brought in some scissors to give him a trim. Diane evened out his buzz cut, and Dad looked great. It was a big step in the recovery process to trim his thick black hair. It would come back just like his ability to move would return.

Each day he was more and more alert. At first, his eyes wandered with an almost worried and confused look, but now he was able to focus better on whoever was talking to him.

When the stroke occurred, I was four months away from going on a mission for my church. I had not yet turned in my missionary application, which meant I still did not know where I would be serving. Dad had served a mission to the Northwestern States Mission, which at that time included Washington, Oregon, and Idaho. My older brothers served missions to Columbus, Ohio, and Buenos Aires, Argentina. Dave and Mike even went to the same mission, which was almost unheard of. Not only did they serve together in the Ohio Columbus Mission, but they were companions for one month. That was extremely rare.

On one of his visits, our bishop, Jim MacArthur, informed us that there would be assistance provided to help supplement the cost of my mission. A donor had offered to contribute $100 a month to help my family. A regular mission at the time cost $350 a month. This was such a wonderful blessing to me and to my family. I asked Bishop MacArthur who the donor was, and he told me our benefactor wanted to keep it an anonymous gift. I was completely blown away by the generosity. That kindness was definitely an entry in our Blessings Book.

With Dad in that condition, I had wondered if I shouldn't postpone my mission until he got better. But I changed my mind following one very energetic phone call from Dave Harvey, a friend of Mom's who was also serving on the Alpine School Board. He said he just wanted to chat with me for a minute. He knew I was preparing to serve a mission and asked if I had submitted my application yet. I told him that I hadn't and that I was thinking about staying with my dad for a few months and helping him learn to walk again before I sent them in.

Dave nearly jumped through the phone. He strongly encouraged me to submit my papers at once. He told me not to wait another minute because my dad would be much more blessed if I was serving a mission than if I stayed to help him. I asked him, "Are you sure?" He was rock-solid sure. He could not have been more emphatic or have urged me more forcefully. He said it in a way that got me off my perch. He was a catalyst in my making the best decision I had ever made. I finished my interviews and quickly sent off my application to Church headquarters in Salt Lake City.

On July 10, Dad began moving his left leg for the first time. He was in the rehab full-time and was showing signs of progress. His therapy sessions lasted all day and were aimed at getting him back to normal or as close to it as possible. They helped him set goals of moving, walking, and working again.

He was still having nightmares and would call late at night needing someone to be with him. I thought it was a lot of fun to drive down at midnight and talk with him until he could fall asleep. One of our conversations was about his remembrances of us as little kids. He told me how much fun it had been being our dad. He recalled the simple phrases that we used to say, and it would bring a smile to his face. He cracked up telling the story of Mike when he went into a friend's house as a three year old. Mike stood in a living room looking at an arched doorway leading into a hall, and after a long time commented, "Somebody ain't got no doors!" Dad got the giggles recalling that unexpected comment.

The slow pace of being stuck in a hospital bed afforded time for many such conversations, and it was fun to get to know Dad better. I loved it.

During the day, he continued to have a great attitude. His jokes and corny sense of humor helped everyone around him. He thought the nurses were a bit too overprotective at times and complained, "They are worried that I will bruise my eyelashes." He also began wearing a hot pink Nike cap given to him by our friends Jeff and Tracy Kimball from Huntington Beach. That pink hat with the Nike slogan "Just Do It" covered his new crew cut but also served to encourage him. He wore it every day and everywhere he went.

His speech therapist, Ann Sumner, worked with him to train his tongue and his mouth how to work properly again. He had difficulty telling time. He would look at the clock and couldn't make sense of what it meant. It was a reminder to my mom how much progress needed to be made and also that the road we were on was going to be a very long one. But when Ann asked him one day to tell her something in a happy way and something in a sad way, he dramatized the sad statement with all the energy and effect of a professional Shakespearean thespian. It made everyone

My dad standing up and sharing a laugh with his friend Tom DeLong.
Enthusiasm and optimism are contagious.

laugh and Mom was able to take a breath and say to herself, "Good, he'll be okay."

He started to have days in rehab where he thought his improvements were 150 percent of the day before, and his therapists were delighted. That was reassuring because we knew that the therapists were seeing hundreds of these patients a year and knew what they were talking about. We had tremendous confidence in them and continued to be amazed at their skill and patience. They would work for over an hour, trying to get some movement in a leg or an arm, and even if no change or improvement was made, they still did their job with big smiles on their faces.

It was a shock to walk into the rehab facility one day and see Dad standing up with the therapists. That is what he tried to do right after surgery, and now he was doing it. The therapists always had a big thick belt around his waist that they could hold on to to help steady him.

By July 15 Dad was able to raise his leg off the bed a couple of inches. What improvement! It would take him a great deal of time and concentration to lift his leg, but when he succeeded, we would all hoot and holler. Even the smallest of improvements brought tons of fun into the room. We laughed and smiled and encouraged him the best we could. Even though it was slow progress, it became one big party. We loved it. It truly was a team effort. The Lewis team.

On July 17, I took him for a trip around the hospital in the wheelchair. We left the rehab section of the hospital and took an elevator up to the top floor of the main hospital. We went to a spot in the hallway that had a big window, and he was able to look out and see the mountains. There was a sense of freedom just truckin' around the hospital. We went past several nurses stations and Dad would say hello to all of them. He was on the move and he liked it, even if he was sitting in a wheelchair.

Something remarkable happened that same night. The members of our ward wanted to do something special for Dad. They decided to participate in a fast and then visit the temple together and pray for his recovery. Eighty-five members of our ward went to the Provo Temple, and we were strengthened by their show of faith, love, and solidarity. We had lived in the same ward for over fifteen years. It was our home. It was our extended family. Our immediate family was extremely moved that they would reach out in a way that Christ taught us—to fast and pray for those who are sick or otherwise afflicted.

When we gathered for family prayer in the hospital that evening, we were feeling extra grateful for the thoughtfulness of our ward members and for the spiritual connection that we felt with them. After our prayer, Dad wanted to show everyone there that he could lift his leg off the bed about six inches. When it was time to show his stuff, he took about thirty seconds to get his mind right. He focused all of his energy and mental capacity on the effort it would take.

When he finally moved his leg, it did not stop at six inches. He raised his leg three feet off the bed into the air, and the effort almost caused him to fall off the bed. We had people on both sides of his bed, and we caught him as he was heading for the floor. We were so happy to see that kind of power and movement, we all started yelling with excitement. Within seconds, the nurses opened the door and rushed into the room with startled looks on their faces. With all the commotion and racket we were making, they thought that he might have had another stroke or some other type of emergency.

I learned an important lesson that day about the power of fasting and prayer. I learned that the Lord listens to our prayers and that when people unite their faith, miracles can happen. It was a miracle to us that Dad was able to move that much and that he was continuing to get better at the rate he was going. I learned to be much more grateful to my Father in Heaven and to recognize His hand and His power in all things. In the critical time that I was preparing to serve Him as a missionary, I was learning more about His loving kindness. My testimony of His reality was becoming stronger each day.

Dad continued to learn how to walk. The rehab center had parallel bars like those used in men's gymnastics. Holding on to those with his good hand, he was able to steady himself enough to take a few slow steps. He was upright, he was taking baby steps, and it was awesome.

On July 26, he walked outside the building and into the fresh air. We had to hold on to his white belt strap to balance him, but it was so much fun to see him take that many steps. His left leg swung in a wide arc from back to front. It was labored and difficult, but it was walking.

The very next day, he walked all over the place. He went from

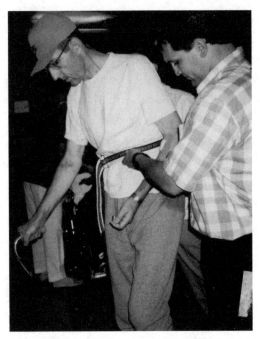

Rehab therapist Mike Fischer (at right) at Utah Valley Medical Center
teaching my dad how to walk. Great day!

his therapy room, out into the hall, to the sports therapy room, outside, back into the building, and all the way into his therapy room again. This was another one of his 150-percent improvements from the day before. His balance was improving, but he still needed someone right by his side. He would stumble very easily and if he did not have a companion, he would go down. But he was making great progress.

That was also the day that my mission call came in the mail. The anticipation had grown each day that my papers were being processed. I was so anxious to know where I would be spending the next two years of my life. I was also very anxious to know if I was going to be learning a new language and living in another country. I had been there when all three of my brothers had opened their mission calls. I had been there when many of my friends had opened their mission calls. I could be sent anywhere from Salt Lake City, Utah, to South Africa.

I personally wanted to go to England or Australia. I figured they would be fun places to live and serve while still speaking English. I decided to open my call at the hospital at 5:30 in the afternoon and whoever had the desire to be there was welcome to join me.

Mormons believe a mission call is determined by revelation and is from the Lord. It is therefore the most anticipated letter any Latter-day Saint will ever receive.

With my family and friends gathered in my dad's hospital room, I opened the letter. It read:

Dear Elder Lewis,

You are hereby called to serve as a missionary of The Church of Jesus Christ of Latter-day Saints. You are assigned to labor in the Taiwan Taichung Mission. It is anticipated that you will serve for a period of 24 months.

You should report to the Missionary Training Center in Provo, Utah, on Wednesday, 24 October 1990. You will learn the discussions in Mandarin . . .

I was stunned. I read the words *Taiwan Taichung* and wondered where on the world's map it was located. I immediately thought I would be living in a culture I did not understand and eating strange food. I knew that everything was made in Taiwan at that time. I was so nervous. Mom and Dad were thrilled for me. I was still developing out of a self-centered kid and my nervousness was part of holding on to what I wanted as opposed to letting the Lord help me serve others.

Soon after I opened the call, I drove home. I was still in shock and my heart was pounding. The second I stepped out of my car at home, my neighbors, Ralph Johnson and Jim MacArthur, were outside and asked me about my call. I told them I was going to Taiwan. They both got the biggest smiles on their faces. They were immediately laughing with delight and shaking my hand. Jim said that I was going to absolutely love Taiwan. He was so excited about Taiwan that my own heart started to pound with excitement instead of fear.

Any anxiety that I had after opening my call was gone. From that second on, I had nothing but great enthusiasm to serve. I couldn't wait to get to Taiwan. I wondered about the Chinese language of Mandarin and if I would ever be able to learn it. I could not stop thinking about Taiwan. It was one of the Lord's tender mercies that my two incredible neighbors were there right when I got home. Their excitement and enthusiasm sparked a fire in my heart. They were the first ones I was able to tell, and they could not have said anything better than what they said.

Remembering the anonymous donor to my mission made a difference in how I viewed every dollar that I spent in Taiwan. It was sacred money. It was well used, well spent, and I was extremely grateful for the help. I bought a Chinese scroll during the last week of my mission for this anonymous person. Since the bishop would not tell me who it was, I at least wanted to say thank you in a special way. The scroll consisted of a hundred different ways to write BLESSINGS in Chinese. After I got home, I asked the bishop to give it to the person who had helped with my mission. I gave it to him in hope that I would walk into a home some day in the future and see that scroll hanging on the wall. The person remains anonymous to this day.

My dad got to leave the hospital for the first time on July 28. He was given an overnight pass. We were all very excited to have him back home. It was another step toward getting ready for life after the stroke. He was doing very well with the slow process of moving in and out of cars, but someone had to stand next to him to make sure he didn't fall. He took his first hot bath, which was against doctors' orders, or maybe just nurses' orders. He said it felt so good to sit in a nice hot bath again.

He stayed pretty busy while he was home. On Sunday afternoon, we took a walk down the street past the homes of our neighbors—the Johnsons and the Heaps—and then turned around at the MacArthurs. Our neighbors were awesome. We were surrounded by greatness, no doubt about it. He had several visitors who stopped by to say hello and see the miraculous progress. Word was out that he was healing very fast. Part of this was deemed spontaneous recovery, and part of it was attributed to an incredible and even miraculous healing.

The neighbors kept bringing in food. I could fill another book with the nice things people did for us. Just to illustrate the kindness showered on our family, and in only a few days' time, here is what our neighbors brought: Evelyn Wentz—salad; Carolyn Maughn—orange rolls; Suzie Dastrup—pop, pizza; Brad Camp family—chicken; Sharon Smith family—cookies and cake; DeAnn and Sharon—soup, rolls, salad, and ham; Karl Tucker family—casserole; Gloria Larsen—lasagna, salad, and bread; Angie Childs—ice cream and pie; Wilde family—punch; Sandi Hirshi—pie and rolls; Lois Poulson—zucchini bread, and apple pie from Mae Roylance; MacArthurs—cookies; Vira Johnson—taco salad and pie; Hoen family—bread; Ortiz family—cookies; Jeana Holt—éclairs; Jeannene Easley—bread and cookies; Bandleys—some of everything.

The generosity was truly overwhelming. As we counted our blessings every night, we found that we could not number them all. They seemed to multiply before our very eyes. My dog, Murphy, even participated in these blessings. One afternoon, while we were at the hospital, a family left a plate of cookies on the porch at home. Murphy somehow got out of the house and helped himself to the whole plate.

Beautiful flowers were sent by many people and many groups

that Dad was a part of, including the Orem Rotary, Alpine School Board and Cabinet, Don Armstrong, Gayle Chandler, Susan Stone, Jenny Barber, Jim Barnes, Alpha Plasma, Porta Medic, Orem Community Hospital, Hawkins and Cloward Accounting, Steve Downey, Nelson Abbott, and Tom Mackay. Each day people took time off of work to stop by and say hello. They went out of their way to do what they could to cheer my dad along and inspire him to keep working so hard. The list of visitors filled up pages in our Blessings Book.

One of the Church hymns that we were very familiar with is "Count Your Blessings." It was part of the inspiration behind my mom focusing our family's vision on the Lord's blessings to us. The words are powerful and poignant. I offer them as a gift to anyone who feels a loss of any kind. Instead of focusing on that loss, take strength and life from the words of this song:

> *When upon life's billows you are tempest-tossed,*
> *When you are discouraged, thinking all is lost,*
> *Count your many blessings; name them one by one,*
> *And it will surprise you what the Lord has done.*
>
> *Chorus*
> *Count your blessings; Name them one by one.*
> *Count your blessings; See what God hath done.*
> *Count your blessings; Name them one by one.*
> *Count your many blessings; See what God hath done.*
>
> *Are you ever burdened with a load of care?*
> *Does the cross seem heavy you are called to bear?*
> *Count your many blessings; every doubt will fly,*
> *And you will be singing as the days go by.*
>
> *When you look at others with their lands and gold,*
> *Think that Christ has promised you his wealth untold.*

Count your many blessings; money cannot buy
Your reward in heaven nor your home on high.

So amid the conflict, whether great or small,
Do not be discouraged; God is over all.
Count your many blessings; angels will attend,
Help and comfort give you to your journey's end.[3]

CHAPTER 5

"DOC ROG" WALKS TO EDUCATION WEEK

My dad had been asked earlier in the year to be one of the presenters at BYU Education Week, an annual conference of hundreds of presenters on a wide range of topics. He'd agreed to teach three classes at the conference. But when BYU heard that he had had a stroke, Max Palmer called from the school and told him not to worry about presenting. Dad responded that he still planned on speaking and delivering his message. They were shocked, but Dad was firm.

On Monday, July 30, Dad was back at work in the rehab facility. His rehab drills were a lot of fun to watch. He stacked cans in order to help strengthen his left arm. He walked in between the parallel bars and focused on strengthening his left knee. He solved math problems and used the phone book to find a name, rode the stationary bike as though he were Lance Armstrong, and continued to fight to get better. He'd graduated to solving a colored block puzzle and practicing finding Waldo. He was getting more movement in his left index finger. He was also walking with a smaller walking cane. Progress was slow, but it was steady.

August 2 was a month since the stroke. It was a great time to reflect on the trauma, the recovery, and the rehab. It was also a great time to remember the dozens and dozens of visitors as well as the countless acts of kindness and service that had been rendered on behalf of our family. We thought of the fasting and prayers, the temple visit, the strength that the Lord had given my dad up to that point. The Blessings Book for that day read:

Past Month of Blessings
1. Our own family closeness
2. Closeness to each other
3. Family prayers
4. Friends and family who have visited
5. Ward friends
6. Cards, letters, flowers, food
7. Increased confidence and commitment to Christ. "My peace I give unto you," one example
8. Confidence that what the scriptures say is true. "All that He has is ours."
9. Blessings of getting better
10. Being able to work with Dr. Lyman Moody, Dr. Karl Douglas Nielson, Rhonda Metcalf, Gordon Heinz, and the good people in the rehab unit
11. Ron Liston's jokes every day
12. Connection with ward family—their prayers connect with Roger
13. We share a big mission together. Like a big school of fish traveling together. Connection is much more profound.
14. Ann Sumner, speech therapist

August 4 was Dad's forty-eighth birthday. At the time, I thought he had lived a great life and that he was fairly old. Oh, how my perception has changed after having been through some of life's ups and downs. He was, in fact, a young man, a very young man, in the prime of his life.

He was given a special weekend pass to go home for his birthday, where he was able to sleep in his own bed again. We held a big birthday party for him, and four of his five brothers, his sister, and their children all came to the house for the big event. Our living room was packed full of people who filled up every available chair and couch, and the rest stood or sat on the floor. We sang songs, laughed, gave presents, and gave our greatest thanks to God for the miraculous healing that was taking place and for the love that we all felt from Him. We gratefully accepted a donation that the extended family had collected for Dad.

On Sunday morning, we all attended church together for the first time in a month. In The Church of Jesus Christ of Latter-day Saints, each Sunday a sacrament meeting is held in which members partake of bread and water in remembrance of Christ's flesh and blood and where assigned speakers address the congregation. One Sunday of the month is set aside as "fast Sunday." In preparation for that meeting, members are encouraged to go without food and drink for two continuous meals. The money saved (called a fast offering) is then donated to help care for the needy. I had been taught from as young as I could remember that fasting and prayer strengthens us spiritually. On fast Sunday, the sacrament meeting is unique. Instead of assigned talks, anyone who has a desire is welcome to stand at the pulpit and express his or her feelings (or "testimony") about the Savior to the congregation.

Having so much to be grateful for, Dad wanted to express his feelings to the members of the ward. At the appropriate time, aided by his four-pronged walker cane, he stood to *walk* to the podium from his seat in the congregation. As he rose to do so, he leaned down toward Mike and said, "Spot me." He wanted Mike to make sure that he didn't tip over as he headed for the stand. Mike walked next to him and helped him climb the three stairs that led to the pulpit and microphone.

Just a month after his ordeal had begun, Dad *stood* and bore his testimony of the divine help he had received in the healing that was taking place. He thanked the ward members for their many visits, their prayers and fasting on his behalf, their generous offerings of food and baked goods, and the love they had extended to our family. He spoke especially of his love for our Heavenly Father and His Son Jesus Christ. Dad was very emotional and cried the whole time he spoke.

Most of the people in the congregation shed tears of their own. They had prayed and fasted for Dad. They had given of themselves in an effort to help him and us in our time of need. They were invested spiritually and emotionally. The outpouring of love and the warmth of the Spirit of the Lord were elements that had contributed to his healing. There may have been some dry eyes in the congregation, but I don't recall seeing any. It was a very tender moment.

Standing, walking, balancing, speaking, and breathing were all miracles manifested in church that day.

Life back at therapy resumed. Each day added new skills to acquire, bad habits to retire, and people to inspire. We were never short on inspiration. Whether it was doing harder math problems or figuring out more difficult living problems or taking on a new exercise regimen, Dad attacked it with so much enthusiasm that it was an inspiration to all of us. The whole scene evolved daily. Every time we looked back at his progress we were amazed.

Mom was constantly by his side with words of encouragement, not just for him, but for all of us. Dave was newly married; Mike was getting ready for fall training camp at the University of Utah; Jason was just back from a mission and waiting to get back in school; I was getting ready for my mission to Taiwan; Todd was

My parents at a Fourth of July picnic, 2004, at the home of a good friend.

preparing for his junior year of high school, going through summer conditioning with the football team; and our mom was keeping us all together.

Everyone agrees: our mom is something else. Dr. Steve Lewis (no relation) stopped by the room in the hospital and told my dad, "I had a chance to talk to your wife recently, and she is just as sharp as everybody says she is." We all shared the same feeling.

My dad's brother Bill and his wife, Diane, were frequent visitors at the hospital. They may have come more than anyone else. Bill is one year younger than my dad and a carpenter by trade. He is a real craftsman and has constructed beautiful wood staircases and rounded archways for some of the nicest homes in Utah. He can curve a staircase or an archway to within a millimeter of the specifications.

On one of his visits, Uncle Bill and I were sitting in the rehab cafeteria talking with my dad about missions. Uncle Bill had served his Church mission in Japan. We started talking about the Far East and about Taiwan in particular. Then, all of sudden, he asked me who my mission president was. I told him that I wasn't sure. He said, "You're going to the Taiwan Taichung Mission?" When I said yes, he slapped his leg and exploded with excitement. A huge smile beamed from his face. He said, "Kent Watson is going to be your mission president!"

I said, "Who is that?"

He said Kent Watson was one of his best friends while growing up in Cedar City, Utah, and rattled off about five stories about how impressive President Watson was. I was already excited to be heading to Taiwan, but that conversation with my Uncle Bill ignited a flame in my heart. I couldn't have been happier to know that a friend of my dad and his family would be my leader for the next two years. Even though Taiwan was on the other side of the world, I was starting to feel more and more that it would be my home.

By August 8, Dad was out of the wheelchair for good. He could and would walk wherever he went, though he still used the cane for help. He was able to get to the bathroom by himself. His left leg was getting stronger, and he was able to get up and down stairs without assistance. He practiced finding words in the dictionary with the speech therapist. He used his mind to work multiplication problems and increased his proprioception (the sense of his limbs in space). He was getting more of that sensory ability through the long hours of rehab.

He continued to use the metal cane for a few weeks—until it nearly cost him his life. He would walk one time around the block at home for exercise. He did so on a rainy evening when the damp air was charged with electricity. As he got closer to home, he felt a strong charge of electricity in the air. It was so strong that by the time he reached our driveway, he was unable to let go of the cane. He was strong enough by then that he carried it for moral support more than anything else, and he was holding it mid-shaft rather than the usual way by the handle. Because of the electricity in the air, it took a great effort to break his grip on the cane and throw it on the front lawn. He said it was doing everything but shooting sparks. That was the end of the cane. He walked with it no more.

In the midst of his miraculous healing, and with the pressure of presenting at Education Week, Dad collected his thoughts and feelings and went for it. He was surrounded by his family, who loved him and believed in him. We had been there with him almost nonstop for the last month and a half as he agonized from one therapy session to another in his efforts to walk again. We were also there with him at BYU Education Week.

August 21 was the first of his three days of presenting. He had practiced his presentations the Friday before in front of the staff at the rehab unit, and he was ready. I remember walking by his side into his assigned room at BYU and being surprised to see how many people were there for his class. It was remarkable how well he performed. As he described his stroke and his miraculous recovery, he was able to connect with his audience in an intimate and effective way.

One of the messages he shared over the course of the three days was about the healing power of beautiful words and music, particularly the "Ode to Joy."

His message was one of hope and redemption. His presentations were enlivened by honest emotion. His story was real. His expressions were heartfelt. They were inspiring, and people related to them and were encouraged to face their own problems. Recalling the love he had experienced during his illness, Dad often wept on the stage as he taught. He affirmed that life is beautiful! Life is worth living!

Right after Education Week, Dad was able to pack up his

belongings, which included his tape recorder, his tape of the "Ode to Joy," and his books, and with his good luck pink Nike hat on his head, leave the hospital for good. He got in the car and came home. It was so inspiring to see the progress that he had made in the nearly two months that he was there. His unexpected survival, the hard work in rehab, and the blessings of heaven were all miraculous to me. It was great to have him home. He would continue to go to rehab every day, but he was home. As I prepared to leave home for two years, it was so nice to have him there with me.

To help raise money and pay for my mission, I was working for Reid and Sue Robinson. Their company, Signature Promotions, was a screen printing and embroidery business, and during the year leading up to my mission, Sue and Reid became two of my best friends. They reinforced everything that my parents had taught me about what it takes to be a good person. They encouraged me to work hard and to be responsible. They became almost a second set of parents for me.

BYU awarded the Robinsons a contract to make ten thousand neckties for the "Ty Detmer for Heisman" campaign the school was marketing. Because I had such high regard for Ty as a person and as a player, I took special pleasure in making those ties. I had never met him, but after making all those ties, I felt I had a connection to him. I did not have the chance to meet him until after my senior season when I was getting ready to select an agent and turn professional.

Michele and I set up a meeting with Ty and his wife, Kim. We met in LaVell Edwards's office and talked for over an hour about all of the things we should be prepared for in beginning a career as a professional football player. It was then that I finally got to tell Ty that I was the one who made all of the ties that BYU gave out during their successful marketing campaign, and it was fun to make that connection. Imagine how thrilled I was to then join Ty with the Philadelphia Eagles my rookie season as a free agent. He threw me my first NFL touchdown pass against the Cowboys on Monday Night Football. He also became one of the people in my life who I looked up to the most. He is a class act, on and off the field.

Reid and Sue were great people to work for, and I was sad to be leaving them. They made work a blast because they were such good and friendly people. Their personalities were such that you could not be sad if you were in their presence. People loved them, including all of their employees.

In that year working with them, I changed my attitude toward work. Instead of drudgery, it was something to be enjoyed. Even the dirty job of cleaning screens was fun because I was doing it for people who trusted me and cared about me almost as much as my parents. I also gained a greater sense of responsibility while working for them. I realized that every minute of hard work was helpful and profitable and that every ruined screen or time spent not working was not profitable.

Even more, their influence helped me want to be a better person. They were selfless in the way that they trained me, guided me, taught me, and loved me. They never once lost their temper toward me when I did something wrong or ruined a screen. To me they were perfect employers and set a standard that would be very hard to beat. Though it was a concept I wouldn't encounter for another year, I see now that in their presence I was surrounded by greatness.

The Saturday before I left for my mission, I attended a football game between the University of Utah and the University of Texas El Paso, a game in which my brother Mike played for the U. The night before the game, we got a call that Kim Johnson, our next-door neighbor and the daughter of Ralph and Nancy Johnson, had been in a car accident outside of Beaver, Utah. She was coming up for the weekend from her first year of school at

Dixie State College of Utah in St. George, and the car she was in struck a bull that was wandering on the highway. She was a year younger than I was in school. Her brother Ryan was my same age and was serving as a missionary in northern France at the time and had already been out for a year.

The phone call informed us that Kim had been seriously injured and was not expected to live. It was devastating news. I felt so sad for the Johnson family. I knew each of their seven children and had known them my whole life. My heart was broken for them.

I attended Mike's game the next day. When it was over, I learned that Kim had been flown to a hospital in Salt Lake City, not far from the football stadium. I went over to see how she was doing. When I got there, the Johnson family had just made the unfathomably difficult decision to take Kim off life support and donate her organs to save the lives of others.

The Johnsons were not actually there by then, but the nurses allowed me to go into the room and be with Kim one last time. It was a horrible reality. Life is often brutal. My heart broke for Ryan, who was in France. I did not want to accept that Kim was dying.

The next day, Sunday, was my designated missionary "farewell," a regular sacrament meeting in which I was to deliver a formal address prior to entering the Missionary Training Center (MTC) the following Wednesday. The Johnsons were in attendance as a show of support for my family and me. It was a humbling, emotional experience to try to convey my condolences and love for them. I was excited to head to Taiwan, but that excitement was tempered by the realization of the terrible loss they had just experienced. It was one of the most difficult settings for a talk I have ever been in. I prayed that they would be comforted and that Ryan especially would be blessed and comforted as he served in France.

My parents both spoke as well. Their talks were just what I needed to hear. I recorded their talks on tape, and I was able to listen to them many times over the course of my mission. Dad was walking pretty well by then. He stood at the pulpit and held up his left hand, which was clutched into a big, balled-up fist. He said that his "clutching muscles" were much stronger than his "let go muscles" and used that analogy to stress the importance of letting go of fear, hate, and any other obstacle that keeps us separated from God. He reminded me that I needed to work on my "letting go" muscles so I could relinquish the things of the world and replace them with the things of God. He counseled me to focus on the light of Christ and to let that light fill up my soul.

Mom talked about the power of prayer. She spoke from experience, and she spoke with great energy and feeling. She described her feelings over the previous four months and said how reliant she had become on prayer to help her get through my dad's ordeal. Her love for me was real. The love she described for our Father in Heaven was a great comfort to me. I was moved by her strength, compassion, and the solid example she had been throughout my whole life and especially over the last few months.

Now it was time to put all these things to work.

CHAPTER 6

THE MISSIONARY TRAINING CENTER

I entered the Missionary Training Center (MTC) on Wednesday, October 24, 1990. I was excited, full of resolve, and confident I would be successful, but at the same time I was feeling the sadness from the death of Kim Johnson. Kim's funeral was held earlier that day, and our whole family attended her service before going to the MTC together. Her passing was heart wrenching because she was in the prime of her youth, and the car accident was devastatingly sudden.

Kim's father, Ralph, spoke at the funeral and said there were two things he hadn't thought he could ever handle as a father. One was to rear a child with disabilities and the other was to bury a young child. He and his wife, Nancy, had a family of seven children. Their youngest child was born with serious physical and mental disabilities. It tore at my heart to hear Ralph speak of the love that he had for his family and the loss he was feeling with Kim's death. He shared how the Lord had blessed him to raise his son with love and patience, the same blessing he would need to deal with this tragedy.

What great faith. What great humility. What incredible

neighbors. I loved the Johnsons after living next to them for fifteen years. I shared their grief. But their faith in God and their commitment to keep trusting in Him was inspiring. It was inspiring because they did not have any bitterness, only love and gratitude. They were not giving up or throwing in the towel but sharing their hope of redemption from sorrow. They believed that Kim was in a better place. It was that faith that gave them hope.

An hour after the funeral I was at the MTC, with my excitement on one hand and heavy heart on the other. I was also nervous to engage in something so huge. I was leaving my family for two years, and two years started to feel like a very long time. The prospect of learning Chinese was daunting, to say the least. But even with the swirl of emotions that I was feeling, I couldn't have been happier and more confident about what I was doing.

The MTC is in Provo, Utah, within walking distance of the BYU campus. It is a large facility, accommodating up to four thousand missionaries at a time, including dormitories for living and classrooms for instruction. The average stay for a missionary depends on the language he or she is to learn. A missionary going to an English-speaking location stays for three weeks. A missionary learning a foreign language (and they don't get more foreign than Chinese) would stay for two months.

I had visited the MTC a few times—three times with my older brothers when they left for their missions and a couple of times with friends. The procedure was the same for all missionaries. After arriving at the front doors, my luggage was dropped off and would be taken to my dorm room. We were only allowed to bring one large suitcase, which held my clothes—mainly dark suits and white shirts, ties, dress shoes, a few articles of casual clothing, and some clothes for exercising.

After dropping off my suitcase, we were greeted by staff members who put a colored sticker dot on my suit lapel, which identified me as a new missionary to all the other people working at the MTC.

We then walked with our families down a main hall and into a large meeting hall. Chairs were set up for groups of around three to four hundred. There were several such halls off the main hall. When one room would fill up, the next room would be used to greet families. In that room we received instruction from one of the leaders of the MTC as to what would be required of us during our brief stay. Mission rules were emphasized, which included obedience to the commandments, daily scripture study and prayer, remaining with our companions at all times, no dating or listening to music, and no swimming. We would be allowed to call our families only on Mothers' Day, Christmas, and in times of emergency. We were allowed to write letters once a week.

When the meeting (which lasted about thirty minutes) was concluded, parents and families were asked to say good-bye to their missionaries, and we each exited the room through different doors—the families through one door and the missionaries through another. The separation was sudden and without ceremony and symbolized the beginning of the two-year mission.

I hugged my parents for a long time. I didn't want to let go. When I hugged my dad, I could feel the effects the stroke had had on his body. There was a part of me that wanted to stay with him and help him continue to recover and regain his strength. It was tough to say good-bye.

After I walked through my door, I was directed to the MTC bookstore, where I picked up all the study materials that I would need to teach the gospel and also to learn Chinese. The large and heavy book titled *Mandarin for Missionaries* was as big as a phone book. Talk about daunting! The weight of what I was embarking on started to add up with each step I took. After the bookstore I was led to my dorm room, where my suitcase had been placed. The small room consisted of four beds, in bunk-bed format, and four desk spaces. There were instructions to eat in the cafeteria and then to attend a six o'clock meeting in a specific room with directions on how to get there.

With wide eyes, I went to the cafeteria and ate my first missionary dinner. It was no different than normal cafeteria food at college. There were hundreds of missionaries with colored dots on their lapels with the same wide eyes as mine. After dinner, I located the small classroom where I had been instructed to go. Slowly the room filled with seven other missionaries, all of whom would head to Taiwan with me in two months. Three instructors joined us.

The instructors began talking to us—in Chinese! Two of them were actually Chinese people, one man and one woman. The other was a Caucasian man. They were all in their early twenties. The Chinese guy kept saying "Wo" while pointing to his nose. I wasn't quite sure what he was doing at first. Then he would point to all of us sitting at our desks and say, "Knee."

He continued doing this for a few minutes. His face was serious and foreign. It finally dawned on us that he was teaching us how to say "me" and "you" in Chinese. Lesson learned! I would never forget how to say *me* (Wo) and *you* (Ni) in Mandarin Chinese.

After speaking only Chinese for what seemed like a very long time, he started speaking in English. Whew! I was beginning to think we would have to learn Chinese by total immersion, or submersion (because I probably would have drowned!). He introduced himself as Brother Fong. He was an American-born Chinese guy who had served a mission to Taiwan. He was finishing his schooling at BYU, as were the other two teachers, and working part-time as a teacher in the MTC. I grew to love Brother Fong and Sister Jyang and Brother Lindsey. The MTC teachers were all former missionaries, and I would spend a lot of time with them over the next two months.

Then the missionaries were asked to introduce ourselves. One of them, Elder Rob Lamb, sat directly across the room from me. He said he was from a nearby town, American Fork, Utah, and he had a familiar face. When he was finished with his introduction, I asked him if he had played football for American Fork High School. He said that he had. We made the connection that we had played against each other. It felt good to run into someone I knew—even remotely.

When I entered the MTC that morning, I had so many emotions running through me. I felt confident about my mission and my purpose. I was resolute in my determination to serve to the best of my ability. Now I was starting to sense how hard it would be. All the confidence I had had seemed to be dissolving. Maybe I wasn't as tough or as strong as I had thought.

We were put into companionships of two and were required to be together 24/7 for as long as we remained companions. My companion was Brian Allred from Seattle, Washington. He was a well-mannered, friendly guy, and after being with him for a day or two, he told me that the happiest people he had ever known were those who were striving to obey the commandments. Because of Brian Allred, I decided that if anyone asked me how I was doing, I would respond that it was the best day of my life and that it couldn't get better. I wanted to be obedient, and I wanted to be happy.

One of the biggest adjustments was being with a companion at all times. It was cool most of the time, but it was awkward for the times when I wanted to just be by myself. It would take some getting used to.

Missionaries were put into small classes of around eight to ten persons. Our three teachers were designated as morning, afternoon, and night instructors. They taught us lessons in language, culture, and how to teach the gospel of Jesus Christ.

We were in class for ten hours a day. Learning Chinese was the hardest part. At times, my brain seemed as hard as a rock. I would look at a page of Chinese words for an hour and not absorb a thing. But other times, it felt as if my brain was a sponge and I could absorb and remember anything put in front of me. I had never prayed as hard in my life as when I was in the MTC, trying to learn how to be a missionary and trying to learn how to speak Chinese. It wasn't long before I realized that I would not be able to learn the language without God's help.

The missionaries all ate together in large cafeterias. It was fun to see those going to other missions, and we would hear them practicing their different languages at mealtimes. We envied the guys learning Spanish. It seemed so easy. But I eventually realized that nothing worthwhile comes easy. To become good at anything requires hard work. Learning Spanish (or Chinese) was no different.

The MTC was run by a three-man presidency—a president with two counselors. The president served for a period of three years. While I was there it was President Kline. He was in charge of all two to three thousand missionaries. Under him, it was broken down into smaller groups of around sixty missionaries. These groups were called branches, and they were each led by a branch president who also had two counselors. These were men who lived in the area who could help lead and interview missionaries one night during the week and most of the day on Sunday. They were also in charge of running our Sunday meetings.

After a couple of days in the MTC, I became homesick. Two years seemed like eternity. I missed my parents, my brothers, and all of my friends. I was overwhelmed by the task of learning Chinese. It was difficult to be with a companion all the time, even though he was a stud. My life, as I knew it, had been turned upside down. The first week in the MTC seemed like a year.

Then I met my branch president, Zane Taylor. I recognized him as one of the Little League baseball coaches for one of the teams in Orem when I was growing up. He coached another team, and I never got to know him when I played, but I recognized him the second he was introduced as my branch president. I didn't know anything more about him.

I found out that first Sunday that he was an Army veteran of World War II and that he had fought for our freedom. He was tall and lean and had a face that was void of hatred and guile. His eyes seemed full of love for all the missionaries in our branch. They were eyes that couldn't hide or cover his emotions. When he spoke to us he often looked as though he was about to cry. He had a tender spirit, and his voice often quavered when he spoke. It made him seem old and wise, but at the same time, he was full of energy and life. Though he was very thin, his shoulders were broad.

He had a love for us that I couldn't comprehend. He had just met us, but he immediately made us feel as though we were his own family. He would hug us and tell us how much it meant to him that we were taking two years out of our lives to serve other people. There was something about him that made an instant bond with me. I loved seeing him on Wednesday nights and again on Sundays.

I remember the first time that he spoke about the war during one of his Sunday talks. He explained how cold he was at different times in the war and described digging foxholes in frozen ground to get away from flying bullets. He spoke about praying and digging at the same time. I was fascinated. I had never been in a life-and-death situation of my own. I had never had to fight for my freedom.

My Grandpa Belden Lewis also fought in World War II. As a young kid, that was one of the things that I loved about him. It made him seem brave and courageous. I was just growing up enough to clue in to the fact that Zane Taylor, my grandpa, and every other person who fought for our freedom in that great and terrible war were my heroes. I looked forward big time to each meeting with Zane Taylor. I wanted to hear more about the war without causing him to open up wounds in his own heart, and I was grateful that he was willing to share some of his stories with us.

As he spoke, I became aware of the sacrifice he had made as a soldier. He and his buddies put their lives on the line so we could remain a free nation. It would have been a lot more fun for them to have been back at home, swimming, playing, dating, marrying, and working. I drew some similarities to the sacrifice that I would be making for the next two years. I would not have bullets flying, but it would be a challenge and a sacrifice. And there was Zane, weeping with gratitude that we were living in a free country and a free world where I could serve a mission or go to school or whatever I chose to do. I was free to serve a mission because of him and others similar to him.

It was strange to me to discover how some people made such an immediate connection and bond with my heart. I don't know why Zane Taylor or other such people through the years have had such a quick and profound impact on me, but I have learned to be grateful for them when they do.

Zane Taylor wrote a book about his experiences fighting in Patton's army. He named the book *Lesser Heroes,* and it is a wonderful reminder to any reader of the sacrifice made by the thousands of young men who willingly put their lives on the altar of freedom for us. They fought through the hell of war so that we could enjoy life and freedom. I hope I never forget their sacrifice. It impressed me that I was standing on the shoulders of giants—my grandpa, my parents and other predecessors, Zane Taylor—those whose sacrifice, love, and service make possible my freedoms. Such men were heroes to me, and I wanted to become more like them.

It was in the MTC that I learned how much I loved getting letters. I couldn't wait to receive letters from my family and friends. They gave me encouragement and inspiration. They added fuel to my fire to work hard and to be my best.

I also learned how important it was to reach out to others instead of constantly worrying about myself. Because my MTC group was so small and self-contained, we began looking for missionaries with whom we could be friends. As we passed other missionaries in the hall, we looked for something that was unique about each of them, and when we saw something, we selected that missionary to be our project. That meant that we would do whatever it took to become his friend. We tried to find a new person each day.

The first person that we chose was Quincy Edwards from Las Vegas, Nevada. We selected him because he was a strong, athletic-looking guy. He looked like a warrior, and we nicknamed him "Iron Mike" after we found out that he had played college football. I walked up to him one day and just started talking to him. Our group became friends with him, and we sat with him when attending large group meetings, which were usually held on Sunday nights. My friendship with Quincy would change the course of my life in the greatest way possible. But I'll get to that later.

We got to know many good people in the MTC because we reached out to them and made the effort to get to know them. We gave all of our projects nicknames. Elder Galbraith was "Gingerbread Man," and Elder Watkins, who was from North Carolina, was "The Walker." It made a huge difference for my group and me to stop worrying about how hard it was to learn Chinese by focusing on others in the MTC instead of on ourselves. Instead of being homesick, we started enjoying new relationships. The goal was the same with all of them—we wanted to make them smile and we did what we could so that they would have a great day. We knew how hard it was to begin a mission, and we knew that most of the guys in there were probably feeling the same way we did.

Within a very short time, our group was saying hello to just about everyone in the MTC.

The other missionaries in my group were incredible guys who each had an impact on my life for the better. They were:

Brian Allred (Seattle, WA)
Timothy Davis (Salt Lake City, UT)
Cody Fowler (Grace, ID)
Don Hill (Richfield, UT)
Rob Lamb (American Fork, UT)
Damon MacDonald (Redmond, WA)
Jeff Nielsen (Richfield, UT)
Chad Pettingill (Kaysville, UT)

We stayed in the MTC from October 24 until December 27. So we were there through Halloween, Thanksgiving, and Christmas. It was actually the best holiday season of my life. I started learning the true meaning of Thanksgiving and Christmas. I felt a deeper love for my Savior and a much greater appreciation for what He has done for every single person who has ever lived. My desire to share His gospel with the people in Taiwan grew every day that I was in the MTC. As an MTC group, we recognized the greatness of others, and they blessed our lives through their goodness.

I was also gaining the confidence to speak and pray in Chinese. Even though it was limited, my vocabulary was growing. I was comfortable with the sentence structure and was progressing quickly. I couldn't wait to get to Taiwan and speak to people for real.

CHAPTER 7

HELLO, TAIWAN

The other missionaries and I said good-bye to our families again at the airport in Salt Lake City. We had gained two months' worth of training and instruction, but it seemed more like a year's worth. Before walking through the jetway and onto the plane, I tearfully told my parents how much I loved them and that I would try my hardest to make them proud. Then we boarded the flight and headed for the Far East. We had a layover in Portland and then a long leg to Seoul, Korea. It seemed like we were chasing the sun and its sunset for hours.

When we finally landed in Korea, night had already fallen. The air was thick and muggy. The world outside the windows of the airport looked very different. Giant fluorescent signs glowed in the humid air. Their writing was unfamiliar. After a short stop, we boarded our final plane for Taiwan. We arrived a few hours later at the Taipei International Airport.

I was anxious to meet President Kent Watson, who I had heard about from my Uncle Bill. President Watson was there with his wife, Connie, to meet us. He was tall, wearing glasses similar to mine. She was much shorter than he and very friendly. Her

Imitating the dragon's face during Taiwan's famous dragon boat races in Kaohsiung, summer 1991.

smile reminded me of my mom's. She hugged each of us as though we were her own kids and said they were excited to meet us.

They were accompanied by three missionaries who were the assistants to the president. Their enthusiasm was contagious. They told us how much we were going to love Taiwan and enjoy serving as missionaries. They looked sharp and bright. If they were any indication of how fun it was to live and serve in Taiwan, I was all for it.

We all fell asleep during the three-hour ride south to the mission home in Taichung. As soon as we arrived, we all crawled into bunk beds and crashed. The time change had us all mixed up and tired. The mission home was an actual home where the Watsons lived with their family. They had some extra rooms equipped with bunk beds for missionaries who would be coming and going. Next door to the mission home on one side was a small office building that had offices for the president and the half a dozen missionaries who helped him run the office. On the other side of the mission home was a Church building where Sunday meetings were held and where missionaries could teach people during the week. The compound was located in the middle of a very busy city full of more people than I had ever seen in one place before.

When we woke up in the morning, we had our interviews one by one with President Watson in his office. It was a lot of fun getting to know him. He let me know during that first interview together what it would take for me to be a successful missionary.

Number one was to write my mom and dad every week and share the mission experience, including everything I was learning, and let them know how much I loved them and how grateful I was to be in Taiwan as a missionary.

Number two was to memorize the six discussions and pass them off to one of the older missionaries. If I was unable to speak the language, it would be very difficult to share Christianity with the Chinese people. Learning the discussions was the best way to start speaking and understanding the language.

When our interviews were finished, we were taken by the assistants to the mission president on a brief tour of the area. We boarded the van and headed south for the city of Chang Hua, which was about thirty minutes away. We went down there to visit a Chinese culture center and also to practice our MTC Mandarin on the visitors at the center. Among other things at the culture center was a statue of Buddha the size of a four-story building. As we were getting close to the culture center, we were taken aback by the waves of scooters that flooded the streets. It seemed as though there was no end to them. They fought for space on the roads with cars, trucks, taxis, and bicycles. They filled every available space when they stopped at traffic lights. They were everywhere.

Our van pulled alongside a traffic accident at a stoplight on a busy corner in the middle of the city of Chang Hua. There was a crowd of people gathered around something. When we got closer, we could see that it was a person who had just been hit on one of the scooters. It was a young woman wearing the clean uniform of a salesperson in one of their shopping malls who had been struck and killed by a truck. It was a gruesome and unsettling sight.

As our van slowly inched by where she was lying in the road, we passed within a few feet of her. It appeared that she had hit her head and had died instantly. There was a lot of blood running down the street, and her scooter was still tipped over on the ground right next to her body. The driver of the truck was there and the police had yet to show up.

We were in shock. We couldn't believe what we were seeing. We were already in the beginning stages of culture shock and now we were suffering traumatic shock. I wondered if we were going to be safe riding our bikes on the streets since that would be our mode of transportation for the next two years. Would we make it home? Those were my thoughts.

After spending a couple of hours at the culture center, we piled back into the van and headed back to the mission office. As we neared the accident site, we noticed there was still a small crowd of people standing on the corner. We figured they must be talking about the accident. But when we got closer, we noticed the girl was still lying in the street.

The closer we got the more disturbing the scene became. Next to her body were smoldering piles of paper money and incense. The blood had dried but it was still visible in the roadway. We were in disbelief. We couldn't figure out why she was still there. Why hadn't she been taken to a hospital? It was confusing and frightening.

This was my first experience in a culture different from that of Orem, Utah. I realize now that it was also my first wrestle with *ethnocentrism,* a mindset that plagues many missionaries in the early part of their missions. The reason she was left in the road for so long was because, in certain Asian cultures, people believe the spirit is still present for a time after someone dies, and moving the body too soon may affect a person's transition into the afterlife. It was an unsettling thing to see, but it was also a strong reminder of the need to drive with caution while I was there so that it wouldn't happen to me. What a way to spend the first day.

New missionaries were called "greenies." Greenies were known to have great enthusiasm for the work. They were also thought to be too young, too inexperienced, and too naïve to know how difficult it was to be a missionary. It was the general perception that after the difficulty of the job settled in, the greenie enthusiasm would slowly wear away. But that process didn't sound too cool to me. I thought it would be great to keep the spirit of a greenie and combine it with the wisdom of an experienced missionary. I had kept the colored green dot that was put on my suit lapel the first day of the MTC, and I stuck it on the back of my plastic missionary badge as a reminder to keep the greenie spirit alive.

The next day, we were invited to go on exchanges with other missionaries who were serving in the city of Taichung. I was paired with Elder Todd Barber from Oregon. As we were crossing the street to find some people to teach, a bird decided that I was a good target. On my first full day in Taiwan, a bird dropped a little bomb directly on my left shoulder. I looked at that mess on my new suit and just started laughing. I was still fresh from the hospital with my dad, and I knew what was a big deal and what wasn't.

That night we attended a meeting in the mission home where we were assigned our new companions. Companionships generally lasted for a month or two, and your first mission companion was called a trainer. He was the most important companion of your mission. My new companion/trainer was Paul Mauerman, a lacrosse player from Columbia, Maryland. He looked like a cool guy, and he had a lot of energy. He smiled and laughed easily. It didn't appear that he had lost any of his greenie spirit.

We were sent to the city of Yuan Lin, where he was already living. It was a small town by Taiwan standards, but it looked like New York City to me. Elder Mauerman turned out to be one of the most incredible guys I've ever met. He had been in Taiwan for a year, and he could speak the language very well. I quickly learned why. He woke up at five o'clock every morning and studied as though his life depended on it. He had a thirst for knowledge that I had never seen before. He attacked the language as hard as my dad had attacked his recovery and rehab. Elder Mauerman had been the valedictorian of his high school graduating class, and it seemed like he did everything at a very high level. He could not have been a better person, companion, or missionary.

He was never afraid to teach me the lessons that I needed to learn. His goal was to turn me into a good missionary, and he was relentless. I started to feel the same feelings I felt when I entered the MTC. Two years seemed like forever; I wondered if I would ever make it home. Instead of being full of confidence, I was homesick. One morning, when I was wallowing in self-pity, he walked into our room and told me to put away all of the pictures of my family and friends that I had been flipping through. He told me that I was just punishing myself by staring at them. I could look at them later, but it was time to get to work, and it was impossible to work if I was homesick all day. Man, was that great advice! I also started waking up early to get a jump on the day. I was surprised how much I could get accomplished by doing that. I think Paul Mauerman earned a special spot in heaven for his diligence in teaching me the right way to serve others as a missionary.

Taiwan is an island three hundred miles long and eighty-nine miles wide. It is south of Japan, north of the Philippines, and east of the southeastern part of China. Taiwan is mostly mountainous

My trainer, Paul Mauerman; a local member of the Church;
and me on the roof of our church in Yuan Lin, Taiwan.

on the east and has gently sloping plains on the west. Its huge
population of twenty-three million people is concentrated mostly
on the western plains.

Taiwan was a lot different from Orem, Utah. There were so
many people that I just couldn't comprehend it. Everywhere we
went, it was as though a football game had just ended and people
were pouring out into the streets. It was like that all the time.
How could there be that many people in one place, I wondered. I
was also taken aback by the distinct odors of the island. It was a
blend of the smell of Chinese food cooking; exhaust from the
thousands of scooters, buses, and cars; and the effluent that ran in
open ditches along the streets.

The food tasted nothing like the Panda Express back home. It
took me two weeks before I started to like the food. The greatest

lesson that I learned during those two weeks (when I cried myself to sleep because of homesickness, culture shock, and food that for me was drastically different) was to never, ever, ever complain about my mom's food as long as I lived. I made a promise to myself that I would learn to eat food that was prepared by my mom or anyone else with a smile on my face, no matter what it tasted like. I realized just how selfish and spoiled I had been. Complaining about food that someone else had taken the time and means to prepare was a clear sign of my immaturity. The adjustment was prying open areas of my mind and personality that I was not aware even existed. I discovered closets of selfishness in my life that I needed to open up and clean out. My house was in need of a major cleaning and renovation.

The first thing I noticed about the Chinese people was the courteous way they treated me. I could barely speak their language, but they were more than tolerant of me even while struggling to understand what I was saying. The people who had absolutely no interest in talking with me about religion were still incredibly respectful and patient. It was a great mirror for me. Was I that patient and kind with others? Did I give others the same respect that the Taiwanese were showing me? I had so much to learn.

I was so far away from home, but I felt closer to my parents and family than ever before. My heart was ready to burst because it was so full of gratitude for my parents. For the first time in my life, I was really starting to understand the kinds of sacrifices they had made while raising my brothers and me. I thought about all of the ball games they had attended, the meals they had prepared, the family vacations we had gone on, the many opportunities they had given me. My side of the ledger started looking pretty bare.

The fastest and cheapest way to get around the streets of Taiwan was on a bike. I purchased a bike the first day. It was a low-end mountain bike that would last the entire two years unless it was stolen. To prevent its premature disappearance, I spray-painted it the most hideous colors possible. It looked worse than a clown bike in a parade. It would have taken pure desperation mixed with color-blindness for a person to want to steal that bike.

We made friends with the little family that ran the bike shop. They were a young couple with a two-year-old boy. We gave him a nickname because he was so fun to see each time we stopped by their store. We called him "Meat" because he was as thick as a brick. He looked like a linebacker in the making. There was nothing small or dainty about him. He was huge and strong, and when he grabbed hold of us it felt like a little bear cub was attached to us. At the same time, he had the most cheerful disposition. He would run up to us and shout, "Ni hao," which means, "How are you?" But he would say it with so much enthusiasm that it sounded like a donkey braying, "Hee-haw!" Every time he said it, we cracked up laughing. Boy, did I have a long way to go before I understood their language.

We would pick him up and his legs would keep running in the air. If we picked him up facing us, he would run his feet right up our white shirts. The only problem with that was that he ran around his parents' bike shop all day without any shoes on. His feet were always black, and we quickly learned to pick him up with his feet pointing away from our shirts. Man, we loved that little guy.

One day, not long after meeting this little family, we stopped in to see them. The parents had the saddest and most mournful looks on their faces. Something else was different—their little boy was not there to greet us. That was the first time that he hadn't come running out to jump on us. When we asked them where he was, they started crying. The father held up his index finger like he was saying number one. Then he slowly curled his finger into the rest of his hand making a fist. I had only been on the island for a few weeks, but I knew that what he was making was the sign for death.

Elder Mauerman and I looked at each other and wondered if we were getting the right message. We asked again where he was. The parents only continued to cry. There was a neighbor lady who used to join in our conversations when we would stop by. She heard us talking and knew that we were confused and obviously not understanding the parents' sad message. After we asked the second time for our little friend, she walked into the store and answered our question. She said coldly and matter-of-factly, with very little facial expression whatsoever, that he was dead.

We couldn't believe it. What had happened and how had he died? She told us that a few days before he died there was a funeral procession that passed in front of their store. The funeral processions in Taiwan had hired mourners who would weep, sing, and wail as they walked down the street following a hearse carrying the body. Special white, yellow, and blue clothes were worn by those in the funeral procession. Some mourners wore hoods over their heads. Believing they would scare off ghosts, people would throw firecrackers on the ground. Loud music would be played on gongs and cymbals. It was a very noisy event.

When this funeral procession passed in front of the bike shop, our little friend got so excited that it startled his parents. Even after the procession went farther down the street and then finally disappeared around the corner, the boy continued to dance around and laugh. The parents couldn't figure it out. They said that the next day, without warning, their little boy turned blue in the face and suddenly died.

It was hard to comprehend what we had just heard. He was our little buddy. How was such a tragedy possible? It had happened so quickly and seemed to have no cause.

We tried to tell the parents we were sorry for their loss. We loved that little boy. The parents could not be consoled. They were

My favorite little buddy, "Meat," and me. He passed away shortly after this picture was taken. I still miss his dirty feet.

heartbroken. I did not understand any of their customs relative to grieving for the dead, but I wanted them to know how much joy their little guy had brought into my life, especially since the first couple of weeks in Taiwan had been so difficult for me. If I was homesick, nothing made me feel better than to see that little kid, have him dirty up my shirt with his feet, and say, "Ni hao!" with all the energy and emotion that he had. I was beginning to really love the people of Taiwan. The more I loved them, the less homesick I felt.

That couple was never the same after that tragic event. We stopped by a few more times, but it seemed as though life was drained right out them. We tried to let them know that we cared about them, but we were met with little response. They clung to the sadness of their child's passing and would not engage in any happiness. I was only in that city for two months, but I never again saw them smile. I was sad to lose their friendship, and I have carried their memory in my heart ever since. I hope they have found happiness in their lives. I would love to see them smile again.

In our mission we changed companions every month or two. We would also change locations every few months as well. I was with Paul Mauerman for only two months and had many other companions after him. Each of them taught me something I needed to know about serving other people. It was not always easy, spending uninterrupted time with each other, and sometimes we had our differences, but these guys each had a major, positive impact on my life. What a blessing they were to me. Here is a list of the fifteen companions I had and where we served together:

Brian Allred, Seattle, WA, MTC
Paul Mauerman, Columbia, MD, Yuan Lin
Travis Christensen, Albuquerque, NM, Tainan
Curtis Hawkins, Salt Lake City, UT, Kaohsiung
Steve Decker, Bountiful, UT, Kaohsiung
Ken Bown, Sandy, UT, Kaohsiung
Duane Andersen, Laie, HI, Feng Yuan
Jean-Michele Wu, Taiwan/France/Canada, Feng Yuan
Russell Stagg, Kearns, UT, Feng Yuan
Jason Smith, Bountiful, UT, Taichung
Christian Nilson, Ogden, UT, Taichung
Lance Jorgensen, Kennewick, WA, Taichung
Rob Lamb, American Fork, UT, Taichung
Cody Fowler, Grace, ID, Taichung
Larry Harmer, Holladay, UT, Taichung

CHAPTER 8

LARRY, ROB, AND PRESIDENT WATSON

Two of the missionaries who I became closest to and learned the most from were Rob Lamb and Larry Harmer. The three of us served in the same city of Kaohsiung for five months. We were not companions at the time, but we worked together nearly every day. While getting to know each other better they became like family to me. I was still missing my four brothers back home in America, but the void was filled with my new friends who became my brothers and were an addition to my family.

I had always participated in team sports while growing up. I thought there were many lessons to be learned in playing on a team, including selflessness, teamwork, team chemistry, sacrifice, and many more. I could see where those things were essential in missionary work. We were a long way from home, and we had to trust each other and work hard to accomplish any of our goals. I started to get a glimpse of what soldiers must feel when they are far from home and have to rely on each other for survival. The idea of being a band of brothers started to make a lot more sense. I would have never understood that concept if I had not left the comfort zone of my home and served a mission.

Rob taught me so much about patriotism, loyalty, and how to love and search the scriptures. He loved history, especially the history of America. He had a horse back home that he named Liberty. As he told me stories about Abraham Lincoln and Thomas Jefferson, I started to appreciate more than ever the history of the United States. He gave history a heartbeat. I could feel it when he talked about it. He loved words and brought the scriptures to life when he shared his favorite passages.

Loyalty was the hallmark of Rob's life. He was loyal to his parents, and he demonstrated that by the respectful way he talked about them. His mom and dad meant everything to him. They were never far from his heart. The Lambs had ten kids, and Rob worked with his dad in their family rental business. They spent hours attending ball games together. He learned how to work from his parents, and he was a bulldog when it came to hard work. He had four brothers and five sisters. Rob had gone to school at American Fork High, where he had been the quarterback on the football team, point guard on the basketball team, and first baseman on the baseball team. His fair skin was just fine at home in Utah, but in the hot and humid conditions of Taiwan, he developed skin rashes that would have sidelined a normal person. They never slowed him down, and he just continued to outwork every one of us missionaries.

Rob's greatest gift was sharing his love for the scriptures. If a passage struck him as true or great or inspiring, he would get so excited. He was anxious to talk about why it made an impact on him, what he gained from it, and why it was worthy of a second look when ample time was available. A lot of times, we opened the scriptures up right then and he would show me what he was talking about. Other times, I would write the reference down and look it up and study it later.

There were some white benches on the Church grounds in Kaohsiung that missionaries would sit on while waiting for

Elder Rob Lamb, one of my favorite local guys, Hank (Liu Han Chi), and me in Kaohsiung, Taiwan.

appointments to show up. Some of the time sitting on those benches would be spent studying the language—either the discussions, the vocabulary list, or the Chinese characters. Some of the time was spent getting to know other missionaries and the local members. And some of the time was spent listening to Elder Lamb expound the scriptures. I never tired of listening to his commentary and insights. Thanks to Rob Lamb for teaching me the power of the scriptures and inspiring me to love, appreciate, and apply them in my life.

Larry Harmer grew up in a big family in Salt Lake City and went to school at Olympus High School, where he was an All-American defensive lineman. He had a scholarship to play at BYU when he returned home.

Rob and Larry both loved life. They loved their families with all their hearts. They made everyone around them better because of their strong, positive personalities and their humility, traits that most missionaries had but that were especially evident in these two guys.

Larry was a big guy and was strong enough that he could have bullied people into liking him or listening to him. But he used his strength and size like a big teddy bear. To illustrate his personality and quick wit, he visited Disney World one year with his family when he was about thirteen years old. At closing time, he and the thousands of visitors all headed for the exits. He and his sister ran ahead of his family a little bit. Once they realized they were by themselves, they turned around and headed back to find the others.

Larry was running outside the mass of exiting people, balanced on the curbing that held the flowers and plants. When he passed a tough-guy high-school kid wearing his letterman jacket and trying to impress his friends, the bully leaned into Larry and gave him a hard shoulder that stopped him in his tracks and knocked the wind out of him. In pain, Larry gasped, "Geez!"

The bully swelled up like a toad and, while sticking out his chest far enough to fall forward, he demanded in his most sinister voice to know what Larry had just said to him. Larry was big for thirteen, but not as big as these guys. He also needed to protect his sister. As the older boy got in Larry's face and tried to intimidate him further, Larry used his hands to simulate sign language and while doing it said in a muffled and only partially understandable voice, "I'm sorry I said 'Geez.'"

The bully was disarmed and disrobed in front of his peers. They immediately started slugging him on the shoulder and chastising him for picking on a little deaf guy. Larry saved the day. The school kids in their letterman jackets walked away feeling very small.

Larry's outgoing personality charmed the Chinese people. They loved being around him. They also recognized his generous behavior. Elder Harmer had a companion named Aaron Battraw, who developed a knee problem. Elder Battraw's condition progressively got worse until he could no longer ride his bike. Larry did not even hesitate to help his companion. He had Elder Battraw sit on the bike rack that all the missionaries had installed so we could carry luggage when we moved or carry other missionary supplies. Week after week, Elder Harmer pedaled Elder Battraw around the city as they met their missionary obligations. They became a familiar sight as they drove through the streets all day. We couldn't go anywhere without people asking about the big foreigner who was carrying the other foreigner on the back of his bike.

It gave us a great way to start conversations with people but also gave me a great role model of service to others. Not only did Larry transport Aaron on his bike, but soon Aaron's legs were so bad that he could not walk the stairs in their apartment to the second floor. Larry willingly carried Aaron on his back up the stairs several times each day. What an example he provided us and the people of that city.

Whenever he could, Larry would talk to me about playing football at BYU. He was excited to play as soon as he got home. He did not want to be without friends, though, and he routinely asked me what I thought about walking on. After talking to him and getting to know him better and better, I started to think that there might really be a possibility for me to do just that.

My brother Mike was still playing at the U of U, where I had thought about playing ball, but I didn't know anything about his new coach, Ron McBride. Jim Fassel had been the coach but had been fired. Before my mission, Coach Fassel had encouraged me to walk on when I returned. Since he was not the coach anymore, my desire to go to the U of U disappeared. My plan was to attend school at BYU and become a doctor, but Larry got me fired up about the remote chance of joining him on the football team at the Y. My brother Dave had walked on at BYU, and I knew the kind of commitment and determination it would take. I also knew that I would be starting lower than the lowest guy on the team. The thought of playing with Larry started to feel pretty good, though. It might be the hardest thing in my world, but so what? It was awesome just thinking about it.

When I played football as a junior in high school I was 6' and 140 pounds, not quite NFL tight-end material. As a senior I shot up like a bamboo shoot. I stood 6'4" and weighed 175 pounds—tall but skinnier than a flagpole. If I turned sideways my quarterback couldn't see me. I graduated when I was seventeen, and by the time I turned nineteen, after my Dad had his stroke, I was 6'5" and weighed 195. I was still in the middle of my growth spurt while serving in Taiwan.

That meant that I was eating like a horse. Well, maybe two horses. One of the most enjoyable moments for me as a missionary was mealtimes. We always ate our meals on the streets with the locals, either from food vendors or in family dining halls. We found a little cafeteria that made a nice meal of breaded pork or breaded chicken with some vegetables and rice. I would ask them to pile my rice as high as they could. They would put an extra scoop of rice on my plate and ask if I would be able to eat it all. I would chuckle because it wasn't very much food to me, and then I would ask them to pile it higher. They would hesitantly put on another scoop and ask me if I could really eat it all. Again, I would ask them to pile it higher. It would often get to the point where they would say that the meal would be free if I could really finish the whole plate. Was I called to the right place or what? I was in heaven when they told me that. I never had a problem finishing my meals in Taiwan.

I grew up in a family with five boys, and if I didn't eat quickly, that meant I didn't get to have seconds. So I was conditioned to eating fast. I could pound down a whole plate of rice in minutes. It was a shocker to my Chinese friends. My appetite served several great purposes. Number one, it made me something of a novelty. Some of my favorite people in each city where I lived were the people who owned and operated food establishments. Number two, it also helped me deal with my hunger. I could consume massive amounts of food, almost as fast as they could place it in front of me. After working hard as a missionary all day, and after riding my bike all over the island, I had an insatiable appetite. And number three, since people were entertained by watching me eat, my meals in some instances were donated.

After the first two weeks of crying about the food, I had learned to love it.

The seven months that I spent in Kaohsiung were a real turning point in my life. Without Larry Harmer pumping me up to play football at BYU when I got home, I never would have thought to walk on. When he started talking about how fun it would be to train together, play together, and win the national championship together, I could feel it all the way down to my bones.

Missionaries were encouraged to exercise daily to stay fit. Biking several miles every day took care of that. But I always did my own push-ups and jumps each morning. I would do a hundred push-ups and a thousand jumps. If I didn't have a jump rope, I would just jump up and down.

We had one day off a week. It was called P-day, or preparation day. That was when we did all of our shopping for the week, wrote our letters home, cleaned the apartment, washed our clothes, and usually played a little basketball. I was a high jumper in high school so I could jump pretty well. People in Taiwan liked basketball, and we made a lot of friends on the basketball court. The Chinese especially loved to see us foreign guys dunk the ball. I was able to dunk even in my street shoes and missionary attire, and it turned out to be a great conversation starter. After a dunk or two, people were very willing and interested to talk with us. Playing also helped me keep some quickness and spring in my legs.

Early in my mission, I was amazed at the ability of my

companions to speak Chinese. It took enormous dedication to learn that difficult language. It was cool to see the people who, previous to their being called to serve in Taiwan, had no knowledge of Chinese, but within a few weeks could speak it fairly fluently. I witnessed the true gift of tongues as missionaries from all different backgrounds with many different native languages learned to speak one of the hardest languages on the planet.

We worked hard to memorize the six discussions, which were lengthy and included a very extensive vocabulary. It was a massive amount of information that needed to be memorized, and we were required to pass them off to the more seasoned missionaries.

I passed off discussions one through three with my district leader, Elder Moulton, in just over a month. The language was so foreign that while studying I would sometimes feel as though my brain had turned to mush. Learning it demanded total concentration. It was hard, very hard, but it was also great. It took me another month or so to pass off the fourth through sixth discussions. After reviewing all of them, I was able to ace the final. I couldn't have been happier. It was a great day in my life.

In addition to mastering the discussions, we were expected to memorize a list of a thousand useful Chinese terms. So there was always something to study. In fact, President Watson liked to say that studying Chinese was a lifetime endeavor. And we all knew that if we didn't become proficient in the language, we would really never be effective missionaries.

I was totally impressed by President Watson. He had a great influence on me and altered the course of my life in many ways. Before he came to Taiwan he was a partner with the accounting firm Price Waterhouse in Salt Lake City. When he received his mission call he knew it would be difficult to be gone three years and then reassume his position in the company. Even though he was putting his career on the line, he answered the call and served with all of his heart, might, mind, and strength.

Visiting the wonderful Lu family with Elder Lance Jorgensen in Taichung, Taiwan.

It was obvious that he loved his missionaries. He showered us with praise when we worked hard and constantly reminded us that we were there to serve the Chinese people any way we could. He taught us to love them as we did our own families. When our service and dedication lagged, he was quick to encourage us to pick up our pace, and when we acted more like nineteen-year-old kids than missionaries, he reminded us that trust was something we had to earn.

In leading us, he could be as bold as Vince Lombardi, but he led us in a way that was inspiring and endearing by simply asking us if we were giving our best effort. Knowing his level of dedication gave him tremendous credibility when he taught us to work diligently and to be obedient to the mission rules.

The climate in Taiwan is hot and humid most of the year. Actually, it isn't enough to say *hot*. I often felt as though the heat would melt the freckles right off my face. After working all morning and then eating lunch, it was not out of the ordinary to get extraordinarily tired in the afternoon. But President Watson wanted us to work hard *all day.* To motivate us, he would often say, "When it starts to get too hot for missionaries in other missions, that's when it starts to get just right for a Taiwan Taichung missionary." I loved that concept, and it settled into my heart. He threw down the gauntlet in front of us and challenged us to *work.*

Later, while playing football, I thought about him every time training camp rolled around. When it was hot and miserable, I thought of him and his mandate to outwork anyone. When things were tough, I remembered how hard I had worked in Taiwan, and it gave me the reason and the will to keep pushing. The work ethic he taught me made it nearly impossible to quit.

He also taught me something about dealing with critics. After I had been in Taiwan for seven months, President Watson assigned Larry Harmer and me to speak in our mission conference. Our assigned theme was Acts 3:6, where Peter and John heal a man who had been lame since his birth. The verse reads: "Then Peter said, Silver and gold have I none; but such as I have give I thee: In the name of Jesus Christ of Nazareth rise up and walk."

Larry's topic was "*Walk* with Your Companion," and he was to suggest ways companions could work in closer harmony. We were nineteen years old, and being together 24/7 for several weeks at a time sometimes put a strain on the relationship. Some guys became best friends, but sometimes it was a challenge to work well together. That was life, and it was a great learning experience.

My topic was "*Rise* Up with Enthusiasm." I tried to imagine how it would feel if I had been lame since birth and were miraculously healed. It had only been a few months since I'd watched my dad experience a similar miraculous healing, and I remembered how I'd felt. Our joy and relief was the same as the man's who was healed: "And he leaping up stood, and walked, and entered with them into the temple, walking, and leaping, and praising God."

In my talk I tried to convey that feeling of walking, leaping, and praising God. I had just witnessed my dad rise up and walk. I had that feeling and it was still fresh in my heart. I spoke with energy and enthusiasm because I could *feel* it.

A couple weeks later, President Watson was back in the city of Kaoshiung where I was serving. We had our regular interviews and then went out for lunch. While on our way to Church's Fried Chicken, he told me that a missionary had been critical of my talk, suggesting that I had been "sucking up" to the mission president. I was certainly trying to do my best, but I didn't equate that with sucking up. I wondered what President Watson thought, and so I asked him in the car.

He said he told the missionary that it was his idea to have me speak on the subject of enthusiasm. And then he recited to that missionary a quote from Teddy Roosevelt. As he drove the car, he recited it again for me and my companion, Ken Bown. The quote has been one of my favorites ever since. Here is what he said:

> It is not the critic who counts; not the man who points out how the strong man stumbles, or where the doer of deeds could have done them better. The credit belongs to the man who is actually in the arena, whose face is marred by dust and sweat and blood; who strives valiantly; who errs, who comes up short again and again, because there is no effort without error or shortcoming; but who does actually strive to do the deeds; who knows great enthusiasms, the great devotions; who spends himself in a worthy cause; who at the best, knows in the end the triumph of high achievement, and who at the worst, if he fails, at least fails while daring greatly, so that his place shall never be with those cold and timid souls who neither know victory nor defeat.[4]

I sat in the car, completely stunned. I was amazed that he could quote something that long from memory. But it was more than that.

97

He delivered it with such power. President Watson demonstrated then and many times thereafter that he was a fighter and a doer, and he taught us to be prepared for the slings and arrows we would confront, not only in the mission field but in the rest of our lives. He inspired us. He was a man we were willing to follow. He was greatness.

President Watson had one particular message that he made sure we understood. It was that we were to avoid being ethnocentric in the way we lived in Taiwan. He taught us that we would do great harm to the people if we tried to tell them that the way we did things back home was superior to the way they were done in Taiwan. He wanted us to be grateful for the wonderful people of Taiwan and to show that in how we talked, acted, and served them. He let us know that it would break his heart if we acted cocky or arrogant in any way. He encouraged us to pattern our lives after Jesus Christ and to try to emulate Him in every way. I loved each interview that I had with him because he reassured me that he knew the work was hard, but he motivated me to step it up and work even harder.

I also looked forward to his talks at zone conferences, where he often quoted inspirational and motivational poems. One of my favorites was "Good Timber," by Douglas Malloch.

> *The tree that never had to fight*
> *For sun and sky and air and light,*
> *But stood out in the open plain*
> *And always got its share of rain,*
> *Never became a forest king*
> *But lived and died a scrubby thing.*
>
> *The man who never had to toil*
> *To gain and farm his patch of soil,*
> *Who never had to win his share*
> *Of sun and sky and light and air,*
> *Never became a manly man*
> *But lived and died as he began.*

*Kent Watson, Michele, and Connie Watson at my induction
to the BYU Athletic Hall of Fame, fall 2007.*

Good timber does not grow with ease:
The stronger wind, the stronger trees;
The farther sky, the greater length;
The more the storm, the more the strength.
By sun and cold, by rain and snow,
In trees and men good timbers grow.

Where thickest lies the forest growth,
We find the patriarchs of both.
And they hold counsel with the stars
Whose broken branches show the scars
Of many winds and much of strife.
This is the common law of life.[5]

President Watson became a second father to me. I loved him with my whole heart. I couldn't think of any better way to start my adult life than to serve with him in Taiwan and learn from his example how to treat others. He was there to shape me through the two years in my life where I grew the most. I never would have been able to play football in college or in the NFL if it weren't for serving a mission and serving with President Watson. He taught me how to work hard and how to work smart.

He told us about growing up in Cedar City, Utah, where his dad ran Cedar Home Furnishings. As a young boy, President Watson was assigned the duty of sweeping up the store at the end of the day. After he was finished, he would report to his dad, who would ask him if he had done a "Cedar Home Furnishings" job. When he answered yes, his dad would walk around the place to see if he had. If he could have done better, his father would point out the deficiency. Sometimes it took young Kent two or three extra times to get it right. It wasn't called a "Cedar Home Furnishings" job until it was done right.

As missionaries, we got the message. We needed to give the work all we had and we needed to do it right. That was the standard. And when President Watson asked us if we were doing a "Cedar Home Furnishings" job, we understood exactly what that meant.

After I had served with him for nearly two years, his three-year term as mission president came to an end. He left us with a final message and a set of fifteen things to do:

1. Increase your desire to be a missionary by expressing gratitude to the Lord.
2. Sell out. (Give it your all, and more!)
3. Be humble.
4. Do a Cedar Home Furnishings job.
5. Remember, all you ever need to know to

succeed in life you will learn here on your
mission.

6. Magnify your calling by doing all that is
expected, and then some.

7. Live by every word that proceedeth forth from
the mouth of God.

8. Remember that when it is starting to get too
tough for missionaries in other missions, that is
when it is getting just right for a Taiwan
Taichung missionary.

9. Be full of love towards everyone, especially your
companion.

10. Have the attitude that if something is going to
get done, I am going to be the one to do it.

11. Don't be content to get by with mediocre
language.

12. Shine your shoes every day.

13. Ethnocentricity of any kind must be
eliminated.

14. Don't be a grebe. (Lose your pride.)

15. Be obedient—if you love the Lord, keep His
commandments.

During our final mission-wide conference, he did something
else that impressed me. There was to be a slide show featuring all
the missionaries, the Chinese people, and President Watson's family. One thing he wanted included was a tribute to his wife,
Connie, who had been his companion in their service. He used
one of my favorite songs, the song that rocked my world after my
dad's stroke, Bette Midler's "Wind Beneath My Wings." It was
meant to show how grateful he was to his wife for her love, her
service, the way that she cared for all of the missionaries, and the
way that she had stood by him. That was a lesson in how to honor
your wife never to be forgotten.

And it was a well-deserved tribute. Sister Watson is a superb lady. She doesn't complain; it is not in her DNA. As a mission mother, she was a solid support and a supreme example. Since she would never toot her own horn, I will say that hundreds if not thousands of people have benefited from her powerful example of humility, faith, kindness, dedication, and love.

It is impossible to exaggerate the impact Kent and Connie Watson had on me, my outlook on life, the way I view hard work, and the values I hold. They are greatness personified.

CHAPTER 9

"IF IT'S TO BE, IT'S UP TO ME"

One of the aspects of a mission that helped me grow up was moving from city to city and changing companions regularly. It began in the MTC, and I always found it a challenge. It was a difficult transition to go from being an ordinary college student to a missionary with a companion whom I was required to be with 24/7.

I found that I got homesick every time I changed companions or moved to a new city. That surprised me the first couple of times. I figured once I got adjusted to the MTC that I would be a man. But the process was only beginning. I had so much to learn. When I left America and landed in a foreign land with a foreign culture, the process started all over again. After two months in an apartment with Paul Mauerman, my good friend Brian Foutz from Arizona, and Elder Moulton, I was transferred a couple of hours south to the city of Tainan to be a companion with Travis Christensen from New Mexico. That pattern was repeated over and over again, and each time the feeling of homesickness, the same feeling that I had when I entered the MTC, returned.

Those feelings didn't last long. As soon as I got involved in the new area, with new people and my new companion, I was okay. I learned that when my focus went from me to others that I didn't feel lonely or homesick. I would have many more chances to understand this process.

There were twenty-four missionaries working in the city of Tainan. After working with Travis Christensen for two months, I was transferred another hour farther south to the huge port city of Kaohsiung, where I would stay for seven months. I was assigned to work with Curtis Hawkins for two months, Steve Decker for three months, and Ken Bown for two months. I fell in love with Kaohsiung and the people there.

Kaohsiung is located on the southern end of Taiwan. It seemed like each mile farther south toward the equator meant another degree hotter. If Tainan was hot, Kaohsiung was boiling. I was there in the summer, and it was the hottest summer of my life. Some days it felt as though I was living on the surface of the sun.

The next stop was Feng Yuan, which was the most northern city in our mission. It was a beautiful city tucked up against the green mountains in the middle of the island. I came to love it, but I again went through the same initial feelings of loneliness and homesickness.

I served there with Duane Andersen from Hawaii and Jean-Michele Wu, who was born in Taiwan, lived in France until he was three, and then grew up in Canada. I also served there with Russell Stagg from Utah. Then it was another transfer to the central city of Taichung with Jason Smith, Christian Nilson, and Lance Jorgensen.

I had those same feelings of disorientation when I walked on to the BYU football team and when I moved to Philadelphia to play for the Eagles. I had them when I moved to St. Louis and played for the Rams and when I moved back to Philly to rejoin the Eagles. But I gained perspective through each move. I learned that the anxiety wasn't permanent. I learned that the sooner I got to work the sooner the feelings would be replaced by confidence, excitement, and enthusiasm for the new challenges. What a gift to be able to learn those lessons as a missionary.

One afternoon in the first area of my mission, the whole zone I was in—all twenty-four missionaries—went on a service project to the small mountain city of Puli. It required an hour or so bus ride to get there. As we arrived in the city, the school kids were just getting out of class and were beginning to flood the streets. They seemed numberless. I don't think I had ever seen so many school kids at one time.

They were all wearing identical school uniforms, which made them appear to be even more numerous. I was in Taiwan to share God's love with the people of Taiwan, and in that instance I realized how small I was and how many people live on planet Earth. I was in a small remote village in the mountains of Taiwan, and there I was caught up in what seemed to be a countless multitude of kids walking down the street.

I wondered how it was possible that God loved each of us just the same. My own smallness was humbly acknowledged, maybe for the first time in my life. I was tiny compared to the earth, let alone the universe. The feeling I had was similar to the powerful sense of endlessness that one gets when looking out at a boundless ocean. I grew up hiking in the mountains, but never until then had I ever associated myself as just one tiny, miniscule tree surrounded by a forest of a billion trees. I started to glimpse eternity when I thought about God's love being total for every single one of us. Serving as a missionary gave me a precious perspective that I needed.

Each week we were required to give at least four hours of community service that had nothing to do with proselytizing or teaching the gospel. We could choose anything we wanted. We visited many orphanages during my time in Taiwan. I loved seeing the

*My good friend Elder Cody Fowler and me dressed as
Santa Claus in Taichung, Taiwan.*

kids smile and laugh, especially knowing they didn't have families
to go home to.

One Christmas, I borrowed a full Santa Claus suit from a big
American man who was living with his family and working in
Feng Yuan. I wore it while visiting an orphanage in Taichung. It
was so much fun. The missionaries gathered from a few cities and
we visited with the purpose of spreading some holiday cheer. The
kids loved it. They wanted us to stay forever and play with them.
For a little while, each child felt needed, included, cared for, and
remembered. Their smiles were the only rewards we wanted. We
considered that priceless. We left the orphanage wealthy in emotional currency.

The most fulfilling service that I participated in was serving
in a hospital of older stroke patients. We visited the hospital at
least once a week in Feng Yuan. We would routinely sing to them.

I didn't have the biggest repertoire of Chinese songs in my head, so my companions and I usually sang John Denver songs, such as "Grandma's Featherbed" or "Country Road" and also Christian hymns. The patients loved it. My companions and I danced and sang the "Hokie Pokie" with them, and the patients had a blast. Some of them would rock their wheelchairs back and forth with us, and we would take turns pushing them around as we "danced."

After visiting there several weeks in a row, I got to know some of the patients' families, and they expressed their gratitude to us for taking the time to befriend their loved ones and help them have a reason to smile. They thought it was unusual that a couple of foreigners would be willing and comfortable enough to hang out with stroke patients. I told them about my dad's experience, which gave them a better understanding of why I loved being with them. I wanted to be surrounded by their greatness.

My time in Feng Yuan provided an intense season of personal growth. I was surrounded by great companions who wanted to work hard. I was also surrounded by wonderful people in the community who opened my heart and filled it with their goodness. The stroke patients in particular left a deep impression on me. It would be easy to think that they had nothing to give; they were in wheelchairs and needed constant care just to sustain life. I had a perfect opportunity to reflect again on my parents and the love they had for me. I would spend one day a week with the stroke patients, and I grew to love them. After a few months, I knew all their names and they knew mine. I knew many of their family members, and we started to develop some strong friendships.

At this important time in my life, I was also inspired by the good words of President Gordon B. Hinckley, who was then a counselor in the First Presidency of The Church of Jesus Christ of Latter-day Saints. He would later become the President of the

*Popping a wheelie with my stroke patient friends in Feng Yuan, Taiwan.
What a memorable time of my life!*

Church, a position that he held with distinction for thirteen years until he passed away in 2008 at the age of ninty-seven.

I found a tape of one of his talks in our apartment. It was recorded in 1965 at BYU and was titled, "Caesar, Circus, or Christ?" As I listened to him speak about making Christ the central figure in our lives, I also made some decisions that would last forever. I decided that I never wanted to watch an R-rated movie. I never wanted to listen to music that was degrading instead of uplifting. In my journal entry for February 24, 1992, I wrote: "My goal and quest is to surround myself with greatness! Friends, thoughts, movies, books—you name it; only greatness will penetrate the walls of my heart!"

I had a stack of small white business cards that I used to write down any Chinese term that I did not understand. At the end of the day, I could go over the terms that I had written down. I wrote on one of those cards: "Surround Myself with Greatness!"

I made that decision when I still had eight months to serve in Taiwan, and I carried that card with me every day until I went home. For years after I got home, I still kept it in my wallet. The idea was that I wanted to gather a pile of great things around me. In my mind I could see that pile of greatness grow. And as it grew, it would eventually lift me up, and I would grow right along with it. "Surround Myself with Greatness" became a theme for my life.

I started to think about the powerful influence of friends, the effects of music, and the ability of movies and videos to shape our thoughts and feelings. Contemplating the power of these three things filled me with wonder and fright. I thought about the impact these three things had had on my life. I was grateful for the friends I had growing up. I was in awe of their patience with me and their kindness and friendship. I felt as though I were the luckiest guy in the world.

I thought not only of my friends but of their parents as well. They cared for me as much as my own parents did. I remembered the years before my mission when I ate about a million pounds of ham sandwiches over at Shawn Bandley's home. We lived in the same neighborhood and had been friends our whole lives. His mom, Greta, who had been so helpful to my family when my dad had his stroke, could make a meal out of anything in two seconds. She had a real gift for cooking, baking, and preparing food, and she opened her home and her kitchen to me and Shawn's other friends. She welcomed us. She cared for us. There was no way my parents could do everything. The only way for me to learn all the lessons of life was to draw from all the great people around me. I reflected on every kind deed she did for me and marveled at her generosity.

I thought of Bryan Rowley's parents and the considerate way they had always treated me. They were not a wealthy family and

Bryan's dad worked a few jobs to make ends meet. As a family, they rallied around Bryan, who was one of the best athletes to ever come out of Orem, Utah. After football games, when his body was bruised and hammered, his mom would care for him with a tenderness and a love that inspired me. She had a soft voice and a loving heart, and when she spoke about Bryan, I could feel how much she loved her son.

When Bryan and I were in junior high school, there was a period of time when we were painfully aware that we were not the popular kids in school. We were very ordinary and anonymous. As we wallowed in and resented our ordinariness, we one day referred to ourselves as "losers." Bryan's older sister, Natalie, heard what we said and reprimanded us. She told us that we were not losers, but that we were cool because of how we were living our lives. We were not into drugs, and she pointed out that some of the popular kids were and that they were going to pay an awful price for it. Bryan's whole family rallied and encouraged not only him, but all his friends, to hold our heads up high and be our best. His home was a safe and great place for me.

As my mind caught hold of this principle—surround myself with greatness—a flood of memories poured in. I remembered a time in high school when a girl told Greg Kennedy's mom, Sylvia, that I was swearing. The next time I was at Greg's house, his mom let me have it with both barrels. She told me she could not believe that I would use such language and that she was very disappointed in me. She said that she never again wanted to hear that I was using foul language and let me know that she did not think it was cool for one second. She hammered me for talking like a slob, and it caught me off guard. I had so much respect for her that I felt like a pile of garbage. And I looked back on that experience with total gratitude. I decided I wanted to be around people like that, and I felt a desire to be that kind of person.

I reflected on other great people in my life, from friends and teammates to coaches and teachers. I thought of great church leaders who had spent hours trying to teach me correct principles. I remembered one of the most influential men in my life, my high school football coach, Tom Rabb, who not only taught me football but many important lessons about life.

I recalled one day when I was in the weight room prior to my senior year. I had a disagreement with one of my teammates over a girl I liked and whom he wanted to take on a date. As we argued, I started acting tough, and it got to the point where we were almost ready to fight. Coach Rabb was observing us from the other side of the room.

He asked, in a voice that I knew meant nothing but business, "Hey, what's going on over there?"

I responded like the coward that I was, "Nothing."

Then he taught me the lesson. Instead of letting me off, he taught me. Instead of not making a scene, he taught me. Instead of thinking that since I was one of the captains and I didn't need getting after, he taught me. Instead of being a weak leader, he roared at me, "We are a team in here. And if you don't want to be a team then get out!"

Coach Rabb was professional in everything that he did. But there was a message he needed to send, and he spoke boldly and with great emotion. His words jolted and embarrassed me. I respected Coach Rabb as much as anyone, and I was stung by his reprimand. I had no place to hide, even though that was what I wanted to do. With my face redder than my hair, I apologized to him for acting like an immature idiot.

I thought of Coach Rabb's way of teaching our team the importance of giving all we had. In the state play-off on our way to becoming state champions, he had us do around a hundred "Green Bays" or "up/downs." That was an exercise where we would run in place until he blew his whistle, and then we would all hit the deck. As soon as we were flat on the ground, we were to pop back to our feet and resume running in place.

He took us through one quarter of up/downs and then gave us a short break. He pushed us until we had gone four full quarters, and we all thought we were ready to die. Then he took us into an overtime period of up/downs. After that, we *really* thought we would die. He had no mercy. He was tough. But we willingly gave our maximum effort because we had *total* respect for Coach Rabb.

After the overtime session, as we were all sweating and trying to catch our breath, he said to us, "If it's to be, it's up to me." Then he explained what he meant. With the sun setting and the light leaving the practice field, we sat on the ground, completely exhausted, and listened to him drive home his point. The smell of the grass and dirt that had been churned up from all of the up/downs imprinted a memory on my senses that I've never forgotten. He taught us that it didn't matter what our role was on the team but that it was up to us *individually* to become state champs. He emphasized that concept so strongly that it became something we all believed.

The only time I saw the field in my junior year was when I played on the punt-return team. As only a role player, I had internalized Coach Rabb's principle to where I believed that I was just as important to our team as our quarterback and state MVP, Ed Chatterly. I felt as needed as our starting receivers, Tyler Anderson and Brad Eldredge. I was as essential to the team as our running backs, Carter Rockwood and Bryan Rowley. If we were to win the state championship, it would be on my shoulders as much as those of our tight ends, Vic Cram and Brock Stoner. I was convinced that my performance on that punt-return team was as vital as the play of our middle linebacker, Jason Gray, or our linemen, Joe Heaps, Dave Allphin, and Troy Willardson, or our fullback, Russ Lamereux!

Coach Rabb made us believe that *each* of us had a contribution to make. But at the same time, we were not individuals. We were a TEAM. We had one heartbeat, and after the up/downs that heart was beating like a machine gun. I did not want to let the team down. I knew I needed to give everything I had on the field, on the sideline, and in practice during the week, in order for us to become state champs.

Coach Rabb was a legend. And at the dinner table, my parents often asked my brothers and me what it was about Coach Rabb that made us love him so much. There were a lot of things. He was a black belt in karate who treated every person he ever met with total respect. He was an accounting teacher at the school and our head football coach. His personality was not that of a marketer or a used car salesman, but a coach. What did he do that earned our supreme respect? He was real. He was honest. He was brave. He was all that, and he was great. *He was great!* I wanted to surround myself with people like him.

As I thought about this idea of surrounding myself with greatness, I remembered one of my favorite movies growing up, *It's a Wonderful Life,* starring Jimmy Stewart. I could feel the power of friendship and love as I replayed the final scene in my mind. Jimmy Stewart's character, George Bailey, was heading for jail unless he could come up with a large deposit of money for the savings-and-loan company, money which had been carelessly misplaced by someone else. He had no hope of getting together that much money by himself, and then the whole town showed up at his home with small bills and change to help pay the debt. It was an inspiring and joyful scene, seldom equaled by Hollywood, one that depicted in an emotional way the importance of family, generosity, and love. Then I thought of the crass, vulgar, or violent movies that I had sometimes seen growing up, and I was ashamed that I had wasted my time and money on such drivel.

I could imagine the contempt that movie makers had for me

as they put together movies with excessive violence and sexual images, which held nothing good for me. I promised myself that I would never watch a lame movie again for the rest of my life. It didn't matter if it was the most popular movie in the world, if it didn't fit my standard of greatness, it was out. I was determined to stand my ground, no matter who or what pressured me to watch something that was not up to my new standard.

I thought of the music I had loved before I was a missionary. It had been such a huge part of my life, just as it was for so many of my friends. I realized that music is a powerful motivator for me—for either good or evil. I thought about the "Ode to Joy" that had been such a comfort and inspiration to my dad. Was that music sleazy? Was that music degrading? Was that music full of words that belittled goodness and hope? Did that music tear down? No. It moved Dad to tears, not because it was full of suggestive lyrics or frantic rhythms, but because it was full of greatness—faith, love, inspiration, and joy.

I made a commitment that I would never listen to sleazy or titillating music again. Sure, I had listened to great music before Taiwan, but I had also listened to stuff that I shouldn't have. I pictured myself sitting in a car listening to musically gifted bums whose songs were filled with filth, hatred, and venom, and I felt guilty. I didn't want some rock-and-roll band dictating my emotions. Now I would choose only music that was great. I would listen to music that would inspire me to do my best, to be grateful, to treat others with kindness, and to create in me the feeling that I could climb any mountain. I decided I would never again listen to destructive music.

I remembered the atmosphere that my mom and dad created in our family. They surrounded us with great music, fun family activities that brought us together, and wonderful people who enriched our lives. I thought of the family night activities that we did once a week and how much love was created there. We would often drive up the canyon and share a plate of brownies, just to be together. Most of the time it was a simple gathering in our living room where we spent time with each other. I loved those times. I loved the atmosphere and the closeness that they created.

I thought of Dad's hospital room. He was surrounded there by great neighbors and friends. To someone looking in from the outside, those people might have looked ordinary. But they were great, and they had hearts full of love, concern, and compassion.

Mom and Dad also gave themselves up to much prayer. If his hospital room had been a laboratory where greatness was tested, it could not have delivered better results. It was a breeding ground for miracles. It was an invitation to anything good. It was welcoming to the Lord's presence. It was the embodiment of what I was feeling when I decided I would surround myself with greatness. That was it. That was exactly what I wanted to do forever.

I decided while still in Taiwan to enroll at BYU after my mission, with the hope of successfully walking on to their football team. I filled out the papers, sent them to BYU, and quickly heard back from them that I was accepted. I was pumped about that. The hope of playing football with Larry was a small seed, but it was there, and I continued to water it here and there by imagining how fun it would be to play football and go to battle with Larry.

As Elder Russell Stagg and I rode our bikes around the beautiful city of Feng Yuan each day looking for people to teach or serve, we noticed a homeless guy who was living on the roundabout in front of the main train station. He was there every day. He was a fixture in that city and was always looking for food. During that winter, he tried to keep warm by burning small fires of trash in a tin can. The fires were usually full of plastic and thus very smoky. His clothes were black with soot. His hair was long and mangled and matted with soot and grease. His life was covered with soot. He wore no socks, only boots that were a few sizes

Cutting the hair of a man who lived at the roundabout in Feng Yuan, Taiwan.

too big. He wore a dark overcoat that matched his hair, his shirt, his pants, and his boots. Everything was black and sooty.

We periodically asked him how he was getting along. We really liked his smile and his friendly wave, and we made it a point to say hello each day. Then we got the feeling that he might want a haircut. We asked him if he wanted us to cut his hair and he smiled and said that he would like that. Elder Stagg and I went back to our apartment and got some scissors and a comb.

We returned to the roundabout and started the work of getting a comb through his hair. It was even dirtier and smellier than I thought. It was the greasiest hair I had ever seen. It seemed like the comb would never make it through the dirt and snarls. But after a few minutes of patient combing, his hair finally succumbed, and the soot and grease started to give way. My hands were covered in black grease when I was finished. But I had never been happier. He looked great. His hair was sharp and his smile was a mile wide. As we were cutting his hair, taxi drivers and others passing by honked and gave us a thumbs up.

I felt as though I was in the right place at the right time. I was happy, and it had nothing to do with money, titles, or fame. We were serving him and that was why I was happy. My life as a missionary was very simple. Our goal each day was to be of service to others. I realized how happy we were when we served other people. Serving others is one of the secrets to a happy life.

But missionary work was *work*. It required giving everything I had, and more. It meant waking up early to study and working all day until 9:30 at night. When we got back to our apartment, we planned for the next day, made phone calls, wrote in our journals, and went to bed. We crashed and then started all over again the next day.

The best sleep I have ever had was in Taiwan as a missionary, except for a three-week period during the summer in Kaohsiung when the air was stifling and all I had to keep cool was an electric fan. It was too hot to sleep. I used to soak my sheets in water before I got into bed. I would drape the wet sheets on top of me and then point the fan toward me in an effort to create a swamp-cooler effect. Instead of a swamp cooler, it felt more like an oven blowing hot air all night. For that stretch of time, I was constantly tired and miserable. Other than that three-week period, as soon as my head hit the pillow at night, I was out like a light.

As a missionary, I learned that life is dynamic. There were good days and bad days, and some middle-of-the-road days, but things were always changing. I experienced great happiness when my friend Mr. Wu from Tainan left a life of alcoholism to walk the path of a Christian. And I also experienced sadness when, in the same month, two of my missionary friends, Shane Wilson and Andy Hogan, both had to leave Taiwan due to poor health. They finished their two-year missions in America. I was sad that they would not be able to continue their service in Taiwan, where we were surrounded by the always fascinating Chinese people, their culture, and their language. There was never a dull moment.

As I got closer to finishing my mission, I got more and more tired by the end of the days. I told President Watson about it and he said that it made perfect sense. He said that I would continue to feel exhausted until I went home because the responsibilities that were on my shoulders were heavy. He reminded me that we were not out there doing light work and that we were there to serve others and teach them the gospel. I was learning how to carry the weight of responsibility.

When President Watson's mission ended, he returned to the United States, where he went back to work for Price Waterhouse in Los Altos, California. It didn't take long for his company to realize how valuable he was. Because of his experience in Taiwan and his ability to speak and write Chinese fluently, his company made the wise decision to compensate him for his time in Taiwan and reinstate him as a partner. After a short time he was promoted to be the CEO of PricewaterhouseCoopers China. His decision to take a leap of faith and head to Taiwan to serve others was one of the great examples that impacted my life.

Our new mission president was Timothy Stratford, but because of his schedule at the US Embassy in China, he would not be able to begin his service for another month. For that short time period, Elder John K. Carmack, a member of the First Quorum of the Seventy, came from Hong Kong, where he was serving in the Area Presidency and became our mission president. We had met him a year earlier when he visited our mission and conducted some missionary training meetings. President Carmack was a former attorney in Southern California. He had a zest for life and an enthusiasm and a love for people that was unmatched. During that month he interviewed every missionary and in doing so lit a fire of enthusiasm and a love that inspired our whole mission. He was sixty-one years old but seemed more like thirty. His memory was phenomenal; he could remember names and quotes from what seemed like any year of his life. And his wife was his equal in every way.

Knowing that we had been away from home for a long time, Sister Carmack painstakingly gathered all the food required for an American-style summer barbeque. For the 24th of July, we had a zone leaders training meeting and a picnic lunch, replete with potato salad, baked beans, potato chips, hot dogs, drinks, and brownies. The Carmacks are wonderful people.

I spent the next three months with President Stratford and his family in Taichung. He and his wife, Robin, had three children, two boys and a girl. He was only thirty-seven years old. I very much enjoyed getting to know them and serving with them.

When they were both younger, they had each served missions in the Far East—he in Hong Kong and she in Taiwan.

They had been living in Beijing, China, for several years and would be in Taichung, Taiwan, for the next three. President Stratford was an attorney who graduated from Harvard Law School. After his missionary service in Taiwan was finished he would go on to serve as the general counsel for General Motors China and then serve as the assistant US trade representative for China. I was amazed at how fantastically talented these mission presidents were and yet how humble they were. There was no pretense about them. They were honest and good to the core. Both Kent Watson and Timothy Stratford were extremely successful in their fields of work. They could speak, read, and write Chinese, and they were dedicated to serving the Lord with all their hearts. Their families were willing to work right alongside them in their service.

I worked with Elder Jason Smith and Ken Bown while I was in Taichung. I had already been companions with Ken Bown in Kaohsiung, and it was a blast serving again with him before we finished. Both of those guys had a work ethic that would not quit. They were patient with me and had a love for the Chinese people that drove them to work harder. They spoke the language with fluency that was obtained through two years of dedicated, hard work. They also had similar personalities in that it was impossible for them to get discouraged. They were awesome.

CHAPTER 10

HOME TO AMERICA, FAMILY, AND BYU FOOTBALL

Before President Watson left for home, I asked him what things were worth buying as a souvenir. He told me not to spend any time buying things but to use every minute in serving the people of Taiwan. He said if I ever needed anything to hang in my home, to go to his house and take anything off the wall that I wanted. His love for the people of Taiwan was what he wanted all of us to feel. Because of that, my companions and I tried to work as hard as we could right up until our time was up.

The missionary group that I came with all went home together. We were called the "Gao" group, which means tall. We piled into the van and headed for the airport. I had become very close to the Stratfords in the three months we were together. At the airport, President Stratford's wife, Robin, pretended that she had lost my airplane ticket and said I would have to stay. I had learned so much from the Stratfords. I loved them and would miss their influence in my life. I felt fortunate as a young man to have worked closely with such accomplished and talented people.

That was it. Two years of service were suddenly over. As I looked out the window of that big plane as we gathered speed

*Flying home to America after two years in Taiwan with Elders Cody Fowler,
Tim Davis, and Chad Pettingill. What an amazing feeling!*

down the runway, memories and emotions flooded my mind and
my heart until there was not room enough to hold them. By the
time we lifted off the ground, tears overflowed and poured down
my cheeks. I looked down at the green rice fields that were falling
away behind us and realized I was leaving a huge part of my soul
there in Taiwan. I was sitting between Tim Davis and Cody
Fowler, two guys who I served with and loved, and we were all
speechless.

A young man serving in the U.S. Navy was sitting nearby. He
was also on his way home. He looked so polished and dignified in
his military uniform. After I regained control of my emotions, I
told him how much I respected him for serving and defending our
country. He was really touched and his eyes filled with tears as he
searched for a grateful response. I was going home a completely

different person than when I had arrived. I was so grateful for the changes.

We had a four-hour layover in Tokyo and boarded another flight for San Francisco. After we got through customs, we saw President Watson and his daughter Melissa running up the concourse to greet us. He was living and working in the Bay Area and they surprised us with their visit. It was so good to see them. They looked even better than I remembered. We visited with them for two and half hours until our flight was ready to go.

I was drained and fell asleep on the flight to Salt Lake City. I woke up as we landed and started to gather my bags. My heart was beating like crazy and I was excited to see my family again. Before the plane came to a complete stop, Rob Lamb raced down the aisle. He was the first one off the plane, and I ended up being the last because I was seated in the back.

My brother Dave was the first person I saw and we gave each other a big hug. He was the first Lewis boy to serve a mission. As the oldest in the family, he had forged the way and blazed a trail for all the rest of us to follow. He had always been "the man with the plan" ever since he used that as his campaign slogan as a sixth grader when he ran for student-body president. His going on a mission helped all the rest of us do the same. Dave is one of my heroes.

Then suddenly I was hugging everyone—Dave's wife, Jonna, my mom and dad, my little brother, Todd, who had grown into a giant, then Jason and his new wife, Angie, who I was meeting for the first time. Unless it is a serviceman's homecoming, there is nothing to equal the emotional return of a Mormon missionary, and I was enjoying every moment of it. Everything was different. My love for my family was deeper. I had more respect for them. There was more gratitude for each of them. I wanted them to know that I understood them better and that I loved them more.

It was especially good to see Mom and Dad. It seemed as

though I had not seen them forever. I looked into their eyes and told them I loved them. They looked younger and better than I could remember. They looked like angels.

I had a new appreciation for home. I had a new appreciation for life. I had grown closer to the Savior as I'd tried to emulate Him in my service to my Chinese brothers and sisters. What a gift it was to serve a mission. It was hard, but it was great. I had been surrounded by greatness in Taiwan—by the wonderful people there and by the missionaries with whom I had served. How could I ever be the same? Being with my family again felt like heaven.

It took some time to get acclimated to living at home. When I began my mission, it was weird to have a companion, and now that I was home, it was weird to not have one. I got busy working with Sue and Reid Robinson at Signature Promotions again. Reid was building his own house, and I spent all of my time helping him with that project. I loved using my body to work hard and going to bed tired. And it was sweet to see his house take shape and know that I was helping it come to life. Reid knew how to do everything, it seemed, and he would give me one project after another until the house was finished.

I paid for school with the money I earned working with Reid. It felt good to be back in school. I was glad that I got straight A's before my mission and I intended to keep up where I left off. I wanted to study like crazy and get the most out of each class.

A phone call from Mom interrupted work one day. She said that Larry Harmer had an accident in Taiwan and was coming home that day. He was playing on a grass field with the other missionaries and broke his collarbone in two places. He was not scheduled to come home for another month, and though he was in obvious pain, it was great to see him again. He was going to need some rehab time on his shoulder before he got into full-time weight training. When he asked if I still wanted to walk on to the football team, I told him that I wasn't sure. What seemed like an exciting dream while I was in Taiwan looked more like crazy hard work and a near impossibility now that I was home.

I did walk on to the track team at BYU as a high jumper. I talked to Mark Robinson, the track coach at the Y, and he invited me to participate. Being on the track team gave me access to the same weight room that Larry would be using with the football team. I also had some friends on the football team who went to my high school, so it was cool to see them and work out with them.

I practiced every day in the Smith Fieldhouse, an old indoor facility that BYU used. It had about twenty-five yards of old carpet that was used for high jumping, and the football team used it during bad weather days. It was so small that when the football team used it they could only have the offense or the defense in there at one time. It was not big enough for both.

As a high jumper, I had some hops, but my form wasn't the greatest. While I was practicing, some of the football players would be playing catch in the same area. Every time I saw them catch the ball I wanted to join them. Tyler Anderson was one of the receivers, and we had played together at Orem High. He was one of the main reasons that we won the state championship in high school. He was the fastest person on the planet and I'm not joking. He and Tim Nowatzke would tease me by saying I should be playing with them instead of high jumping. They had no idea how much I wanted to play with them.

While I was going to school and high jumping, Larry would ask me every week or so about trying out for the football team. I couldn't commit. I was more scared than anything. I was intimidated by the whole process. I was still as skinny as a bean pole and wondered if I would ever be big enough or strong enough to play.

One day, Larry changed the course of my life forever, as if he had not done that already through his friendship. He asked me again if I was ready to walk on to the football team. I gave him the same weak answer that I wasn't sure. Then he did something that he had never done with me before—he got very stern and said that it was time for me to find out for myself if I could cut it. He was sick of my timid answers. His rebuke caught me way off guard.

I wondered where his passion came from because it was definitely out of character for him. He told me that it was time that I prayed about this decision and got an answer from heaven about what I should do. He was so forceful with his eyes and his words and his tone of voice that I committed to him right then that I would do as he said. I would go home and pray about it. I would find out for myself if I should play football at BYU. It was now or never. I was nervous, but I was exhilarated that I was finally going to make the decision.

I started to pray as if my life depended on it. I prayed harder than I had prayed for anything in my entire life. I knew the mountain of hard work that would be there if I chose to play. I started not to care about the size of the mountain, only if I were supposed to climb it. I wanted to know. I had to know. The decision was too big not to get divine assurance. Day after day I prayed and asked God to let me know if I should play. Day after day I did not receive an answer, but I continued to pray with faith. Larry knew I was giving the decision all the time, thought, and attention that I could muster.

Then one night as I was lying in bed, the answer came to me. I had a feeling that came over me and I knew I was to play football at BYU. I knew it! It was as strong an answer as I had ever received. I felt a confidence and a fire growing in my heart. Any fear I had about the difficulty of walking on was gone. It evaporated. I didn't have all the answers but I didn't focus on that. I focused on the possibilities of making the team, playing well, and earning a scholarship. As I lay there on my bed looking at the ceiling, I decided how I would act upon this answer to my prayers. I would

Meeting with my hero, BYU head coach LaVell Edwards,
when I was 14. Also pictured is Devin McCann.

talk to Coach Chris Pella the next day. He was the recruiting co-ordinator for BYU and also happened to be the tight-end coach.

I did it. The next day, I walked into the football office and asked if I could meet with Coach Pella. I filled out a walk-on form and gave it to Shirley Johnson, the longtime secretary of Coach Edwards.

I had been in that office before, when I was fourteen years old. My neighbor Dale McCann was the executive director of the Cougar Club. He asked if I wanted to meet LaVell Edwards and possibly pose in a picture with him marketing the jerseys that were to be given to all the members of the Cougar Club. I was thrilled with the invitation. LaVell was *the* coach. We watched all the BYU games, and he was a fixture on the sidelines with his stoic face and grim demeanor. I had watched his teams and I had admired him for many years. I couldn't believe that I was going to get to meet him. My brother Jason and I were both invited to take some photos with him. It was a great meeting. I was in awe. He was kind and generous and funny. I still have the photo that we took together. I had no idea that was not the only time I would meet him.

Coach Pella said that I was free to walk on but I would need to talk to Coach Chow to see if he'd agree to my starting to catch passes with the guys as they prepared for spring ball. I spoke with Coach Chow the next day. He had been behind the BYU offensive juggernaut for years. The first thing he asked me was if I was "Big Mike's" little brother. My brother Mike had just finished his college career with the University of Utah by playing in the Copper Bowl in Tucson, Arizona. He had blown out his knee on the second play of the game when an offensive lineman on a screen pass had hit him low, at knee level, while Mike was not looking.

Coach Chow knew about Mike from playing against him and the U of U every year. After making small talk about Mike, Coach Chow gave me the green light to join the team on Tuesdays and Thursdays in the indoor practice facility. He let me know there were a lot of tight ends but that I was welcome to show what I could do. That was all I wanted. I just wanted a chance.

I told Larry about the conversations with the coaches, and he could not have been happier for me. After all the talking and dreaming we had done in Taiwan, we were finally going to play on the same team. Without his encouragement, it would have never happened. He and my brother Mike were the catalysts that started my whole football career. Those two had more to do with my playing football than anyone else. Without them, it never would have happened.

The first day I got to throw with the BYU football team it was nice to have Tyler Anderson, my high-school teammate, there with me. I also met some guys who were to become some of my best friends. I met Tom Young, Bryce Doman, Hema Heimuli, Greg Pitts, and a host of other studs. They were guys who I had really looked up to. I had played against Hema and Bryce in high school. They were both the best players on their teams. Bryce was a receiver and Hema was a running back, and I found out after thirty seconds of talking with them that they must have been the best *people* on their teams as well. They were incredible.

After kidding me about my big glasses, they took me right in. I had so much adrenaline that I ran routes like Carl Lewis, not Chad Lewis. I was flying (at least I thought I was). I felt fast. I didn't remember being very fast at all when I played football in high school. But then, all of sudden, I felt fast. It was a cool feeling. I thought it was a combination of riding bikes every day for two years in Taiwan, playing a lot of basketball since I had been home, and, most importantly, that my body was finally beginning to mature. I was 6'6" and 205 pounds.

I still looked more like Clark Kent than Superman. Coach Chow pulled me aside after catching balls that first day. He asked me how I felt running around with the guys. He then told me to be patient with the process of walking on and seeking a scholarship. He said some of the guys had to wait a few years before they got one. I was so excited to be talking to him that it didn't matter what he said. I was glad that he noticed something in me worth talking about. I knew I had a shot.

Tom Young was the returning quarterback, and he could not have been more encouraging to me. He kept telling me that I was running nice routes and that I had sweet hands. I was so pumped up that I wanted to strap on the pads and play that day. As a walk-on, I can't overstate enough how important it was for me to have the support and friendship of the leaders on the team. Not only were they some of the best players, but they were the best guys. Football teams are made up of players with different talents, skills, sizes, and personalities. Because of my desire to surround myself with greatness, I wanted to be around the best guys on the team. That was more important to me than being liked. Tom, Bryce, Hema, and Greg opened the door of friendship and invited Larry and me into their lives.

I loved working out with the guys. I loved being with Larry and getting ready to play football again. It had been a long time since I played. Spring ball was right around the corner. Under the NCAA rules, we were able to have padded practices for three weeks. It was a chance for coaches to evaluate the players prior to summer camp. It was also a chance for someone like me to let the coaches know what I could do. The whole team was tested in the forty-yard dash the week before spring ball. I ran a 4.66, which was the fastest time for all of the tight ends. I was very encouraged by that. My confidence kept growing, and the effort that I was putting in to lift weights and work hard was paying off.

The first day of spring ball practice didn't start anything like I wanted. After wearing glasses for the last two years as a missionary, I needed to get contact lenses. When I went to buy contacts, they told me that I had an astigmatism and would not be able to wear soft lenses. I leaned on their understanding and went ahead with the purchase of hard lenses, which took some getting used to. As I was getting ready for my very first practice, I took my contacts into our equipment manager's office to put them in my eyes. His name was Floyd Johnson. He was a legend at BYU because he was the nicest person who ever wore shoes. He is still revered by thousands of athletes who have passed through the halls of BYU.

Floyd invited me to use his sink and mirror to put in my contacts. I was both nervous and afraid of being late to practice, and I accidentally dropped one of the contacts in the sink. To my absolute horror, the contact shattered. I had no idea it would break like that. I did not have any spares and practice was only minutes away. I could not and would not be late. I thought about just using one contact, but my eyes felt more cross-eyed than anything. It was worse than just trying to squint.

I decided that seeing the ball well enough to catch it was more important than looking like a nerd, so I made the infamous decision to wear my great big Clark Kent glasses behind my face mask, at least for that first day. I hoped that nobody would notice.

Yeah, right. As soon as I started warming up by catching passes from the quarterbacks, Tom Young noticed my glasses and cracked up. He called me Bob Griese. Griese was the quarterback for the undefeated 1971 Miami Dolphins, and he wore sweet glasses while he played. Another QB was John Walsh, and he couldn't keep a straight face, either. By the time our third QB, Steve Clements, noticed what I was wearing, I felt like a big enough nerd that I thought it was better to drop a couple of passes than continue with the abuse.

If I squinted hard, I could see pretty well, and I was able to catch all the passes thrown to me that day, which was a huge relief. I got a new set of contacts in time for practice the next day.

After my freshman year I switched from wearing hard contacts to soft contacts. I always had a couple of extra contacts on the sideline because even the soft contacts would pop out. It would usually happen once a game. The worst part of my contacts getting knocked out was when they would stick onto the eye black on my cheeks. I would peel the contact off the eye black, stick it in my mouth to try to get all of the black goo off it, then put it back in my eye as soon as I could so that I could get back in the game—not the best way to keep my eyes clean but it was the fastest.

One of the best things that I ever did for my career and life was to eventually get Lasik eye surgery. When my Eagles teammate Bobby Taylor had Lasik done on his eyes, I asked him where he had gone for his surgery. He told me that he worked with Dr. Siepser in Philadelphia, and I gave him a call. Steven Siepser got me in for an evaluation. Even though I had an astigmatism, he said I was still a candidate for Lasik. I was glad to hear that. I was also glad to interview him and see the quality of his machines. The last thing I wanted to do was put my eyesight in the hands of someone who was unqualified and who did not have the latest technology.

He was able to take care of my vision troubles in the off-season. It was a miracle to see my clock radio without any contacts. I could see the football like an eagle. No more contacts. No more missing plays because I was fussing with my contacts.

Having them mess with my eyes during the procedure was as disconcerting as anything I had ever experienced, but from that next morning on, my eyes were eagle eyes. What a miracle. I was thankful for the technology that could give me near perfect vision. We live in a day of miracles.

I wish I could say that I never dropped a pass. Later, that first week of practice at BYU, we had a brief, full-contact scrimmage. During one play I dropped a wide-open pass along the sideline, right in front of group of defensive guys. Tom Young threw a perfect pass that went right through my hands and straight to the ground. It was embarrassing. All the defensive players on the sideline were laughing at me and saying that I was too scared to catch it. Maybe I was. I know I was pretty nervous. But my blood was boiling as well. I did not like dropping a pass, and I did not like being laughed at. It was a feeling that ripped my guts out.

When I got back to Coach Chow, he was half laughing at me and half angry, and he reminded me that the goal was to CATCH the ball, and he emphasized the word *catch* so that I would never forget it. I never did, even if I dropped a few passes along the way. I could always hear Coach Chow in my mind saying, "The goal is to CATCH the ball!"

Coach Chow was famous at BYU for his most memorable coaching point or saying. He drilled into us that "Difficult catches are routine, but the impossible ones just take a little more practice!" No wonder BYU was known for players making unbelievable and even impossible catches. That was the standard. Coach Chow would not accept anything less.

One more catch stood out in my mind from that crucial time. The very next week we held another scrimmage to finish practice. One of my favorite all-time guys and coaches, Lance Reynolds, was in the huddle calling the plays. He called "Red right 65." I loved that play. If the defense was in man-to-man coverage, my job was to run straight upfield for ten yards, freeze the defender with a hard head fake, plant my foot, and sprint out of the break toward the sideline. If it was zone coverage, I would run a "sail." Instead of breaking out to the flat at the ten-yard mark, I would turn my shoulders to the outside at ten yards, but I would continue to drift vertically into the zone and give the QB an easy target.

The play was money. The defense was easy to read for a tight end and for a quarterback. During that scrimmage, Lance called the play, knowing that it would probably be thrown to me. He and the other coaches were trying to see if I could take the next step in my football progression and become a player who could be counted on. The scrimmage was very spirited. The defensive guys were whooping it up and trying to create as much pressure and intensity as they could. And there had already been a few scuffles.

I ran my route into man-to-man coverage. I was double-teamed from the top down by the strong safety and from the side by the outside linebacker. Tom Young was the quarterback. Once I broke out at ten yards, he threw the ball high and away where either I would catch it or it would fall incomplete. I jumped as high as I could with the two defenders draped all over me and somehow came down with the ball. I don't think a pass had ever felt sweeter in my hands. I was immediately tackled, but I had made the play. I was on fire. I ran back to the huddle and my teammates slapped me on the helmet. It was a big play in the middle of an intense scrimmage.

When I stood next to Lance and looked in his face, his eyes were saying that was a job well done. He said, "That was big-time!" As a player fighting to earn a job, those words were more valuable than anything, and they were all I needed to keep digging in and working my hardest.

Lance Reynolds was a key figure in my football schooling. Along with Coach Chow, he had an impact on my every perception of the game. In an effort to help me become a better blocker, he invited me over to his house where we practiced some drills in his backyard. Talk about taking work home with you. He went above the call of duty in his efforts to teach me how to play the game.

I loved listening to his stories of playing at BYU when he was in college and with the Pittsburgh Steelers in the NFL. He had played with all my childhood heroes—Lynn Swann, Franco Harris, Jack Lambert, Rocky Bleier, and Mean Joe Green. I sat next to him on many bus rides, listening to him tell great football stories. He understood the pressure I was going through and always helped me keep my attitude up. He would later introduce me when I was inducted into the BYU Athletic Hall of Fame. He and his wife, Leslie, treated me like part of their family.

While I was walking on, I did feel pressure from some of the other players. But pressure and the feelings of intimidation were never a reason to quit. I found that those were the times I needed to strengthen my resolve the most and those were also the times where a good friend like Larry made all the difference. There were eight tight ends and I was number eight. Some of the other guys were already an established part of the team. They had their friends, and I was the new guy encroaching on their turf. The starting tight end was Terrance Saluone, and he was tight with the starting QB, John Walsh.

I didn't want to mess up their relationship or become their enemy, but I did want to play. It is impossible to describe all the social and relationship dynamics that go into team sports. Since they were dynamic, they were always changing. Luckily, for me, Terrance could not have been a cooler teammate. He never acted threatened by me and he was always helpful as I tried to master the playbook. He was cool about teaching me the subtle nuances of running routes and getting open. I will be forever grateful for the generous way he tutored me. His example was the basis of how I wanted to treat a teammate in a similar situation in the NFL when the roles were reversed.

I scored my first touchdown in the final spring scrimmage, called the Blue and White game. Paul Shoemaker, the prep school phenom quarterback from Longmont, Colorado, threw me a perfect "66 Y Bench." It was a simple five-yard down and out, and he hit me in stride and I scored a big confidence-boosting touchdown. I wanted so badly to make some waves, to get noticed, to get on the coaches' radar screen, that I was overjoyed to catch that ball. Even though it was in a scrimmage of little importance, that is still one of the all-time favorite catches of my career.

At the end of spring ball every player had an interview with his position coach and also with Coach Edwards. I was excited for both. I wanted to know if I had made an impression worthy of a scholarship. When I met with Coach Chow, he said that I had done a great job. He reminded me to be patient and even asked me how long I would be able to pay for school and remain a walk-on.

I was well aware that some players on BYU's team were seniors and they were still walk-ons. I had already decided that I would give football my heart and soul for one year. And that was what I told him. I said that if I deserved a scholarship after giving everything I had for one year, then I wanted one. But if he and the other coaches didn't think that I deserved one after a year, to please let me know and I would be gone. I told him that I was paying for school by myself and it would not be possible to go any longer than a year if I did not receive a scholarship. He was really cool about my answer and reminded me again to be patient and that he would do everything he could do for me.

Like many coaches, Coach Chow had a commanding presence. He was big for being half Chinese and half Hawaiian. He didn't talk that much and wanted players to fight to earn his respect. He was a tough coach who demanded greatness and expected exact execution and was the driving force behind the success of the BYU offense for many years. Receivers had to run routes at the correct depth every time. We had to cut our routes off at the exact same spot every time. We had to have some pop out of our breaks—and we had to catch everything! He never settled for trying hard and coming up short. He expected us to play like BYU receivers. The standard was very high, and he let everyone know that we had to meet it. Coach Chow was the reason I was given a chance. His greatness as a coach has proven itself over many years.

Coach Pella was my tight-end coach. Facially, he looks like Marlon Brando in his role as Superman's father in the movie *Superman*. His silver hair was sweet. He was the coolest coach in the world because he was always positive. It didn't matter if I just dropped a critical pass, he was always positive. Always.

Coach Pella came to BYU after being the head coach at Utah State for a few years. I don't think it was possible for him to get mad. He would always grab my hands with his and physically show me where my hands needed to go when I was blocking. He would also have me crouch down into the exact position that would help me be successful in blocking and getting out of breaks on pass routes. He was unique that way because he was so demonstrative with his coaching style. He would patiently work with me until I could feel exactly what I was supposed to feel in a certain position. He took me straight from the streets of Taiwan and taught me at BYU how to play the position well enough to make it in the NFL.

During my interview with Coach Edwards he told me that he liked my effort and liked the way I was catching the ball. He said there were a limited number of scholarships and that being a walk-on required patience. I was so glad just to be in his office. We talked about my brother Dave, who had walked on a few years previously and also about my brother Mike, who had just finished his career with the U. Then Coach Edwards remembered a phone conversation he had with Jim Fassel.

When Jim Fassel was fired by the University of Utah, in a parting phone call he had with LaVell, Coach Fassel told him to keep his eye out for Mike Lewis's younger brother who was on a mission. As we were talking, Coach Edwards remembered that conversation. It was great to know that he made that connection with my family. There was still a chance for me to get a scholarship—I could feel it.

LaVell Edwards was the best coach in college football because of where he coached, how he coached, who he coached, and what he was able to accomplish. He and his staff were able to turn a skinny kid from Orem, Utah, with no scholarship, into a three-time Pro Bowler and nine-year NFL veteran. That was coaching.

One of his greatest lessons to us players, and one of the secrets to his winning the conference championship year after year, was his repeated encouragement to give a full measure of ourselves for sixty minutes. He said that before every single game. It was his mantra. He assured us that if we did that, everything would work out. He taught us to give that same measure in school by saying, "Be where you are supposed to be, when you're supposed to be there."

It was simple. Maybe even too simple to comprehend for

those people who wonder how he could have been so successful. He changed the lives of thousands of football players with those messages because he lived them, taught them, and believed them. LaVell's greatness was subtle. If a person looked too hard to find out why he was great, they would miss it. His greatness was to be found in his simplicity, genuine goodness, charitable kindness, self-deprecating manner, and Christian values.

Not a day of my life would pass when I didn't feel grateful for the chance I had to learn from LaVell and play for him at BYU. What an honor it was for any of us who knew him to be associated with him. His wife, Patti, stood as his equal in every way. She never tired of letting us players or our wives know that she loved us. She held wives' dinners at her home where she focused on them. She always encouraged the wives to love their husbands with all their heart and soul because that would help them be better men, students, fathers, and football players. What wise counsel.

Together, LaVell and Patti brought BYU greatness for decades. And now they have an army of loyal friends who would answer any call or any request that they ever made. They are some of the best people I have ever known.

My interview with LaVell was very encouraging. I knew that I had a chance to make the team and earn a scholarship. It would still be a major challenge, but there was hope.

CHAPTER 11

MICHELE AND BYU

While I was training during that summer, I met a girl who changed my life. Her name was Michele Fellows and she was an All-American volleyball player at BYU going into her senior year. She was beautiful, friendly, kind, tall, and my dream girl in every way. The football and volleyball seasons coincided, and we met for the first time in the training room at the athletic facility.

She was talking to Rich Pearson, who was playing football with me and happened to have served his mission in Las Vegas. He and Michele were chit-chatting, and I butted in and asked Michele if she knew a guy named Quincy Edwards from Las Vegas. She did! I asked her to say hello to him the next time she went home. She was going home that very weekend and promised to say hi if she ran into him.

About two weeks later Michele was back in the weight room and said that she had seen Quincy and shared my greetings. She said he was excited to hear from me and said hello as well. After that, Michele and I continued to talk to each other whenever we were in the training facility. The volleyball team had a glass enclosed bulletin board with pictures of each player, and I stopped to stare at her photograph every time I passed it. I have that photo and still keep it on my desk and look at it more than any other picture.

After talking with her and getting to know her a little better, I realized that she was the most beautiful person I had ever met. Her blue eyes were full of light and I loved the way they sparkled. I loved the kind way she treated her teammates. For an All-American she sure was down to earth.

Our first date was an outing in Provo Canyon with her twin brother, Mark, and his future wife, Becky. Their friend Hartman Anderson also came with us. We ate Subway sandwiches and just hung out and had a wonderful time getting better acquainted. Michele was fun because she was easy to talk to and was comfortable being outdoors. I was also very impressed by her brother, Mark. He was a sharp guy and had just returned from serving a two-year mission to Korea. We all had a lot to talk about and the evening was perfect. We were both getting ready to start our two-a-day practices and would not have very much time for dating.

Our football meetings began at the same time her practice started. I used to sit outside of our meeting room before we started and watch Michele practice. I became the biggest BYU volleyball fan around.

I continued to work my guts out leading up to camp. I caught passes from the QBs anytime they were throwing. Tom Young was the QB whom I practiced with the most. He was a hard worker and we enjoyed being around each other. It was fun making friends, especially since Tom was a humble guy. Even though his older brother, Steve Young, was tearing things up in the NFL, Tom never acted as though he was entitled to anything.

When summer camp finally started I felt fast and fit. I was confident with the playbook and my role in the offense. I hoped to make the field that year so that I could force the coaches' hand into giving me a scholarship. After doing pretty well the first three days, I was moved to second string for practice on Thursday. I was so excited that my heart nearly popped. That meant I was getting noticed. It also meant I would be playing with the starters. It also meant that the chances of earning a scholarship were increasing. After so much hard work, things were coming together for me.

After practice on Thursday afternoon, Coach Edwards called the team together for some quick announcements and then a yell. I can remember only one of the announcements that he made. He said that he wanted to see Chad Lewis in his office after practice! I wondered if I'd heard that correctly. Did he ask to see ME? Larry, Tom, and Bryce were all smiles, wondering what that was all about. As I walked off the field, Coach Chow said to me, "If this is what I think it is, you owe me a steak dinner!"

I can't explain how grateful I felt at that moment. I loved Coach Chow and wanted to prove that his confidence in me was going to pay off. I loved Coach Edwards and felt so honored to be around him. I wanted to play for the Y so much I could hardly think of anything else. I was humbled to associate with all of the great guys on the team. I don't think I had ever wanted anything more in my whole life.

I floated from the practice field to the locker room. A million thoughts ran through my head as I showered and then headed for LaVell's office. I thought about the price I had paid over the last eight months for the chance to make the team. I remembered the hours of weight lifting and the miles of running. There were faces of my new teammates and friends that flashed through my mind. There was the vivid memory of being in Taiwan talking with Larry about the possibility of playing football together at BYU.

I also thought about the cost of tuition that I had just paid, which completely wiped out my savings. If I didn't get a scholarship, I would not be able to play after Christmas because I would be out of money. I thought about my parents, who did not have any extra money to help pay for school since my dad's stroke. I thought about the chance to play on the field where I had seen my heroes play all through my growing up years. I had given it everything I had.

While still in this train of thought, I sat waiting outside of Coach Edwards's office. When it was my turn, he called me in.

He told me that he really liked the effort that I was putting in and how I was catching the ball. He wanted to make sure that I would keep working like that no matter what. He said that he had decided to go ahead and put me on grant-in-aid, but he stressed again that he did not want to see my effort slip at all.

My first reaction was to wonder if grant-in-aid meant the same thing as full scholarship. I felt too dumb to ask the question so I just sat there and smiled as if I were seven years old and had been told I was going to Disneyland the next day. When I asked him what I should do about the tuition I had just paid, he told me to go ahead and get it reimbursed. Could this be happening, I wondered? Was it a dream? Was LaVell Edwards really telling me that I was on his team and that I had earned a scholarship that would pay for my schooling for the next five years? I don't know how I kept from fainting as I sat there in front of him.

I didn't walk for the next several hours, I just continued to float. The trip up to the administration building to get reimbursed for my tuition was better than trick-or-treating in the rich neighborhoods that gave away big candy bars. The check seemed huge when I wrote it, but getting it back seemed as though it had doubled. I could appreciate how much money that was and what it meant to my life. It was like solid gold. Not only did I not have to pay to go to school anymore, but the school was going to start giving me money for food and room and board. That was a dream come true.

My parents wouldn't have to worry about my schooling. I felt so grateful for that. It also meant that I could keep some money in the bank. It also legitimized, to some extent, who I was as a football player on the team. As a walk-on, like it or not, there was always a feeling that I stood on the outside of the circle.

When I got back to the locker room, I was issued the shoes and gear that were given to those players on scholarship. The Nike Pegasus shoes that were issued to me probably cost $25, but they felt like million-dollar sneakers on my feet. Larry and I had talked so many times about the slim chance of getting a scholarship and playing together, and to think that it had actually happened was almost too much for me to take in.

The rest of that day was spent celebrating with my family and friends. I called Michele and shared the good news with her. Since she was an established athlete, she knew how important it was to me. There was a lot of luck, timing, hard work, desire, effort, and divine help that went into getting that scholarship. I promised myself never to let LaVell down for believing in me. I wanted to make sure that he was satisfied that he had made the right decision.

I've never heard LaVell speak of another person with disparaging words. Of all the great people I met playing football at BYU, LaVell was the best. The longer I was with him in the program, the more I understood how awesome he was. His genius was loving people. He cared about each of us players in a way that made us want to give everything we had on the field for him. He was not a man of big speeches or motivational talks. He rarely got emotional. But I do remember his love and his affection for all of us. He was greatness personified.

He and his wife, Patti, were a team that was fun for all of the players to be around. He never acted as though we were little people and that he was the big dog. He always made us feel we were important in his eyes and that he was happy to be around us. If we rode the elevator with him at the hotel he would often crack a joke that always seemed even funnier because his sense of humor was so quick and dry.

Once, after a Friday walk-through in the stadium, after we had gone over each offensive and defensive situation as well as each of the special teams assignments, we gathered in the end zone to give a team cheer before we got on the buses and headed for the hotel. Just then, Coach Edwards's cell phone went off. Normally he would have turned it off, but he answered it. We could tell it was his secretary of many years, Shirley Johnson. She had never married, and everyone knew she was perfectly loyal to LaVell and Patti in every way. His conversation was short and when it was over, he waited long enough so that we all knew the connection was terminated, then, with a twinkle in his eye, he deadpanned, "I love you, too. Good-bye!"

It was a classic Coach Edwards's moment, and the whole team cracked up. He is one in a million.

If it was exciting to make the team, it was even more exciting to play in the games. Our first game that year was against New Mexico in Albuquerque. It had been four years since I had been in a real game—my high-school state championship game. And I was pumped.

Pete Whitbeck was the "get back" coach for BYU. Every football team assigns a person on staff to keep the players back from the sideline. If players and coaches standing on the sideline get on the field, they can incur a penalty. Pete was the assistant athletic director, and he spent most of the game yelling at me to get back into the players box on the sideline. I was so excited that I couldn't help it. The game was very close and we came out on top. I was the backup to Terrance Saluone, but Coach Chow put me in at tight end for the last two minutes. I was very surprised when he made that move. It caught me off guard. My heart was beating like a hummingbird's. I knew that Coach Chow had a lot of confidence in me and I was glad that he threw me into the fire on my first game.

After four wins to start the season, we traveled to Los Angeles

to play against UCLA. They torched us for four quarters. Their receiver, J. J. Stokes, seemed like an octopus with a helmet. He must
have had eight hands because he caught everything thrown to him.
He was dominant. I was happy to make my first catch at the end of
the game during "mop-up" time. I was so glad to be out there running around. Tom Young was the quarterback and he looked my
way a few times in the one drive that we had. He called "69 H
Option," which was my favorite route. I started next to the offensive
tackle on the right side and angled across the field, getting to a
depth of eighteen yards at the far hash mark. Tom hit me in stride,
and I was pushed out of bounds. It was a meaningless catch to any
fan still watching the blowout, but not to me. I had thought about
that for a long time. It felt even better than I had imagined it would.

Tom marched us down inside the UCLA ten-yard line. Coach
Chow called a fade route to me on the left side. The play was basically a jump ball situation since I was several inches taller than
the cornerback who was defending me. The play worked just like
we planned. Tom threw the ball high and I was able to jump up
and catch it. Even though we were getting creamed, Tom and I
congratulated each other like it was a game winner.

I got my first start in the seventh game in a home contest
against the University of Notre Dame. Tom Young was the starting QB because of an injury to John Walsh. We had practiced
hard all throughout the off-season and we were excited to be playing together. Notre Dame was one of the top-ranked teams in the
country that year. They beat us, but the thrill of starting and
catching some balls got in my blood. I wanted more of it. From
then on I got to play more and more.

The best thing that happened that freshman year was learning
the power of having a great *dream.* My dream was to jump over a
tackler in a football game. It would combine my past as a high
jumper with that of a football player. And I wanted it bad.

As a tall football player, I got tired of the defensive backs going low and tackling my knees out from under me. I thought it would be sweet to hurdle over a defender and keep on running. I thought about it a lot that spring as I was trying to make the team. To say that I thought about it a lot would not be correct; I thought about it *all* the time. When I caught passes in the summer, I thought about it. When I went to bed at night, I thought about it. When I went anywhere, I thought about it. I became obsessed with how great it would be to jump over someone in a game.

When I started dating Michele, I shared my obsession with her. She grew up watching football with her dad and her brothers Steve and Mark, and she knew enough about football to think I was a little crazy. It was not a common move and the risks were obvious. She wondered why I wanted to jump over someone so bad. I couldn't explain it; I just did.

I used to lie in my bed at night thinking about how cool it would be to jump over someone. I would get so excited that I could not sleep. Instead of counting imaginary sheep, I would envision jumping over defenders, which had the opposite effect on my sleepiness. I would get so excited that I couldn't sleep. I would lie there and stare at the ceiling and imagine how sweet it would be to do it in a game. I could hear the crowd and feel the rumblings from their cheers. I could see the reaction from my teammates. I would literally laugh thinking how fun it would be.

My dream finally became reality later that freshman season. It happened in our last home game of the year, against UTEP. It was a cold, sunny day in Provo, and I was wearing tights under my pants and an extra long-sleeved shirt to keep warm. I heard John Walsh call the play, "Red Right 63, on one." I was not thinking of anything except running my route, which was ten yards straight ahead and a cut across the middle of the field.

I ran my route and when John hit me over the middle, I caught it in stride and turned to run upfield. Sam Rogers, their defensive back, ran toward me to tackle me, and when he did, I jumped right

Courtesy of Mark A. Philbrick/BYU

*Mark Philbrick's award-winning photo, "Bronco Rider." Jumping over UTEP's
Sam Rogers for the second time in the game my freshman year at BYU.*

over the top of him. It was crazy. He didn't even touch me. I ran
another ten yards up the sideline before being pushed out of
bounds. Ironically, it happened right in front of my brothers Dave
and Mike, who jumped up from their field-level seats in the stands.
I raised my hands into the air and exploded with emotion. I ran
around the field like I had just won the Heisman Trophy. Bryce
Doman finally caught up with me and hit me on the head over and
over to celebrate the play. That was my great dream come true.

I tried to jump over Sam later in the game as well, but that
didn't go nearly as well. I caught a pass and ran up the field in
Sam's direction. When I got in front of him, my legs kicked into
dream mode again, and I tried to jump over him. He was ready
for my little trick that time and when I was right above him, he
stood up and caught me in midflight.

I ended up riding his shoulders to the ground like a bronco rider in a rodeo. BYU photographer Mark Philbrick snapped a perfect picture of the play. Luckily, I landed without any harm done, and Mark ended up winning first-place honors in the sports category at the University Photographers Association of America's annual competition with that photo, which he titled, "Bronco Rider."

Because of that experience, I realized the power of my thoughts; visualizing something can actually make it happen. Up until that moment, I hadn't understood how important it is to have a dream. I found out that if I believed something was possible and thought about it long enough, it would happen. I let that dream sink so deep in my heart and settle so deep in my brain that it became a natural reaction when a situation presented itself.

When I was running with the ball I did not think about jumping over the defender. It just happened. I did not think about setting up my steps in preparation to jump, it just happened.

Even now, many years later, I can still feel myself flying over that defender, and I smile because that dream came true. Since that first jump, I have jumped over defenders more than a dozen times in college and in the NFL. Some jumps have turned out just the way I wanted; other times I have been smashed. But each time I have jumped, I have fulfilled that initial dream. I loved it.

During my career and through the years that followed, I have occasionally been asked to share with youth groups, school children, and church and civic gatherings some of the things I have learned through my experiences. One of the things I have shared is the importance of having a dream. Thinking ahead and planning are essential. When we do so, we are prepared when opportunities arise. Then our reaction is instinctive.

The same is true of avoiding bad situations. I think of youth who are confronted with the choice of attending a party where alcohol or drugs or pornography will be consumed. If a decision has already been made to avoid those destructive things, then the choice is easy. If you wait until peer pressure is being applied to make the decision, it is too late. The choice to stay away from sleaze and smut must be made *previous* to its presentation. The decision not to drink alcohol and not to use drugs needs to be made *before* distractions drown out wise judgment. The right time to decide to run away from pornography is *well in advance* of running into it.

Playing football at BYU got better every day I was there because the quality of guys who played there was second to none. My freshman year came to a close in San Diego at the Holiday Bowl in a game against Ohio State. Since we entered the game with only a 6–5 record, it was important to us to make a good showing and prove we were a better team than our record might indicate. It was the first game after I had jumped Sam Rogers while playing UTEP. The image of that jump wasn't just in my mind anymore. It was on the highlight reel, in photographs, in my memory, and a part of my game. I was excited to use it some more. I couldn't wait to get on the field and catch a ball. I promised myself that the first time I had a chance to hurdle a tackler again, I would.

Early in the game, Ohio State was running all over us. They were leading in the second quarter 21–7. We put together a nice drive and were getting ready to score when I had the chance to jump someone else. We faked a run to the left and John Walsh rolled out to the right. I was the tight end on the right side of the line of scrimmage. I blocked for a count or two and then released into the flat as the first option for the play. John got me the ball and I turned up field. I saw their cornerback ahead of me and I ran straight at him. When I got close to him I jumped, planning to go over the top of him. What I didn't see coming was Lorenzo Styles, the middle linebacker, bearing down on me. As I jumped over the cornerback, Lorenzo hit me from the side, knocking me even higher in the air and cartwheeling toward the ground.

Lorenzo and I would be teammates on the St. Louis Rams, and we later talked and laughed about that play.

I loved the grass at Jack Murphy Stadium, where the game was played. It was fast and smooth. And I also found out that it was hard as rock. I came down on my right shoulder and instantly was breathless. My eyes got wide as I tried to deal with the pain. I rolled to my knees and ran off the field.

I never liked it when players lay on the ground hurt when they could have gotten themselves off the field. I don't think I was able to take a breath until I got to our sideline. Hema asked me if I was all right as I ran toward our bench, but I couldn't speak. As soon as I got to the sideline I collapsed in pain. The trainers couldn't figure out what was wrong with me, and I couldn't help them because I was still gasping for air.

It took me a few minutes on the sideline to get my wits about me. I had separated my right shoulder when I landed. I think a week's worth of breath got knocked out of me at the same time. Our team called a play that involved me, but I was AWOL, lying on the ground trying to find some oxygen.

We had to call a timeout because of all the confusion. That gave me enough time to start breathing again and go back into the game. I was glad, because on fourth down on the eight-yard line, John Walsh threw a perfect pass over my shoulder that I caught with one hand for a touchdown. I had so much adrenaline and excitement running through me that I didn't feel the pain in my shoulder for a while. I recalled that catch for the rest of my career as a positive reminder of the plays I could make. I used that memory just as I used my dream to jump over a player. I would replay it over and over so that my brain would bend to my desires.

Not only did the jump move teach me the importance of having a dream, but I also learned that wisdom is a necessary part of football as well. I couldn't use the unusual ploy every time I caught the ball because it would have been too dangerous. But it sure was a fun move.

CHAPTER 12

MARRIAGE, FOOTBALL, AND A BABY GIRL

Michele and I continued to date throughout that season. At the very beginning when we were going out, I found out I had plenty of competition. Since she was the most beautiful and eligible bachelorette, I had my work cut out for me.

I knew that I wanted to be with her more than anything else in the world, but I did not want to pursue her so aggressively that I would push her away. My mom encouraged me to give her some of her famous chocolate chip cookies and let her know that I cared about her. She was leaving for a weekend volleyball tournament so I dropped off the cookies at her apartment. She wasn't there, but I left them on her kitchen table.

Along with the chocolate chip cookies, I left a note that read: "Michele, good luck in your tournament this weekend. I hope you have fun and do your best. Either way, I think you are the greatest. Chad."

I meant it: she was the "greatest." Whether she chose me or someone else, it had been an honor and a privilege to go out with her. Thank goodness things worked out in my favor. She responded well to the plate of cookies and the note, and we continued dating.

I felt like the luckiest guy in the world. We still credit Quincy Edwards for giving us a reason to get to know each other, and I am so grateful that I gained Quincy's friendship as a missionary in the MTC. In the case of Michele, it certainly paid off to reach out to others in friendship.

Michele and I saw each other almost every single day after that. Talk about surrounding yourself with greatness! She helped guide her team to the final four that year in Madison, Wisconsin. Her team was defeated in a tough match against Penn State. She was named to the All-American team and was asked to speak at the All-American banquet representing the athletes that year. Not only was she one of the best volleyball players, but she was the best girl I had ever met. I was in love. It was time to look for a ring!

Because I grew up just five miles away from BYU campus, I lived at home with my parents through that first year of college. And since I earned a scholarship, I was able to save some money. I actually saved every penny that I could. I finally had enough to walk into Payne Diamonds in Provo, Utah, and pay cash for a simple but beautiful ring.

My neighbor Dale McCann, the same person who introduced me to Coach Edwards when I was fourteen, was still the executive director of the Cougar Club. We had occasion to speak at different functions together. As we drove to those events, he would tell me how important it was to save money as opposed to spending it. In his opinion, it wasn't necessary to go into debt for anything except a house. He not only drove me to the event, but he drove home the importance of being financially wise. What some people thought was tight, he thought was wisdom. He made a huge impact on my life and my pocketbook. Dale would later pass away between my first and second seasons in the NFL, but not before he impacted many, many lives for the better. I am grateful for the time that I had to be with him. His fiscal philosophy still rings in my ears today.

Standing with my beautiful fiancée, Michele Fellows, at Squaw Peak overlooking Utah Valley, a few days before we were married.

Michele and I got engaged on Valentine's Day, and I didn't think life could get any better. The experience of getting on one knee and looking into Michele's eyes while asking her to marry me was better than anything I had experienced before. Thankfully she said yes. We planned a May wedding in Las Vegas in the beautiful Mormon temple that sits on the east side of the valley at the foot of Sunrise Mountain.

Both our families were excited and supportive. I was caught off guard when one of my coaches thought it was the worst thing I could do for my football career. I had a serious disagreement about that with him in the weight room one afternoon. He thought that when a football player got married, that he also got soft and never had the same desire to compete. It was a backward notion and went counter to my belief in the power of surrounding yourself with greatness. If I had followed his advice and hadn't gotten married, I would have missed the greatest part of my life. One of the problems with giving someone bad advice is that you don't have to live with the decision. Thank heavens I did not take his advice.

I found a similar philosophy in coaches throughout the years. There were always a few of them who thought that if a guy was a good citizen or too nice, he could not be a dominant player. I am glad it was only a small number of people who thought that way, but I knew that I had to live my life the way that made sense to me. There would always be critics.

We got married on a beautiful spring day. It was the best day of my life. Michele radiated beauty, and I was ecstatic that she had agreed to marry me. I fell in love with her family as well. Her parents are wonderful people, and they immediately treated me as though I was someone special to them. Her father, Doug, was a school teacher at Bonanza High School in Las Vegas, where he taught Spanish. He was raised in Preston, Idaho. After having served a mission where I worked with several missionaries from Idaho, I gained a great respect for people from Idaho. It seemed to me that they could do anything or fix anything. Doug was no different. While Michele and I spent time in Las Vegas during that off-season, I saw firsthand what Doug's students thought of him. Several times while we were driving together with Doug, students would see him and honk like crazy to say hello. Both current and former students would holler, "Hey, Señor Fellows, how is it going?"

Michele's mom, Geneva, was a full-time nurse who worked at an obstetrics clinic and was the most service-oriented person I'd ever met. She was not only the most generous person north of the South Pole, she was also hilariously funny. She was raised in southern Alberta, Canada, in the small town of Cardston. The people there are known for their incredible work ethic and their great sense of humor. If I had to describe her in one word it would be *selfless*.

Michele had an older sister Christine, who was married to Kent Gunnell, and they lived in Idaho. They had two girls, Brooklynn and Camille, and would later have two boys, Bridger and Landon.

Michele's older brother Steve was married to Jenny. We did a lot of stuff with them while they were still in school at BYU. They would later add three daughters to their family—Eliza and twins, Abigail and Alivia. Steve served a mission to Pusan, South Korea, before they got married. He graduated in accounting and would work for Arthur Anderson in San Francisco after finishing school. Following a few job changes he ended up working in Las Vegas for Pacific Coast Steel as one of their accountants.

Michele's twin brother, Mark, married Becky during training camp of my sophomore year. He and Becky would add five children to their family after they left BYU: McCall, Parker, Carson, Gracie, and Bayden. Mark was a serious road-bike racer before serving a mission to Pusan, Korea, the same place as his brother Steve but a couple years apart from each other. Mark traveled across the country competing in bike races. At 6'5" he was one of the biggest racers. He competed against Lance Armstrong and many of the world's best racers. He would graduate with a master's degree in public administration and currently works in northern California.

It was a joy to be married and to spend each day with the person I loved. Michele made everything in my life better. Football was better and so was school. Being married only increased my desire to do my best and to work hard.

Our football team started the next season with high expectations for ourselves. We had a great year and finished with a record of 10–3 and were ranked tenth in the nation. We beat the University of Oklahoma in the Copper Bowl in Tucson, Arizona.

Even though we had enjoyed a successful year, the same coach who didn't want me to get married gave me the silent treatment for the whole season. That was miserable. We talked only once or twice that year. No one is immune to difficulties in athletics. I am good friends with that coach today, and I know that he only wanted me to succeed. He was famous for getting after players, and it worked for him because he got several of his guys into the NFL. But I also know that it was difficult to work with him. That was a tough year in my life.

I began to really enjoy the cyclical nature of football. Every year posed new challenges and every year was just as difficult as the previous one. There was no hiding from the hard. There was no way to duck the difficult. The process of getting in shape was imminent. There could be no faking that. Training camp was always tough. Each year was an opportunity to work from a clean slate. There was always room for improvement because there has yet to be a perfect football player. The cycle brought around the new and the fresh just the same as it brought the impossible. I loved the game. The smell of the freshly cut grass always reminds me of football season and the nostalgia I have for the game—its sounds, big plays, team camaraderie, the competition, and the excitement of playing in front of huge noisy crowds.

I wish I had space to write about all of the great teammates I had at BYU. I would at least like to name some of them. After he served a mission to New Zealand, Itula Mili returned to BYU, and we joined forces to give our quarterbacks two big targets and defenses two big fits. I got to play with him for the next three seasons. We made a nice two-tight-end package for BYU.

Itula is from the North Shore of Hawaii. He attended Kahuku High School on Oahu, which routinely produces several division I football players a year. Itula was big and fast with hands like sticky glue.

Sometimes it happens that two good players at the same position quarrel over playing time or the number of catches or rushes.

*Shaking hands with Coach LaVell Edwards after BYU
beat the University of Utah my senior year.*

It was not that way with me and Itula. We became close friends
and supported each other. We celebrated together after good plays,
we learned how to open each other up on pass patterns, and we
both liked jumping over defenders. He was extremely quiet and
shy off the field, but he played with great emotion and passion
during the games.

I was glad that I had Tom Rabb for a high-school coach because he taught me to be a team player. I was also glad that I
served a mission where Kent Watson taught me to serve my companions in Taiwan, to love the people, and how to buckle down
when the going got tough. And I was glad that LaVell Edwards
was my college coach because he taught through his own example
that if you don't care about the guys next to you, you won't be as
effective as you can be.

All of my coaches prepared me to embrace playing with Itula

instead of fearing it or being jealous of his many talents. I am grateful that Itula had such a cool attitude with me. He happily shared the glory and the catches that went with being a tight end at BYU.

We both owe some of our success to Patti Edwards. There was a stretch during our sophomore seasons when we were not getting very many passes. We wanted to be more involved, but sometimes that's the way it goes. After one of the games where our team could have done better, Patti told LaVell that if he wanted to have more success, then he should throw it to the tight ends more. After that, Coach Edwards got us more involved in the games. When things were going better for our team and especially the tight ends, Coach Edwards told us that it was his wife's coaching from the sideline that helped get us more involved. That's just one more reason I will always be a big fan of Patti Edwards.

After seven games during my junior year, I was leading all tight ends in the nation in number of receptions. In a game at home against the University of Hawaii, I caught a short pass on the left side of the field, made some moves, and started heading upfield. I was hit by three of their players at the same time. In the resulting pileup, one of the player's full weight landed on my right ankle. The pain felt as though someone had shot me with a gun. I was helped off the field and taken in the back of a truck to a nearby hospital. I was anxious to find out what happened and get back into the game.

The X-rays were negative. No broken bone, just a painful ankle. I was relieved and excited to get back to the game for the second half and make some more plays. It really hurt to walk, but I thought if I taped it up really tight I could make do. When I got back to the sideline I had one of the trainers tape my ankle super tight. It felt like a ski boot. The pain was worse than before, but I still wanted to play.

When Coach Edwards saw what I was doing, he told the

trainers that he did not want to put me back in the game. We were well ahead and the game was already out of reach. Coach Edwards was inspired with that decision.

Unbeknownst to me, my dad was in the stands suffering with severe flu-like symptoms. It was a very warm and sunny autumn day, and his body was on fire. As soon as the game was over, we met as a family by the locker room. My mom and dad thought his endocarditis had returned, and we all went to the hospital to see a doctor about my dad's condition.

While we were there, the training staff at BYU requested that I get an MRI taken of my ankle. I was reluctant for a couple of reasons. I hated the idea of being stuck in that small tube and dealing with claustrophobic feelings for an hour. I also didn't want them to find anything that would force me off the field. But I did have the MRI. As soon as it was finished, I met my mom and dad on the other side of the hospital. Since the X-rays on my ankle had been negative, I was trying to walk on my foot to promote quicker healing.

While we were visiting with the doctor about my dad's condition, I heard my name announced over the hospital intercom. I was told to call the hospital information line. When I did, it was George Curtis, the head trainer, who told me to make sure I was not standing on my ankle. I was. I asked why. He told me that the MRI showed a long hairline fracture of my medial malleolus (ankle bone). Everything turned out to be okay with my dad, but with four games remaining, I was finished for the season. I would cheer on my team from the sideline. If it were not for LaVell's wisdom I would have tried to play. The doctors said that I would have for sure displaced the hairline fracture and required major ankle surgery.

I was not the only physical casualty. Everyone who plays the game gets hurt at some point. Larry Harmer severely dislocated his elbow and was not able to finish his football career because of it. The person who talked me into playing with him would not be able to play himself. I was disappointed that we would not be able to spend so much of our time together lifting weights, running, practicing, traveling, and playing. He took everything in stride and entered the graduate program of organizational behavior and received the top job out of school when he left. Larry went on to have a fabulous career in business, where he excels today.

Steve Sarkisian came to BYU as a Catholic from Southern California. He played quarterback at El Camino Junior College and then transferred to BYU. I had heard a lot about him from John Walsh, who was his good friend. John left BYU a year early to play in the NFL and Steve came in to take his place. Steve fit right in with the team, the city of Provo, and the unique culture of Utah. He was humble but full of confidence as well. He made friends easily and never acted as though he was cooler than anyone on the team. He respected the coaches and earned their trust very quickly with his quick mind.

I was impressed the first day of practice by how well he was able to pick up the BYU offense. I found out about his field smarts on one specific play during spring ball that year. I ran straight down the field on a seam route and he threw me a pass that pushed me away from the safety a couple of yards instead of straight into him and into a gigantic headache. It was a small thing that a fan might not even notice during a game. But for me, the one putting my life on the line in certain vulnerable situations, it meant everything. He could have made an easier throw by throwing into the hole that I was running for, but that would have led me straight into a train wreck with the safety. Instead, he threaded the ball perfectly up the field to where I could catch it and run past the safety or take a glancing blow.

The second he threw that pass to me, I knew that I could trust him with my life. I would go after any ball he threw because I knew he could read the defense and he knew what he was doing.

The excitement and anticipation to get on the field again for my senior year almost killed me. Our team was stacked with "ballers" at every position and they played with selfless awareness of each other. That selflessness did not stop with the players; it carried over into their families. It started with Sarkisian's parents. They came to every game and cheered us on. They loved BYU. Steve's dad, Seb, was Armenian and his mom was a blonde with blue eyes from Ireland. They were some of the nicest people I have ever met. They were a Catholic family that embraced BYU and its family-friendly, clean environment. They had no airs of arrogance whatsoever.

Steve's positive attitude and unselfish demeanor had a great effect on our team. It brought us all together like family. We knew that Steve and his parents cared about every one of us. He never acted as though we were not pulling the weight for him or that we had let him down. If we lost a game, we lost together. If we won a game, we won together. The feeling the Sarkisians brought to the team was infectious. It spread to all the players and all the parents.

Shay Muirbrook was our standout all-conference middle linebacker. He had a knack for making big plays and a toughness that made him a perfect middle linebacker. He also had parents who were as committed to our whole team's success as they were to Shay's personal success. I received a good-luck call from his dad before every single football game. If I wasn't available he would leave a message on my phone that inspired me to play with all I had. I kept some of his messages on my phone for over a year because they meant so much to me.

That a parent of one of my teammates would go out of his way to encourage me meant that we were on a real team. We not only cared for each other, but we cared about each other's families and they cared for us. Team sports are successful when the players act like a team. Team chemistry was even stronger when the extended family shared that same sentiment. Selfishness is the

Picture day with my quarterback, Steve Sarkisian, before our senior year.
Steve was awarded the Sammy Baugh trophy that same year for being the nation's
top passer. He is now the head coach at the University of Washington.

great destroyer of team chemistry. We had very little of it on that team.

One of my highlights that season was getting to play with my little brother Todd. He served a mission to Oklahoma City, and when he returned he walked onto the football team. It was fun watching him work so hard to make the team. It reminded me of the struggle that I had gone through a few years earlier to make it as well. We loved playing together. Since I was three grades older than he was in school we were never on the same team growing up. Todd was an outside linebacker and he played defense against me all year in practice. It was awesome. We were able to lift weights and run together. So much of our lives revolved around football and we grew closer doing it together.

But the best part of that senior year was the birth of our first child. Our daughter, Emily, was born in the middle of the season. After finishing her playing career at BYU, Michele got a job as a math teacher at nearby American Fork High School. Her pregnancy went very well and she delivered a ten-pound baby. We were in heaven until the baby did not make any sound at all. There was no crying, no fussing; she was just quiet and blue. It was frightening.

In tears, Michele asked if I would bless our little girl. The delivery room was filled with doctors and nurses who had been instantly alerted to our child's condition. They moved aside for a few precious seconds, and I gave my daughter a blessing, similar to the blessing that Jason had given to my dad during his stroke. I was overwhelmed by the amount of love that I felt for this newborn baby. My heart was consumed with compassion such as I had never felt before. The blessing took only a few seconds to pronounce, and when I finished the doctors rushed Emily into the newborn intensive care unit.

She stayed in NICU for three days. The problem was that the umbilical cord had wrapped around her neck, and she had also ingested some amniotic fluid into her lungs. She had the best care and rapidly got better. We took her home on her third day, and I had never been such a cautious driver. I wanted to put a big bubble around our car so that she would be safe. Having a little girl caused a dramatic life-change. She was precious and beautiful and the beginning of our surrounding ourselves with wonderful children.

A month later we celebrated Halloween at my brother Dave's home. Michele dressed up as a football player with my jersey and eye black and little Emily was dressed as a football. It was so cute. I was very happy to be a dad.

Another highlight that year was how we finished. We beat the Wyoming Cowboys in the first ever WAC Championship game in Las Vegas. While we were there, my roommate was John Tait, our left tackle. He was the best offensive lineman who ever played at BYU and would go on to have a long career in the NFL with the Kansas City Chiefs and the Chicago Bears. When we checked into our hotel for the bowl game, our room had only one bed. We laughed when we opened the door and then went back to the front desk and had our room changed to one with two beds.

The next morning at breakfast, we were told that Coach Chow wanted to see John and me and that he was not a happy camper. We wondered what he was mad about. When we saw him, he wanted to know why we were not in our room for bed check the night before. It took a second to remember that we had switched our room and he was probably not aware of the change. John and I cracked up thinking about that whole misunderstanding, because we probably went to sleep earlier than anyone else on the team.

College football at the time implemented the much maligned Alliance Bowl system to determine a national champion. Even though BYU had won eighteen conference championships and had one of the best records in college football at 13–1 and was ranked fifth in the nation, we were not invited to play in one of the Alliance Bowl top three bowl games. It was a letdown not to be included, which only verified for us the corruption of the process.

We *were* invited to play in the Cotton Bowl in Dallas, Texas, against the Kansas State Wildcats. It was the first ever New Year's Day bowl game for BYU, and it was the desire of every player to win that game for LaVell. Our duty as players meant rising up and winning for the greatest coach in the game. We represented three decades of players who had battled for LaVell. This was our turn to stand on their shoulders and give LaVell a historic win. I think we wanted it more for him than for our selves.

Even though we had wanted an invitation to one of the Alliance Bowl games, we were honestly grateful to be there because it was the Cotton Bowl and that meant something to us. Great players through the ages had played in the Cotton Bowl. Coach Edwards would have been embarrassed if any of us had acted with anything other than gratitude for being there. The Cotton Bowl people treated us with over-the-top Southern hospitality. They did such a fine job that they made us want to move to Dallas.

We beat Kansas State in one of the best Cotton Bowl games in history. It was a back-and-forth contest that went down to the last play. Our two defensive backs, Tim McTyer and Omar Morgan, and our middle linebacker, Shay Muirbrook, saved the game on the last drive with incredible plays. Shay got a huge sack and Tim pushed their receiver Kevin Lockett out of the end zone after he had jumped to make a sweet grab. His feet were going to come down inbounds, but as they got about an inch from the grass, Tim pushed him out of bounds.

Then, with only seconds on the clock, Kansas State drove down inside the red zone, threatening to score. On the last play of the game, Omar picked off a pass to seal the victory for our team. The game was attended by swarms of Kansas State fans all wearing purple and outnumbering our fans three to one. But in the corner of the north end zone we had a special contingent of fans. There were about two hundred missionaries from the Dallas area, wearing their dark suits, white shirts, and ties. They were given permission to come to the game and cheer us on. Knowing for myself just how hard they work and how dedicated they are, it was cool to have them there supporting us.

As soon as the game clock ticked down to zero, our whole team ran across the field, stood in front of them, and saluted them with waves, high-fives, handshakes, and pictures. It was a monumental victory for LaVell and BYU. What a way to end a terrific season.

When the season was over our record was 14–1 and we were still ranked fifth.

The Alliance Bowl system came under fire when the Senate Judiciary Committee held hearings to determine if they were in violation of anti-trust laws. I was sent to Washington, D.C., to represent BYU in the hearings. It was a new experience to testify before that body and lend my voice to the effort to change the system.

My main point was that their system eliminated about half of the teams in the country from having any chance to become national champions before the season even started. They were crushing the glass slipper for all of the so-called lesser teams before the invitations to the dance were even made. Their arguments in favor of the exclusivity of the Alliance were sounding more un-American all the time.

With the pressure from the Senate, the system was changed just enough to create the Bowl Championship Series, which carefully skirted the anti-trust laws in question but still runs counter to the common sense of the American people. The University of Utah would twice go undefeated and twice crash the BCS party by winning their bowl games in convincing fashion, but still not be crowned national champions because they did not belong to a blueblood conference. The way the BCS was put together was clearly not what inspired the first Americans to leave England and hack out a life on the soil and the frontier of this great country. Pedigree should not trump performance. Champions should always be determined within the lines of the field, not in the courtroom.

CHAPTER 13

THE NFL

As I prepared for the draft, I had some help from some NFL veterans. Steve Young and Lee Johnson lived close to BYU in the off-season, and I got to know them through Steve's younger brother Tom. They were both still playing at the peak of their careers. Steve had just won the Super Bowl with a record-setting performance of six touchdown passes in the 49ers victory against the San Diego Chargers in Super Bowl XXIX. Starting with my sophomore year at BYU, those guys had encouraged me and even invited me to train with them.

Their help turned out to be more beneficial than I could imagine because I found out what made them such good pros. They had a determined commitment to hard work that was beyond anything I had seen. When we would run sprints together in the summer, they would go longer than I thought possible. They attacked their workouts with a vengeance. They made everything we did competitive. If we were doing sit ups, they would push me ten times farther than I would have gone without their help. They had so much energy and made working out a game in itself.

No wonder Steve would later go into the Pro Football Hall of Fame. He had a desire that wouldn't quit, plus he could still roll. He could still run the forty-yard dash in 4.5 seconds at the end of his career. I told him that I would throw with him anytime, anywhere. It didn't matter if he wanted to throw at midnight, I would make myself available. A few times I was checked out of my classes by the athletic department only to find out that it was Steve wanting to throw.

As I got closer to the draft, Lee would pretend to be a trash-talking linebacker and would get in my face and call me a red-headed freckle-faced punk and challenge me to either dominate or quit. He tried as hard as he could to get me ready for the League. He played the part of an intimidating linebacker pretty well, and it was great rehearsal. As it turned out, I never had to deal with anyone in the NFL who got in my face any worse than Lee did. He was a great help in preparing for the professional game.

Getting ready for the NFL draft was a new adventure. It started as soon as the college season was over. All during my senior year I got letters from agents who wanted to represent me. I threw all of them away because I knew there would be plenty of time to select an agent when my college career was over. That was one way that I was able to stay focused during that last year. College players get bombarded with those letters, and I think many of them let the attention turn into a big fat distraction. It could also turn into real trouble if an agent offered any services before college eligibility was finished. All of the potential sticky situations were completely avoided by throwing the letters away.

The NFL Combine was another major milestone in the draft process. The Combine took place in Indianapolis, Indiana, and was the annual cattle call for football players. The careers of many players have ended before they ever began with a poor showing at the Combine. John Walsh was predicted by draft guru Mel Kiper to be one of the top three picks of the draft. It turned out that

John was not drafted until the end of the seventh round, after it was reported that he ran a very slow forty-yard dash at the Combine. Things like that can cause a player's draft stock to plummet. There were other cases where a great Combine propelled a player into the first round. Such was the case with Mike Mamula, who dominated the Combine with speed and power and was the sixth player selected in the draft. Mike and I were teammates for several years in Philly. I knew how important it was to make a good showing at the Combine, and I wanted to do just that.

It was a nice honor even being invited to the Combine, because there are only just over three hundred players invited and only 224 get drafted. I was selected along with five other teammates from BYU. It was good to see them out there as we passed each other at meals or drills. We were outfitted with special Combine sweats and workout gear, which was clearly marked with our position and a number. I was TE #13.

The first thing we did when we got to Indianapolis was take the Cybex test to determine knee strength and stability by measuring the strength of hamstring and quadricep muscles. To take the Cybex test, a player sat in a chair with his leg strapped onto a lever that allowed it to move up and down, bending at the knee. When the trainer running the test gave the go-ahead, the player moved his leg up and down as fast as he could for about thirty seconds. Both legs were tested. Even though the test was relatively short in length, it was tiring. Some players felt as though it would hurt their forty time and boycotted the test. The NFL did make sure that we had thirty-six hours between taking the test and running the forty. That was why we took the test as soon as we got to Indy.

Mealtimes were cool at the Combine because the best players in college football were there. I enjoyed meeting many of the guys I had played against over the years.

My Combine group was made up of tight ends and some linebackers, and my assigned roommate was Matt Russell, the linebacker from the University of Colorado. He ended up playing for the Detroit Lions, where his career was cut short by a knee injury.

After dinner the first day of the camp, our group went to the hospital, where we were X-rayed for everything imaginable. We were there for hours; I was amazed how many X-rays were taken for each of us. When we finally got back to our hotel room, Matt joked, "When we turn the light off to go to sleep tonight, we're going to glow!"

Players feared that with all of the required medical tests, a doctor might actually find something that would prevent them from playing football. Such was the case in the 2009 Combine when a doctor discovered that Northeastern tight end Brian Mandeville had a non-life-threatening heart abnormality. He was told that he would never play football again. That was a rare exception, but it was not out of the realm of possibility. We figured if they looked long enough, they would eventually find something wrong with each of us.

Back at the hotel, teams conducted interviews with players they were interested in. I met with several teams. Sometimes it was with the whole staff and sometimes it was with just a coach or two. I thought the two coolest coaches at the Combine were Andy Reid, who was the quarterback coach with the Green Bay Packers, and Juan Castillo, who was the tight-end coach for the Philadelphia Eagles. Andy was cool because he was a former BYU player and just seemed so down to earth. I knew from following the buzz on football coaches that he was an up-and-coming coach and that he would possibly be a head coach one day. Juan was cool because he had the best smile and because there was a mix of humility and fiery determination that I could sense when I visited with him.

Along with the interviews, many teams required players to

take psychological tests. The Giants' test was notorious. It had 465 questions and took about three hours to complete. Some of the questions were off the wall and seemed to have little to do with football. An example was, "Do you like flowers?" I was more than happy to take the test because I wanted a job with an NFL team, but I did wonder how I felt about flowers might reveal if I could play ball or not.

The next day we went through all of the football drills on the field. Our flexibility was tested with a yardstick, measuring down to the centimeter, just how far we could bend. We were stretched in every conceivable way. After that small exercise was finished, I felt like a pretzel.

Our group performed the broad jump, the vertical jump, and the bench press. The bench press revealed how many repetitions you could do, lifting 225 pounds. There were several timed running drills, including the forty-yard dash, twenty-yard shuttle, sixty-yard shuttle, and the three-cone drill. I ran the forty in 4.84 seconds at the Combine. It was always an issue if guys were going to run the forty at the Combine since the times were often slower than expected. Tony Gonzales, the tight end who would have a Hall of Fame career for the Kansas City Chiefs, ran the exact same time I did. I thought that was good company. When I ran for the scouts at BYU, my best forty time was 4.56.

The variety of running drills provided a way to evaluate every player with the same measuring stick. Tight ends also caught passes, ran pass routes, blocked against a coach holding a bag, and blocked against a blocking sled.

Along with the on-field drills, each player was poked and manipulated by the team doctors and trainers. Every part of our bodies was measured and tested for possible injuries, exact size, and dimension. If a doctor or trainer had a question about any part of our bodies, additional X-rays would be taken. We also stood on a platform in front of a camera wearing nothing but small shorts.

We were filmed, front and back, so that each team had a copy for later use. Our fingers were measured for length; our arms were measured for wingspan. At the end of the three-day Combine, I wondered what I was getting myself into.

Draft day was much anticipated and much talked about. I had thought about it for years during my career at BYU. I was excited each time someone I knew was drafted and felt bad when others who hoped to be drafted were not. The draft is broken up into two days. The first day is composed of the first three rounds. The second is for rounds four through seven. Even though I was not anticipating getting drafted on the first day, I still followed the happenings on TV. On the second day of the draft, my family gathered at our parents' home and we watched closely where I would get drafted. My friend Carter Rockwood also hung out with us for the draft. He was one of my high-school teammates and a huge NFL fan.

The rounds went by, one after another, without so much as mentioning my name. I was disappointed but I wasn't shocked. I was prepared for anything and everything. Michele and I always said to hope for the best but prepare for the worst.

Michele and I had also talked about the possibility of not getting drafted and not being selected as an undrafted free agent. I had always viewed education as the best foundation for my life. During my senior year, I was named to the 1996, twenty-four-member, Scholar-Athlete Team by the College Football Association. I had also been awarded a post-graduate scholarship from the NCAA, and if playing professional football turned out not to be an option, I wanted to continue my schooling.

Luckily for me, the worst-case scenario was never realized. Even though I was not drafted, I was contacted by fourteen teams during the draft, and they all invited me to their first mini camp. Ironically, not being drafted had some unique benefits that are not well-known. The obvious benefit of being drafted was there would be a signing bonus of some sort. If a player was drafted in the first round, that signing bonus would likely number in the millions of dollars. If a player was drafted in the seventh and final round, that would likely amount to $100,000 or thereabouts. While it would be great to get that money in a signing bonus, it would not amount to much if the player did not fit the system or the coach who drafted him.

No player had any say as to what team he would play for. He was obligated to the team that drafted him, without any choice in the matter. The ironic part was that, as an undrafted player, I had a total say in what team I would play for, if there were more than one team interested in signing me. A team could have around eighty-five players on its roster for the off-season. That number would need to be cut down to fifty-three to start the season. Each team would draft around seven players each year and sign another ten or so players as undrafted free agents.

Previous to the draft, I had talked with my agent, Don Yee, about the teams who were likely in need of a tight end and what teams fit with the skills that I brought to the table. With his help, I narrowed the decision down to a few teams, each of which ran the West Coast Offense. Philadelphia was at the top of my list. For one thing, Ty Detmer was the Eagles' starting quarterback. I had watched him play for BYU when I was in high school, and even though my brother played for rival University of Utah, besides Mike, my favorite player was Ty. Jon Gruden was the offensive coordinator for the Eagles and was considered one of the top, up-and-coming coaches. He was also quite a likeable character when I spoke with him on the phone on draft day.

The first person to call was Juan Castillo. Juan let me know that the Eagles really wanted to sign me, and we talked about the small signing bonus they offered. Some of the teams offered up to $20,000 for a signing bonus, but the Eagles only offered $5,000, the lowest of any team. After talking with Juan for a minute about what I thought was a very small offer, Jon Gruden jumped on the phone. The first thing he told me was how much he wanted me on the Eagles. Then he told me that he loved me! It was in that out-of-the-blue declaration that I learned I was one of John's favorites. He was so excited and spoke with so much energy and passion that it got me fired up. I signed with the Eagles. Anyone who has ever played for Jon Gruden has heard him say, "I love you, man!"

At the very first mini camp after the draft, which lasted four days, Jon Gruden was very complimentary of my style of play, my effort, and what I could offer the team. He asked if I would be able to stay in Philly instead of heading home after the mini camp. Because of an NCAA rule, I was not able to stay in Philly until after the second mini camp in June.

During the second mini camp in June, John showed even more interest in me. Two of the veteran tight ends were injured, and Luther Broughton, the other rookie, and I were the only healthy tight ends. Coach Gruden thought I could have an immediate impact on the team. While walking out to practice one day during that mini camp, he declared in his uniquely loud voice, "Chad Lewis, you are Rocky Balboa right here in Philly, man! You are coming from nowhere and you're going to the top!"

I was somewhat embarrassed since he said it loud enough for the whole team to hear, but grateful too that my offensive coordinator recognized my ability to catch the ball.

Two months later, during training camp of my rookie year, Jon Gruden taught me one of the most important lessons I would learn in the NFL. We were talking after practice one day, and I was very interested to know how I was doing and if I was going to make the team. My wife and daughter were at home hoping and praying that I would stay healthy and play well enough to make it. I thought about making the team nearly every second of that training camp. I will share more about what training camp is like in a later chapter.

John told me that I was playing well and that if I kept it up, I would make the team. Then the lesson came. He asked me how old I was. He knew that since I had already served a mission to Taiwan for two years, I was older than every other rookie. When I told him that I was twenty-five he looked at me with one of his great facial expressions—his eyes squinted a little bit, his lips pressed together in almost a crooked grin—and said, "You are an old rookie, man. You have spent a couple years in a foreign country teaching people whatever you taught them. You have had experiences that other rookies haven't. You are older and wiser. You need to act like it. Don't act like every other rookie. You don't have time to do that. You need to play like an old rookie!"

He couldn't have said anything better. When I got back to my room, I thought a lot about that, not just with football, but with everything I was doing in my life. I really didn't have time to act like a rookie. I needed to always remember what I had done in my life, and not take it for granted, and not forget about it, but remember who I was. I needed to carry my experiences with me in everything I did. I needed to be an old rookie. I needed to be aware of my strengths and abilities and my weaknesses as well.

The highlight of that training camp for me was catching a touchdown pass in our preseason game against the Jets. It couldn't have come at a better time. I knew the coaches were debating if they were going to keep me around or not, and I knew that I needed to do something to tip the scales in my favor. The play was "2 Jet Double Swing Post." I always loved that play. I ran a swing route, which was a flat route and up, meaning I ran from my position at tight end almost straight to the sideline, only gaining three yards of depth by the time I got to the sideline. But just before I reached the sideline, I ran straight up, along the sideline and into the end zone. Our second-year quarterback, Bobby Hoying, threw me a beauty of a pass and I held onto it for dear life.

When the final roster was posted, my name was on it! When Lewis and Clark overcame every obstacle on their nearly impossible expedition and finally succeeded in reaching the great Pacific Ocean, one of them exclaimed, "Oh! The joy!" That is how I felt. I never wanted to count my chickens before they were hatched, and I knew the final roster wasn't final until it was final. Even after it was finalized, teams still made changes to their roster because of players who were cut from other teams at the same time. I got used to never feeling all that comfortable about my job security, but making the team, oh, the joy!

Our first game was against the New York Giants in the Meadowlands. I caught a couple of passes late in the game and even tried to jump over their safety Tito Wooten, but it wasn't as successful as some of my jumps at BYU. I would have to do a better job of picking my spots. But I loved being out on the field for a real game; it reminded me of my first college catch against UCLA.

John Gruden loved to put in formations for each player on the team. In my case he named one particular personnel grouping "Cougar Chad." The cougar was an obvious reference to the BYU mascot. John loved to call out his personnel groupings with energy. Each time he called out that grouping, it was a signal to me to rise up and dominate. He did not want me going into the game in a critical spot only to get weak-kneed and flub up. Everything he said, he said with gusto, including the personnel groupings. He wanted us to play with that same confidence. He always coached us to be dragon slayers.

It started in the meeting room when we installed the plays. He would announce to the team what the personnel would be for a certain play. He was basically announcing to the offense who would be running that play and also who wouldn't. He meant to motivate all of us when he did it. I always took it as such. I felt privileged to be included in our red-zone offense. He let me know that when the game was on the line he wanted me in there.

He did the same thing on the practice field. He would shout out the personnel groupings as loud as he could. He tried to increase the pressure during practice to simulate the pressure of a game. All coaches did that in their own way. John prepared me mentally for the pressure of the tight moments in the contest, when everything is on the line. His approach to the game and the things he told me stayed with me through out my career.

Ray Rhodes was my first NFL head coach. He was always referred to as a "players' coach" because he used to be a player and understood a player's mentality. I will always be grateful to him because he took a chance on me and gave me my first job. He also used to love to talk a little trash with the players during practice. Every so often he would brag that he could cover me like a blanket and that I would never catch a ball if he were defending me. He really enjoyed doing that; it was his way of getting close to his players.

Ray made sure that I did not miss the birth of my second child. Michele was due just thirteen months after our first little Emily was born. Since football was in my blood, I guess it was fitting that our children were born during the season. I was nervous that she was going to deliver while I was on the road. That would not have been good.

Michele started to feel contractions the day after we played the San Francisco 49ers on Monday Night Football. I went to work knowing that I could be called at anytime to go to the hospital. Maybe it was the excitement of the game that helped Michele's contractions get started. That game was memorable for several reasons. It was always sweet to play on Monday night because, as the players would say, "The whole neighborhood is watching!" It was also a challenge to play a team that had been as dominant as the 49ers. Steve Young was still throwing the ball better than anyone.

The game was mainly noteworthy because of the countless fights that broke out in the stands. There were so many fights that the news covered them for a week or more. One unruly fan actually shot a red flare across the stadium. It lit up the night even with the many lights that illuminated the playing field. I followed the trail of fire back to where it came from and the guy was calmly reloading and preparing to fire another round when the security guys pulled him out of his chair and hauled him away. The game was madness.

It was so crazy, in fact, that Philadelphia set up a courtroom in the basement of Veterans Stadium. There was a real judge who held court during every game for the remainder of that season. That was not a proud moment for the city. What it did was reinforce the idea that an opposing fan should carefully select his wardrobe before entering the Vet.

Toward the end of the game, I was called on in the red zone to make a play. It was the same play that Steve Young and I had worked on together back at BYU during the summer. The play was, "322 Y Stick Nod" and will be described in greater detail later.

Steve said that he and Brent Jones, the great 49er tight end, were both yelling from the sideline that I was going to run the stick nod. But they could not get the attention of Merton Hanks, the strong safety who was defending me, before the ball was snapped. Our third quarterback that year, Bobby Hoying, threw a perfect pass to me and it was good for a touchdown. It was the first touchdown pass of Hoying's NFL career.

After the game, Steve and Brent grabbed me and shook me in jest for scoring a touchdown against them on a play that we had worked on together. Even though I scored a touchdown, I tasted the bitter pill of defeat. Losing games in the NFL seemed caustic. Losses could become habit forming. As a tight end, I had so much

Catching a pass on Monday Night Football against the San Francisco 49ers. My friend Derek Smith (#50) is tacking me.

Courtesy of the Philadelphia Eagles

to improve on if I ever wanted to be an every-down player. At that point in my career, I was only getting playing time in certain passing situations. I needed to become a better blocker.

Thinking about the birth of our next child was much better than focusing only on what I needed to do to better my career. I was in meetings with the offense when I was informed by Carol Cullen, the longtime secretary for the Eagles, that Michele was in labor. Ray told me to get out of the facility and to go to the hospital and be with my wife. I am glad that he was cool about it because it took a lot of pressure off my shoulders. I shot out of our facility in the basement of Veterans Stadium like a rocket.

I was there in plenty of time to witness the birth of our second beautiful daughter, Sarah Lewis. Sarah weighed ten pounds, the same as Emily had. I was amazed that Michele was able to deliver such healthy babies. Sarah was our cute little bear cub. She would snuggle up to us really tight like a baby bear and was so fun to hold. Emily loved her little sister. We were so grateful to have two little girls. The three girls that surrounded me were the brightest spots in my life.

After calling our parents, I called Ray to let him know that everything went well and we were blessed with a healthy baby girl. I asked if I should head back to the facility to catch up on what I had missed. He started laughing and told me to relax and just enjoy being with my wife and newborn. He said there was no need to come back that day. Since I was still a rookie who was fighting for my job each week, I was surprised that Ray was that cool about everything. I cherished being able to stay the rest of the day with Michele and Sarah.

The defensive coordinator my rookie year was Emmitt Thomas. He was inducted into the Pro Football Hall of Fame in 2008. He had played defensive back for the Kansas City Chiefs and worked his way up the coaching ranks. The first day that I was in Philadelphia with the Eagles was a day that I will never forget. I arrived at the facility where we were going to have some preliminary meetings before we met as a whole team. I was meeting with Juan Castillo, my position coach, and he stepped out of the office for a moment. I was left alone looking around the place, wondering what I had just gotten myself into. At that moment, a tall man with glasses, a mustache, and a lower lip full of chewing tobacco stuck his head into the doorway, tilted his head down so that he could see over his glasses, and proceeded to query me.

He said, "Hey, Utah!?"

I said, "Yeah!?"

He said, "Are you a Marmon?"

I chuckled at the pronunciation and said, "Yeah, I'm a Marmon!"

He said, "Are you a good Marmon?"

I said, "I don't know. I try to be."

He said, "Do you smoke?"

I said, "No."

He said, "Do you drink?"

I said, "No."

He said, "Yeah, you a good Marmon!"

And then he walked off as fast as he had appeared. I didn't have any clue who he was or where he came from or where he went. He knew what a Mormon was, and he also knew what a good Mormon did and did not do. With that brief and hilarious introduction, I knew I could trust him as a coach. Whoever he was.

Juan soon came back into the room, and I asked him who that man was who had just popped his head into the room. He thought it was Emmitt Thomas. I asked him who Emmitt Thomas was. And he told me that he was our defensive coordinator and future Hall of Fame member. I felt pretty stupid that I had not done a better job of studying who all of the coaches were for my own team and was embarrassed that I didn't know Emmitt.

I grew to love Emmitt because he loved the players, all of them. He loved every player in the locker room and every person in the whole facility. I knew that because of how he treated people. He was polite and respectful with everyone, and I mean *everyone*. His eyes twinkled when he spoke with players and when he coached us. He coached from a wealth of knowledge and a lifetime around the game as a player and a coach. He was revered by all of us because of how he treated us. Looking back on that first exchange, Emmitt didn't waste one minute telling me that he was the defensive coordinator, or that he was one of the league's best all-time defensive backs, or that he would probably go into the Hall of Fame one day. I would figure that out soon enough. The first thing he did was strike up a friendship with me, one that would last forever. I think that all of his friendships will last forever because he treats people with so much class and respect.

Emmitt took care of me. He always gave me small pointers in practice, such as when I was leaning into my breaks or when I was telegraphing my intent. He would tell me not to give away where I was going to run by changing my speed or gait. He had an eye for football and was a genius as a coach.

More important to me than his coaching tips was his friendship. I was a white "Marmon" kid from BYU, and he treated me like I was one of his sons. He loved me—I could see it in his eyes. He cared about me as a person and a player. I don't think I was unique in that way; he was that way with all of his players. But I was surely grateful. There were a few times when a negative statement was made about the Mormon Church, and if Emmitt ever heard it, he would smile, point at me, and say, "He's a good guy."

When I went to Hawaii for my first of three Pro Bowls, the Minnesota Vikings coaching staff was coaching that game. The Vikings were defeated by the Giants in the NFC Championship game, and so they were to coach the game. I was thrilled with that because Emmitt Thomas was at that time the defensive coordinator of the Vikings. It gave me great personal satisfaction to run up to Emmitt on the field before our first practice and thank him for teaching me, coaching me, and helping me in so many different ways in my rookie season with the Eagles. I could not hold back my emotions and my eyes filled with my feelings. He knew what I was talking about because he had probably heard the same thing from dozens of athletes. It meant so much to me that he had given me the genuine Emmitt Thomas treatment.

When I listened to his induction speech in Canton for the Hall of Fame, I cried a bucket of tears. It was one of the most heartfelt speeches that I have ever heard from an inductee. I got a copy of it off the Internet and sent it to all of my family and friends and encouraged them to watch it, the whole thing, because it was so good. I loved Emmitt then and now. He is a Hall of Fame player, coach, and person.

Juan Castillo was my first NFL position coach. He could not have been a better fit for me. Juan was the tight-end coach under the notoriously early rising Jon Gruden. It was routine for John to get into the office at 4:00 A.M. John was the offensive coordinator under Ray Rhodes at Philly. In his attempt to let Gruden know that he was ready to work, Juan would often show up to work earlier than John. It was like a game. Juan took it seriously, too. He would tell me and the other rookie tight end, Luther Broughton, that he beat John into work that morning. Luther and I loved Juan and we would tease him for showing up so early. Even though we would talk a little smack with him for competing in such a crazy game of lack of sleep, we had tremendous respect for what he was doing to prove his worth to the organization, the other coaches, the players, and his family. He made sure he added value every day he was there.

Juan broke down more film than anyone in the business. If he wanted to teach us something, he would scour the tapes of other games and other players until he could find exactly what he wanted to show us. He went the extra mile on a daily basis so that we understood the concepts he taught. He came to BYU to work me out before the draft. I knew then that I wanted to play for him because he was a hard-working family man. At the time we first met, he had two little boys whom he just loved. When he spoke about them, he would beam and his smile would light up the room.

Juan was also the most courageous coach I had been around. He would always take the heat from the head coach for a mistake that I made. Then he would make sure that I never made that mistake again. That was a quality that was rare in the coaching world. A lot of coaches would have no problem selling their player down the river after a mistake. They could easily say to the head coach that they had gone over that in meetings and the player should have known better. That was not how Juan worked; he would take the heat, take the blame, accept full responsibility, and then he would show me what I needed to do to fix whatever was broken.

Juan also constantly worked to build my confidence. He would push me to my limit on the practice field, in the film room, and anytime in between, but then he would get clips of my best plays and he would show them to me to remind me what I was capable of. He would even find a play or two from college and put that on his highlight reel as a reminder to me that I could catch anything. With that kind of commitment, I knew that he cared deeply and that he didn't look at coaching as just a job. He took it to another level. He would often keep me after practice to work on my blocking, since that was what I needed most to improve my game.

As a rookie, I could not have had a better position coach. Any success I had that year I attribute to his great coaching in preparing me. Even that first year as an unrestricted free agent, Juan inspired me that I could be a Pro Bowl tight end. He made a tape with every catch the Pro Bowl tight ends had made the year before. He would then ask me if I thought those guys were better than I was. He would ask me if they had done anything that I couldn't do. He raised my sights to the top even though I was one of the lowest guys on the League's totem pole. That was greatness.

I enjoyed playing for the Eagles my rookie year. I found out just how tough the NFL was and how many small injuries I would need to play through to stay on the field. I was grateful to have a good-paying job and grateful for all of the associations that I was making. I learned that the NFL is all about toughness. I needed to play whether my legs felt like wet noodles or not. If a hamstring or a hip flexor was bothering me, I needed to manage it myself during practice. It wasn't acceptable to take a day off. The training room became a place that you wanted to stay out of.

Ty Detmer was the best teammate a guy could ask for. He was a team leader as well as the team prankster. What impressed me about him more than anything else was his ability to hold his head

Courtesy of the Philadelphia Eagles

Running with the ball in a game at the Vet. The often-maligned and much-revered Veterans Stadium was imploded March 21, 2004.

up in the middle of disappointments and media pressure. Ty was a man's man because he never made excuses or placed blame on anyone else. The game that stands out to me more than any other was when we were beaten by the San Francisco 49ers on Monday Night Football.

Ty threw three interceptions in that game and was grilled by the media directly afterward. He stood and took each question like a man. He never blamed the rest of us for not doing a better job. He could have picked out several guys who didn't play well, but he didn't. He was a class act even with the hot spotlight of blame on him. Rodney Pete, another veteran quarterback, was the same way. He and Ty went back and forth as our starters that year. They could have used the media at any time to air their grievances, but they chose to walk the high road. I loved playing for them because I could trust them. I knew they had my back.

CHAPTER 14

THE MOST POWERFUL
MAN IN PHILADELPHIA

With less than a minute on the clock, the time ticking down, and a light rain continuing to fall as it had the whole game, the Eagles were driving on the Cowboys and preparing to score the go-ahead and game-winning touchdown against our most bitter rivals. This was not just any game. This was a chance to pay the Cowboys back for our week-three, Monday night, last-second loss in Dallas. We had a chance to win that game with a chip shot field goal from the four-yard line with four seconds left. But something happened with the hold, the ball was fumbled, and we ended up losing a heartbreaker. Now was our chance for redemption. We were on the eight-yard line, and the frenzied Eagles crowd was going bananas.

When you are down by six with forty-five seconds left, with the ball on the eight-yard line, you are so close to victory you can taste it. As a fan, all of the screaming and yelling for the last three hours is about to be rewarded. For a player, all the film prepara-tion and practice, not only during the last week, but for the last year, now seems worth it. The line between winning and losing in the NFL is razor thin. You learn how true the adage from the wise farmer is: "Never count your chickens before they are hatched." In this case, the Eagles' egg was rocking back and forth, cracks were starting to appear, and the bird was as close as could be to popping out of the egg.

To drive home the background and feeling behind the Eagles–Cowboys rivalry, there was a recent survey taken in Philadelphia in which the fans chose the 1981 Eagles–Cowboys NFC Championship game, won by the Eagles, as the greatest game in the history of the franchise. In that survey, the current fans chose that single victory over their own NFL Championships of 1948, 1949, and 1960. That was a very telling survey. The fans loved beating the Dallas Cowboys at home, in the old Vet (Veterans Stadium), for a ticket to the Super Bowl, more than they can remember how sweet it was to win the Championship game in 1960.

Even after losing in the NFC Championship game for three straight years and then finally beating the Falcons in 2005 to head to Super Bowl XXXIX in Jacksonville, Florida, against the Patriots, the '81 Cowboys–Eagles game is still what makes Eagles fans' hearts pound with the most joy and satisfaction. Just ask any coach for the Cowboys how much ire this game can elicit. Ask Jimmy Johnson about the snowballs sent his way from the fans in the Vet. It takes courage mixed with a dash of stupidity for anyone to wear a Dallas Cowboys jersey in the stands for a home game with the Cowboys. As a rookie, the first thing you find out from the fans about Eagles football is how necessary it is to beat the Cowboys.

When we were on the eight-yard line, the Vet was a powder keg of emotional energy. I was just as excited as the fans, watching our team drive down to the eight. During this particular game, I had not played in a single offensive play. Up until this point of the season, I had mostly been used only in red-zone situations. The red zone is the twenty yards extending from the opponent's goal line. And we were in the heart of the red zone.

Suddenly, Ted Williams, our running backs coach, turned and yelled for me to go into the game. All the players loved Ted. One of the things that we loved about him was the high-pitched yell he made when calling in the personnel. His voice took on such a high pitch that even if he was yelling at you in anger, you didn't know if you should smile or be worried.

My heart skipped a couple of beats when he called my number. We had already lived through the effects of a disastrous last-second defeat to these same Cowboys. I did not want to make a mistake out there and lose it for our team.

When I got into the huddle, Rodney Pete, our quarterback, looked across right at me when he called the play. It was "West Right F Left, 322 Scat Y Stick-Nod!" It was a perfect red-zone play for a tight end. It requires a double move, which was the best call for that rain-slick field.

When the ball was snapped, I was to run straight forward for five yards and then break to my right for about three steps toward the sideline, hopefully just long enough for the strong safety to bite on my route and come down hard from the secondary. After three hard steps to the sideline, I was to turn back for the middle of the end zone on an angle toward the goalpost, and if all went according to plan, Rodney would throw the ball between the 8 and the 9 on my jersey and we would win the game. Simple.

The ball was snapped, I got a clean release off the line of scrimmage, and made my first break toward the sideline. When I broke back toward the goalpost, the strong safety slipped on the wet turf, and I ran free and clear into the end zone. I was wide open. Rodney threw the ball and hit me exactly between the numbers and I held on to it for dear life. The play had worked to perfection, and I had a smile on my face as big as the crack in the Liberty Bell. Rodney jumped into the air and ran toward me. The

Courtesy of the Philadelphia Eagles

*Catching a touchdown against the Dallas Cowboys' Dat Nguyen in "The Line."
All Philadelphia Eagles' home games are played at Lincoln Financial Field.*

whole team was jumping up and down like little kids. That is one of the things I love about football: it reduces or raises (you decide which) big tough guys into little kids.

While my teammates were running toward me, I threw the ball up into the stands as far as I could. I knew that was the game winner! I knew we were going to beat the Cowboys! I knew that was the biggest catch in my life! And I knew that I was not going to get cut anytime soon! As a free agent, you work your hardest every day so that there is no reason for your team to get rid of you. Making a play like that against our biggest rival, at home, with the game on the line, meant that my name plate was going to stay on my locker for the rest of the season!

I ran to the sideline and hugged every person on the team. I was going crazy. After playing football my whole life, that was the greatest play that I had ever been part of. I could not contain my excitement and relief. All the work that I had put in to make the team as a free agent was paying off. The year-round wind sprints. The endless practices. The thousands of catches. The countless weights that were lifted and the blood, sweat, and tears shed while playing the game made this moment not an accident, but a reward.

In the middle of their elation, the crowd began singing the Eagles' fight song, "Fly, Eagles, Fly." It is without doubt the best pro football fight song out there. Once it gets into your head, you can't get it out. If you haven't heard it yet, I think you should get on the Internet right now and listen to it for yourself. Just type in the words: *Eagles fight song, fly eagles fly.* Here are the words:

> *Fly, Eagles, fly, on the road to victory!*
> *(Fight! Fight! Fight!)*
> *Fight, Eagles, fight, Score a touchdown 1 2 3*
> *(One, Two, Three)*
> *Hit 'em low,*
> *Hit 'em high.*
> *And watch our Eagles fly.*
> *Fly, Eagles, fly, on the road to victory!*
> *E A G L E S—Eagles!*[6]

This is a fun story, but it is only the first half, and the second half is the best part.

On Friday of that week, I had stopped in the ticket office to pick up tickets for my wife, parents, and my Aunt Geneve and Uncle Mark, who were all going to be there for the big game. The ticket office was run by Leo Carlin. I didn't know it at the time, but over the next nine years I would get to know why Leo Carlin was the most powerful man in Philadelphia.

Most people think it is because he holds the strings to getting the best seats for games, concerts, and other events. That is only part of the reason. The real reason is that he has a perfect heart with no guile. The guy is incredible.

Leo is a little man by football player standards. But by a wise man's standards, he is a giant. He has graying hair, big ears, little muscles, and the biggest smile you have ever seen. For exercise each day, he would run around the concourse of the Vet and then shower in our locker room. He would usually jog in clothes similar to those worn by Rocky Balboa when he ran through the streets of Philly. They consisted of gray sweats and, when it was cold, usually a towel around his neck.

He fit right into our locker room because after thirty years on the job, he had earned respect and friendships with coaches, players, and management, and had gained all the confidence in the world to be there. An NFL locker room is an intimidating place for most people. You earn the right to be there, or you are an invited guest. You can't be an imposter and stay there for any length of time. Most people would be self-conscious if their physique was not that of an NFL player. Not Leo. He would walk through the locker room in nothing but a towel with not a care in the world that he was not a hulk. He loved all of us players. I think that is why he was so confident among us. He had no enemies, and his only desire was to help us with whatever he could. That is the kind of life to pattern oneself after.

Leo didn't always personally give us our tickets at the ticket window. But for some reason, he was there to give me mine. He was smiling and happy as always. He was also wearing this really cool dark blue rugby shirt with the NFL shield on the chest. As we were chatting, I thought I would have a little fun with him. I asked him if he would be willing to give me his shirt if I scored a touchdown against the Cowboys.

He was incredulous. I don't think he quite knew what to say. He responded with a typical Philly wisecrack, "Fuhgetaboutit!"

Without missing a beat, I said, "Well, what if I score the *winning* touchdown?"

Now he gave me a look of exasperation, and he tilted his head to the side and said, "If you score the winning touchdown, you got it, kid!"

That was the end of the conversation. I picked up my tickets and left. That was also the last I thought about our exchange.

That is, until I was throwing the ball up into the stands after catching the game-winning touchdown! While celebrating with my teammates, I remembered our conversation, and in my mind could see the face of Leo Carlin. My only thought was, *What is that guy's name?* I had met Leo a few times, but I did not remember his name.

After the game was over, we shook hands with the Cowboys. I gave Rodney a big hug while he was getting interviewed on the field and then I ran to the edge of the field and held my Eagles helmet up to the crowd and yelled with total elation, "That's what I'm talking about!" Then I ran into the tunnel and up the ramp to our locker room.

While our team was congratulating each other, Ty Detmer, with his big Texas grin, told me that I had just written a check for $500. I asked him what for, and with his classic chuckle he told me that I would get a fine from the league office for around $500 for throwing the ball into the stands. A minute later, our linebacker, Willie T (Thomas), from Texas A&M told me that the fine was actually $2,500. The price of this fine was going up at an incredible rate.

I was asked to do some interviews out in the lower concourse hallway just beyond the locker room door. While answering questions from the reporters, I saw Leo walking toward me from down the hall. He was grinning from excitement that we had just beat the Cowboys, and from disbelief that he was going to have to cough up his favorite NFL shirt. I broke off the interview in midsentence, grabbed Leo, and we laughed and giggled like third graders. It was such an improbable and almost impossible situation that just happened between us. It took the definition of unlikely and stretched it to its limits. I can still see this unique scene unfold in my mind in vivid detail. His face, his look, his happiness, his total surprise—it all jumbles together in this wonderful memory and joyful moment that continues to bring a smile to my face.

It sure felt good to walk out of Veterans Stadium that day. The players did not have a special parking lot at the Vet. We could park close to the doors because we were the first ones to arrive at the stadium, but our cars were mixed in with those of all the fans. This meant that when you left the stadium after a game, you were hailed and high-fived as a hero if you'd won and called out on the carpet if you'd lost.

The walk to your car could equal the intensity of the actual game if the win was that exciting or if the loss was that disappointing. The Eagles always offered the companionship of security personnel if you felt a real need. That being said, I loved the wins. I loved to see all the kids wearing Eagles jerseys waiting around after the game for an autograph or to request your gloves or anything else they could take to show their family or friends that they were there.

I floated through the parking lot that night, back to my Gary Barbera minivan. Gary Barbera ran a couple of car dealerships in Philly with his brother Geno. I became friends with them through Vai Sikahema. Vai introduced me to them, and they were kind enough to outfit my family with a car, which was very uncommon for a player of my stature—an undrafted free agent. They had a new car for me to drive the entire eight years that I played in Philly. And in the off-season, when I would fly in for mini camps, they would always have a brand-new car of some sort waiting for me at the airport. Their generosity was an example of the way I was treated in Philly.

That win over the Cowboys was the first NFL football game my parents had ever seen, except on TV. They couldn't have come to a better game. I thought about flying them in to every game if they were going to bring that kind of luck. They were somewhat familiar with the area, having lived for a couple years at nearby Fort Dix in New Jersey. My dad had been a doctor in the Army.

It just so happens that I was born at Fort Dix in the same year that Veterans Stadium was built. I always felt a touch of ownership to that place and considered myself, in some respects, a local boy. The stadium was imploded in March 2004 to make way for the new football stadium for the Eagles, called Lincoln Financial Stadium, and the Phillies' baseball stadium, called Citizens Bank Park.

The day after the game we went to the Sage Diner near our home in Mount Laurel, New Jersey. We were surprised and my mom was delighted to see my picture on the front page of some of the papers. Mom bought a copy of every single paper.

She is incredible because she has enormous reservoirs of love for all her kids even when that love might not be deserved. She has always been that way. I was the skinniest kid in school through my junior-high and high-school years. My goal was to at least look like a football player. I wanted to be bigger. I ate like a hungry wolf and lifted weights but still remained as skinny as a bean pole. My mom would always tell me how much she loved me and that one of my gifts was to be able to run well. It rings in my ears: "You can run. You are so fast. And you have long legs!"

Why is it cool for some of us in junior high and high school to act as though a compliment from our parents is not cool? What is up with that? I tried to act as though my mom didn't know what she was talking about. But on the inside, I was soaking up every single nice comment like a sponge sitting in the desert catching some rain drops for the first time in months.

I love my mom and I am proud that she put a house mortgage worth of quarters in the newspaper dispensers to buy copies of those papers. She was in Philly because she loved me. She bought the papers because she loved me. I never wanted to let that junior-high, tough-guy mentality creep back into my relationship with my parents. That I may always remember to honor and love them is my desire. I hope to be like them. I hope that if my kids have that same tough exterior in junior high or high school that I can have the same patience that my parents had with me. I always knew that they loved me. I could see it, I could feel it, and I could hear it in their prayers and kind words. Even an NFL football player who thinks he is tough stuff for catching the game-winning touchdown to beat the Cowboys needs the love of his parents. I am so lucky that I had it. I hope with all the energy of my heart that I can share the same love for my beautiful kids.

Later that morning, when we had our team meeting, Coach Ray Rhodes had a special presentation for the team and for me in particular. He reminded us that in my exuberance after catching the TD from Rodney I threw that ball into the stands and gave it away forever. Then he told us something that had taken place the night before.

It seems our linebacker coach, Joe Vitt, had a cousin named Guido, who somehow found and purchased the touchdown ball in a bar after the game.

The story went that Guido heard some guys popping off about how they had caught the ball that I threw up into the stands. Guido knew that the Eagles would want the ball and so he paid the guys some money and gave it to Coach Vitt. Coach Vitt gave it to Ray, and Ray presented it to me in front of the whole squad. What luck! How did that happen? What perfect and unlikely timing for Guido to be there! I got the ball back and had a permanent memento of the game.

By Monday night, the story of this ball's recovery was part of the media's coverage of the victory over Dallas. During some interviews, I related how the ball left my hands, was caught by some fans, was purchased in a bar, and was back in my hands Monday morning. Incredible!

That story was not nearly as incredible as another story that began to surface. It turns out that an eleven-year-old boy from South Jersey named Johnny Giordano was telling his friends that he was at the game and that he was the one who caught the game-winning touchdown ball that I had thrown into the stands. Imagine his reaction when he heard on the news that I was now reunited with the touchdown ball that he said he had caught. Wanting respect from your friends is not unique to school kids in Philly, but with the emotionally charged situation following a huge win over the Cowboys, that was not a time to be disrespected or caught in a big fat lie.

Johnny went to work to save his good name. He made a call to the Eagles' front office and let them know that they were somehow mistaken. He told them that he was the one who had caught the game-winning touchdown ball and that he was holding it in his hands while he was talking to them.

He alleged the ball I had was a fake. He wanted to prove it so bad that he was willing to give the ball back to me. He had tickets to prove that he was sitting in the seat where I threw the ball. He also had enough fire in his voice that he was not going to be turned away as just some kid with a wild story who wanted to meet one of the Eagles. He convinced the Eagles that he was the real deal and that the ball was no hoax.

I was contacted by someone in the public relations department who told me this unfolding story. They asked if I would be willing to meet this kid. After hearing the whole story, I thought it

*My brother Mike, wearing the Eagles shirt, listens to Leo Carlin
tell the story of betting—and losing—his shirt.*

would be criminal if I didn't meet him. I was informed that
he would be in the locker room with his extended family and
the media on Tuesday morning, the regular day off for NFL
players.

Johnny Giordano was a great kid. He had the spunk that it
took to convince anyone who would listen that the story he was
telling his friends about the ball was true. I loved meeting him.
One of the news stations thought it would be cool to reenact the
whole play in the stadium. So we went out into the Vet and did
just that.

Johnny took his seat about fifteen rows up in the south end-
zone section of the stadium. I simulated running the route, catching the pass, running across the end zone, and throwing the
ball up into the stands again where he caught it. If catching the

touchdown wasn't enough, Johnny Giordano brought twice as much media attention to the catch, the win, and the moment.

When we left the field and went back into the locker room, we were surrounded by cameras and reporters. We congregated in front of my locker to finish the interviews. The Eagles' staff presented Johnny and his family with more Eagles paraphernalia than they would be able to fit into their car. They were given hats, shirts, sweatshirts, banners, balls, and two tickets to the Monday Night Football game against the 49ers with a limo ride to the stadium. That kid was in heaven. After getting all of that loot, he was more than willing to part with the football and offer it to me as a gift.

It was at this moment that Leo Carlin, the most powerful man in Philly, made his celebrated entrance back into the story. He made plenty of noise as he strutted with a great big smile and all sorts of confidence towards my locker. We all looked in his direction. The reporters turned their cameras on him while he started talking about his famous shirt that he was proudly wearing.

With as much pomp and circumstance as he could muster, he took off his shirt right there in front of all of us. He gracefully handed it to me and said that it was mine, that I had earned it. It was classic Leo Carlin.

For the next couple of days, the story of the shirt took life on the pages of newspapers in Philly and around the country. Leo said that he got calls from his family members living in cities all across the United States who couldn't believe that he made their papers with this wild story of the shirt. He said that he had been the ticket man in Philly for thirty years and had never received press like that before. His kids and relatives enjoyed calling him and teasing him that he was now a superstar.

I still have the shirt hanging in my closet. I have pictures of the game and the sweet memory of catching the game winner. I even have the football, once lost, now found, sitting in my office.

But what means the most to me in this whole fun story is the dear friendship of Leo Carlin, one of the greatest guys in Philadelphia.

My family makes sure that a visit with Leo is part of any trip to Philly. Even now that I am living in Utah, Leo and I still exchange phone calls on a frequent basis. That most unusual conversation and succeeding game-winning experience have bonded our hearts together in such a way that we have become lifelong friends. In the long run, that means much more to me than catching game winners.

My memory will fade and the ball will gather dust and eventually crumble, but I know that Leo's good heart will continue to beat with kindness and charity forever. I am a better person for knowing Leo Carlin. Every person who has ever met him feels the same way. That is what makes him the most powerful man in Philly.

CHAPTER 15

FRIENDS

It is as vital for us to surround ourselves with good friends as it is for a fish to live in water, especially in our teenage years. It is critically important to our lives, our future, our health, and our safety to be around positive influences, people who don't tempt us but rather help us make good decisions. A friend who sees the good in us and encourages us to be our best self is worth more than his weight in pure gold. Just to give some perspective, gold is about $900 an ounce.

I am grateful to have been blessed with great friends throughout my life.

Is it any less important to have good friends when we are older? Consider this wise counsel from Proverbs 13:20: "He that walketh with wise men shall be wise: but a companion of fools shall be destroyed." That is the truth!

One of the reasons for the success that I had with the Philadelphia Eagles was being able to learn from Vai Sikahema and his family. Vai was one of the all-time great BYU football players and helped BYU win the National Championship by beating Michigan in the Holiday Bowl in 1984. He went on to have a distinguished career in the NFL, playing for the Cardinals, the Packers, and the Eagles. With his shifty moves and his fearless courage he was selected to the Pro Bowl twice as a punt- and kick-returner.

To be an effective return-man you have to have the heart of a lion, because while the ball is in the air, there are ten guys running at you like laser-guided missiles at full speed, and they are looking at only one thing—the bull's-eye on your chest. If you get distracted by their approach and take your eye off the ball to sneak a peek at the mob of approaching assassins, you will most likely fail. The ball will be fumbled and as it bounces around on the turf you will get smashed. That is not good! Every one of us who has played football has ultimate respect for the punt- and kick-return men. They don't get as much credit as they deserve, but as an insider to the game, I want you to know that they have the admiration of every person in the locker room.

Vai won the hearts of Philly fans everywhere when he took a punt to the house against the Giants in the play-offs and, after scoring, made a beeline for the goalpost. That was where he did his best Rocky Balboa impression by jabbing and slugging the protective pad until his teammates showed up. After his career was over he transitioned to TV and became the sports anchor for NBC10 News in Philadelphia, where he has become one of the most popular sports anchors in perhaps the most sports-crazed city in the United States.

Before I made the Eagles team, I had met Vai only once. It was during my senior year at BYU at our homecoming game victory against UNLV. He came into the locker room after the game and we visited for a few minutes. He made it a point to talk with Itula Mili and me. We were both having a great year as tight ends on a very good team that finished 14–1 and ranked fifth in the country. He encouraged us to keep working hard and to prepare ourselves to play in the NFL by working on every part of our game while we were still in college.

The first NFL mini camp was held either the week following the draft or two weeks following, depending on the team. It consisted of two practices on Friday, two on Saturday, and only one practice on Sunday. It was a crash course in that team's playbook, the organizational structure, and getting familiar with the coaches and other players. We went so fast and so hard that by the end of the mini camp my head was swimming. I will never forget flying home after that first mini camp, feeling physically and emotionally spent. The second mini camp was a month later. We learned the same things at the second mini camp, but this time we were not drinking out of a fire hose. The coaches slowed things down a bit. We even had spare time after practice to see the city and get our bearings.

Fortunately for me, I had two friends on the team who had gone to BYU, Ty Detmer and Morris Unutoa. Those two guys were such a gift as I started my career in Philly. Morris and I played together at BYU. He grew up in Los Angeles and was one of the best long-snappers in the game. He was as tough as football players come, but off the field he was one of the most gentle and humble guys I've ever met. We were roommates for my first mini camp. Morris could snore like nobody's business, which worked to his advantage because he always got his own room. I wanted to room with Morris for the mini camp. I thought being roommates with Morris was more important than worrying about anyone snoring.

Morris was a great teammate because he was a true friend. We had been through many battles together when we played at BYU, and we were excited to go through more with the Eagles. Everyone on the team loved Morris. They called him "The Cat," because of Morris the cat. He won everyone's heart and friendship with his all-American personality.

Ty was one of the truest class acts the NFL has ever seen. Whether he'd just won a game or suffered a humiliating defeat in front of millions, he was the same person, a pillar of character. He was Texas tough, and that was instilled in him by his great parents, Sonny and Betty Detmer. I felt that if someone met the Detmer family once, they were better just because of it. The NFL and every teammate, especially other quarterbacks, who Ty has played with were greatly benefited by his fun personality, honest desire to help others become the best they could be, and locker-room leadership. Along with being one of the biggest pranksters on any of his teams, he was one of the best guys to ever wear an NFL uniform.

Ty made sure that those who sat by him on the plane stayed on their toes. If someone happened to fall asleep, and his mouth fell open, Ty would roll a paper towel up into a long point and use it to tickle his uvula. The sleeping player would always wake up choking and gagging to the laughter of all the other guys who were watching. Ty had a bag of tricks that had no end.

He and his wife, Kim, invited me over to his house one of the nights during that second mini camp. He knew the value of getting away from the facility. We just hung out, talked about BYU and the Eagles, and had dinner. Over the last decade, I have come to understand what an honor and a privilege it is to have Ty for a friend.

On one of the other nights of that mini camp, Vai had Morris and me over to his home for dinner. We had a fun evening talking about BYU football, the Philadelphia Eagles, the gospel, and our families, themes that would run through all of our conversations over the next decade.

Over the years, Vai and his wife, Keala, have taught Michele and me as much about life and gratitude as our own families have. They have made us feel as though we were part of their family. We were not special in that regard. Most people who meet the

Sikahemas feel the same way. Their generosity and friendship made no distinction between race, religion, or financial status. Spending time at their table talking about great things was a little slice of heaven.

One off-season, the young men and women of our church were making a drive down to visit the Washington D.C. Temple. As the bishop of the ward, Vai was responsible for that group, to ensure their safety and that they had a nice experience serving others. Vai had a huge appetite for American history and made it a point to share that same hunger with others. So he planned a stop for a sack lunch in Baltimore at Fort McHenry. It was during a battle there in the War of 1812 that Francis Scott Key wrote our national anthem.

Vai was born in the island nation of Tonga. He moved to Arizona as a child, where his parents made a home for him and where he was taught to love and appreciate this country. He had just become an American citizen a few weeks before our visit to Fort McHenry. As we watched a presentation on the history of what happened there and listened to an inspiring rendition of "The Star-Spangled Banner," sung by the US Naval Academy choir, I felt we were standing on sacred ground. I looked at Vai's face just then and saw the tears running down his cheeks and was taught a lesson in gratitude and patriotism that I would not have experienced in any other way.

As a football player, I've always thought it was an honor that we were allowed to stand on the field before every game, our toes lined up to the sidelines, while singing the national anthem. For a minute, we are united with the crowd and our opponents. During that song we are one, a oneness that is born of gratitude for those who sought to establish this nation and who have fought for our freedom.

I had an unforgettable national anthem experience before my biggest game. It was the 2004 NFC Championship game when the Eagles beat the Falcons for the right to play in the Super Bowl. It had snowed a foot the night before, and the temperature was below freezing. Timmy Kelly was chosen to sing the national anthem. He was a young boy, only ten years old, from the Philadelphia area whom I had met a few months earlier. Under those circumstances and in absolutely freezing-cold Northeast weather, he sang the anthem loud and proud, in a way that rivaled Whitney Houston's famous Super Bowl performance.

Timmy was born prematurely at only twenty-six weeks. He was diagnosed with cerebral palsy. If that weren't enough, he was also blind. His disease did not affect his voice, though, and he could sing as well as anyone I had ever heard sing that song. His performance was unbelievable. He was just a little kid, but he made the walls of the stadium shake. And when he finished, the place just erupted with cheering and applause.

After hearing that, I couldn't hold back my emotions. I began walking from the sideline toward Timmy and his father, and I noticed that Jevon Kearse, our defensive end, was doing the same thing. Timmy was surrounded by a dozen men and women representing every branch of the armed services. They had stood at attention right behind him as he sang. The NFL knows how to put together powerful visual effects, and the field was covered with *dozens* of uniformed servicemen and women.

After the song, Timmy's dad lifted him onto his shoulders, and as we got closer to them, I could hear his father describing the scene that was unfolding in front of Timmy's sightless eyes. He said, "Chad Lewis and Jevon Kearse are walking toward you."

When we reached Timmy, Jevon and I both tried to tell him how his performance had moved us, but we were too choked with emotion to say anything. We both had tears filling our eyes as we reached up and hugged him. *We* were trying to thank *him*, but he thanked *us*.

Javon and I returned to the sideline, and I stood at attention

Courtesy of the Philadelphia Eagles

Congratulating Timmy Kelly, who is riding on his dad's shoulders, after an unforgettable rendition of "The Star-Spangled Banner" before the NFC Championship game against the Atlanta Falcons in 2005.

as the military personnel who had attended the flags began to leave the field. There I was, ready to go to battle against the Falcons, and I felt like hugging every one of the men and women who marched past me on their way off the field. I think they knew by the look on my face just how I was feeling and how grateful I was for them. Many of them snuck a peek out of the corner of their eyes at me as they marched by.

By the time the final person passed me I was ready to explode. The last guy was a Marine who looked as dignified and honorable as anyone I had ever seen. He had a tear streaming down his cheek that shone and sparkled on that freezing-cold day.

While I am writing this, I can still feel the emotion I experienced watching him march past me. I wanted to reach out and

Lending a hand to one of my great Eagle teammates, Charles Johnson.

An unforgettable moment with my brother Todd
after taking State my junior year in high school. I was 6' and 145 pounds.

Todd and me years later as teammates at BYU.
Playing together with him was one of my highlights at BYU.

Standing arm in arm with Rob Lamb, Scott Hardy, and Larry Harmer, missionaries who had just dedicated two years of service to the people of Taiwan.

Having fun "street surfing" with one of my all-time favorite kids in Taiwan for Chinese New Year in Yuan Lin, Taiwan.

This photograph of Michele hung in BYU's Smith Fieldhouse. I stared at it every time I walked by, falling in love with her.

Michele is still the best athlete in our family. Here she is hitting against UCLA's All-World player Natalie Williams.

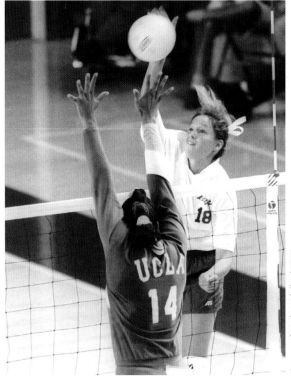

Celebrating the Cotton Bowl victory on New Year's Day 1997. The #88 on my helmet was for Itula Mili, who had been injured in the previous game.

Standing with Michele in front of the beautiful Laie Hawaii Temple. Families are forever!

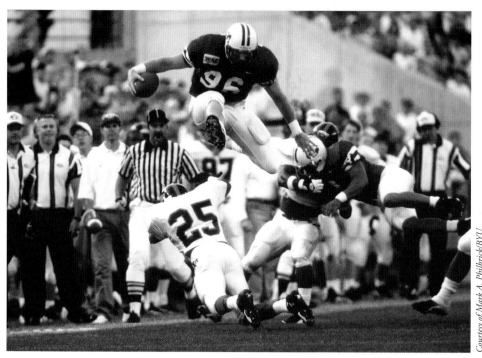

Hurdling over an Arkansas State defender in 1996.
(Notice the incredible sell-out block from my teammate Levi "K.O." Kealaluhi.)

Catching a pass against Pittsburgh Steelers safety Troy Polamalu.

*Sharing some Daddy-daughter time with Emily on Christmas Eve 2000
after the Eagles defeated the Cincinnati Bengals.*

*Running the field with my girls Sarah (left) and Emily (right)
on Christmas Eve 2000. This was the real game!*

Surrounded by two of the best quarterbacks to play the game,
Steve Young and Donovan McNabb.

Left to right: Koy Detmer, Jeff Thomason, me, Dave Akers, and Tony Stewart.
The best teammates a guy could have.

Struggling for yards against the Jacksonville Jaguars.

Donovan McNabb placed this ball perfectly over the head of Giants linebacker Michael Barrow. I love catching the football.

Thanks to tight-end coach Tom Melvin's consistent use of a sideline drill, I was able to keep my toes in bounds on my first touchdown.

I broke my left foot on this touchdown catch in the NFC Championship game against the Atlanta Falcons. Knowing that the Eagles were going to the Super Bowl was the thrill of my career!

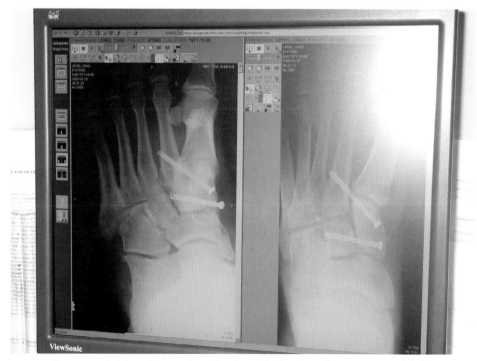

Two screws held my foot together after I tore the Lis Franc ligament in my left foot.

Spending Valentine's Day at the White House was an unforgettable experience. We had our picture taken in the Red Room with President George W. Bush and First Lady Laura Bush.

Introducing President George W. Bush in Bucks County with teammates and friends.
Front row: Reno Mahe, Mike Dougherty, President Bush, Dave Akers, Sara, Emily.
Second row: Paul Grasmanis, Hank Fraley. Third row: Jeff Thomason, Corey Simon,
Vai Sikahema, Dirk Johnson, Mike Bartrum, me.

*Presenting then-Beijing mayor Wang Qishan a Philadelphia Eagles shirt
that I had signed in English and Chinese.*

*Part of the BYU/Philly connection:
Justin Ena, Vai Sikahema, Ty Detmer, and me.*

The majestic scenery of Zion National Park at the top of Angel's Landing with my brothers Dave, Todd, Jason, and Mike.

The Fellows family gathered to celebrate Michele's induction into the BYU Athletic Hall of Fame. Left to right: Steve, Christine (Gunnell), Michele, Geneva, Doug, and Mark.

*One of our "Brother's Trips" took us to the bottom of Walter's Wiggles
on the famous Angel's Landing hike in Zion National Park.
Left to right: me, Dad, Mike, Jason, Todd, and Dave.*

*A family photo in Alpine, Utah. I am holding Maxwell, Michele is holding Tanner and Todd,
and our other kids are standing in a row: Jacob, Jefferson, Emily, and Sarah.*

Throwing a football to a boy at one of my football camps.

hug him and tell him how much I loved him for fighting for me and for my freedom. But that didn't seem appropriate.

However, when he was just a couple of steps past me, I could stand there no longer. I ran after him and grabbed him by the shoulder. I wanted to tell him that I loved him, but nothing came out. I was too choked up to speak. My words got lost somewhere in the tears in my eyes and the pounding of my heart. But he knew exactly what I was trying to say and what I was feeling. We just looked at each other for a second in mutual appreciation and gratitude. We were free men on free soil.

I have a photo hanging on the wall in my office at home to remind me of that emotional experience. It is a photo of Timmy sitting on his dad's shoulders, wearing his Eagles coat and hat, a scarf, and a pair of sunglasses, and he is reaching out to me without being able to see me. I am reaching up to him, just touching his shoulder with my glove-covered hand and taped wrist. Javon's big, glove-covered hand is in the picture, too, reaching for Timmy. Both Timmy and I have our mouths open as we thank each other. My eye black is on my face and the stadium in the background is full of screaming fans. It is a permanent reminder of that moment, that day, and the profound feelings that I had.

I'm not ashamed to admit to these kinds of emotion. When I see the flag and hear "The Star-Spangled Banner" sung, I'm reminded that our nation was founded on the courage and sacrifice of patriots. I have no problem crying in the face of these symbols of our freedom. When Timmy sang and while I stood next to Vai at Fort Henry, I was grateful to be an American. Here, in this blessed nation, we are surrounded with greatness.

CHAPTER 16

THE ST. LOUIS RAMS

During my rookie season I was fortunate to catch four touchdown passes. Even though we did not win enough games to earn a trip to the play-offs, I considered that season a victory in my life. Making the team, contributing by catching touchdowns, and earning the respect of my coaches and teammates constituted that victory feeling I had.

My second season did not turn out nearly as well. I broke my left ankle while blocking on a kickoff return against the Atlanta Falcons in the second game of the year. I hated walking off the field injured. I couldn't stand thinking that because I was injured in the line of fire, I could be on the chopping block. What a bummer.

I went to the locker room to find out exactly what had happened to my ankle. The first thing I did was cut the tape off my foot. That offered much relief since the tape was putting enormous pressure on the injured part of my foot and ankle. Once the tape was cut off I felt almost as though my ankle was better and that the restriction from the tape was what had been causing the pain. Most of that was wishful thinking.

I wanted my foot to be okay. I tried as hard as I could to tell myself that I would be fine, but I knew better. I also knew some of the realities of injuries on a team and that my status as an Eagle was now in jeopardy. I had sustained an injury that would keep me out for about ten weeks. Not only was there a small bone broken in my ankle, but I'd also suffered a severe bone bruise to my talus, the main weight-bearing bone of the foot. What did that mean? That meant that my "money makers" were bankrupt for a while. Players called their feet and legs their money makers. You could play with a lot of pain and injuries to the rest of your body, but when your lower half could not carry your body with a lot of speed, you were done.

I was miserable on the flight back to Philly. My foot and ankle ached and throbbed the whole time. Trying to walk with crutches and carry my bag while boarding the plane and squeezing down the aisle did not go very well. When your team loses, there are not too many helpful hands to go around. People closed up and the ride on the bus and the plane became very quiet. Losing was horrible. When our plane landed, Coach Danny Smith carried my bag out to my car. That was a cool gesture on his part. It helped me to be able to crutch down the aisle and then down the stairs to my car in the parking lot. Small acts of kindness like that go a long way in life.

When we were back at the Eagles facility the next day, as much as I tried to ignore the trainer and coaches discussing my injury, I could tell that my days were numbered. I sat on one of the training-room tables while getting treatment and watched in slow motion as this football brain trust contemplated how they would let me know that I was gone. I was in the bottom of a gully with a large avalanche coming right at me and I had nowhere to go.

Different people from the staff would come in to visit with my trainer. He would discuss my injury with them and they would periodically look in my direction. With each look my way, I was that much closer to losing my job and heading home. It was one of the most stressful situations I had ever been in.

If there was ever a time when I wanted to be surrounded by greatness it was then. I was vulnerable and hurting—physically and emotionally. I didn't want to get cut. From the whispers and the looks to the reality of my injury, it was inevitable. As a player, you can see it coming from a mile away, and it doesn't feel good.

I was finally brought into the office by a member of the management and informed that I was being cut. It was brutal, realizing that my life in the NFL was over for the time being. I had played for one year and two games. I didn't like having this conversation. I didn't like being told I was being cut. It hurt to know that I had just been excused out of the locker room and away from my teammates. That experience of growing up was tough. But, like many experiences in life, it was also one of the best things that I ever went through.

The best thing in my life has always been my family, and I am so grateful that I was able to call my wife, Michele, and process this painful information. She told me she loved me and assured me that everything was going to work out right. She told me that we would get through this disappointment together and that we would be fine. She was a rock-solid support for me as she has continued to be throughout our marriage. Having Michele as a partner is the epitome of being surrounded by greatness. I believe in the principle of marrying *up*. She is my superior in every way, even in athletics. She was a two-time All-American volleyball player at BYU. Even though I was an NFL football player, she is the best athlete in the family! How about that? I love it. What a blessing to be able to lean on her in such a difficult time.

If an NFL player is cut from the team due to an injury, there must be an injury settlement negotiated with the team. My agent, Don Yee, helped me work through that process. He has taken care of me with professionalism since I left BYU. He helped me get another job both times I was cut. He was a tremendous resource during that particular time. He carefully guided me in the negotiation process by walking me through which papers I should sign and which ones I should avoid. He had integrity. I always trusted him. That is the most important characteristic in an agent. I can say with great confidence that his expert guidance brought a huge level of stability to my life and career. Every player should be so fortunate.

Michele and I packed our things and headed back to Provo, Utah, where I would be able to rehab at BYU with George Curtis. The BYU coaches were very accommodating with my treatment. They let me rehab every day until I could run again. Coach Chow even asked if I wanted to run some seven-on-seven drills so that I could get back up to speed. They knew I was committed to working as hard as I possibly could to get back into the mix, and they responded in kind.

A lot of people thought my career was over. Some even encouraged me to get back into school and move on. But Michele and I were comfortable in our belief that my career was not over. We believed strongly that I would get another shot, if not with the Eagles, on some other team.

She even acted as my quarterback during the long weeks of rehab. She threw me passes on the BYU practice field so that I could keep my hand-eye coordination sharp. She threw the football like a real quarterback. Don't laugh. She had a gun for an arm, and we loved playing catch together. She was a tomboy growing up and she always played football with her two brothers. Needless to say, she was my favorite quarterback in my career!

Michele stayed incredibly positive as we went through that rehab transition. She always kept her head about her and never got down. She encouraged me to work as hard as I could and get healthy as fast as possible. She let me know that she loved me

*Celebrating a wonderful night with Michele at the BYU Athletic Hall of Fame.
She was inducted two years before I was. She is still the best athlete in the family!*

whether I played football again or not. She said it, and she meant it. She never panicked. She never lost hope. She was solid as a rock. Since she was not a shopper we were never burdened with the pressure to buy things or keep up with the imaginary worldly goals that are so common. She was genuine and beautiful. She was determined to stay out of debt at all costs and so she was content not buying a new car until our third year in the NFL. If we didn't have the money for something, she didn't want it. Her focus was to save everything we made so that we could take care of our growing family and take care of our parents if they ever needed our help. Her balance and steadiness were what gave me strength and direction.

While I was in rehab, Don Yee let me know that several teams were interested in working me out when I could run. That added fuel to my fire. I was in a hurry to get better. The bone bruise was the most painful part. It felt as though the top of my foot was being pinched by the weight of my body. It was the worst when I tried to run. But I went on several workouts with teams even before I was 100 percent. I didn't want to wait any longer.

I worked out with the Denver Broncos and then two days later with the Jacksonville Jaguars. The Jaguars workout went very well. They even agreed to sign me. I was asked to wait in the training room for the papers to be prepared. I waited for over two hours without hearing a word. Then a team representative finally told me that I was not going to be signed and I had a new flight home that would be leaving in just a few minutes. Someone at the facility told me that I had been put in the ice box and left to wait to hear my fate. I wasn't a big fan of the "ice box."

I also worked out for the San Diego Chargers, the San Francisco 49ers, and the Green Bay Packers. While I was visiting with Mike Holmgren, the head coach of the Packers, he took a phone call. It gave me a chance to visit with their quarterback coach, Andy Reid. We had a great visit. I thought he would be hired as one of the next head coaches in the NFL. He told me that there was no room on the Packers roster at that time, but they did get a good report of my workout. He urged me to keep working hard and to stay positive. I guaranteed him that I would.

I had two more workouts, one with the Tennessee Titans and the other with the St. Louis Rams. The Titans said they liked me but did not have any room for me on their roster at that time. I was off to St. Louis for my workout there. Lynn Stiles was the assistant head coach and tight-end coach for the Rams. He started his career with Rams head coach Dick Vermeil on the Philadelphia Eagles staff that went to the Super Bowl in 1981. He spent several years with the San Francisco 49ers, where he helped coach Brent Jones, one of the best tight ends in the game. He said that he really wanted to sign me on the Rams.

But I had heard some horror stories about Coach Vermeil, and I wasn't sure if that was what I wanted. Earlier that season, the players staged a mutiny against Coach Vermeil. They were fed up with his three-hour-plus practices. I had a nice workout and really liked Coach Stiles. He was a no-nonsense, tough coach who seemed very optimistic about their team, even though they were not winning many games. They did not have an opening on their roster, either, but he said he would stay in touch as the season went on.

Two weeks later, Coach Stiles called back. The Rams wanted to sign me that afternoon. Michele and I were visiting her parents in Las Vegas. I did not have a lot of clothes but that didn't matter all that much. I could wear what I had for the remaining three weeks of the season. I flew immediately to St. Louis and signed with them.

That first week I was there, Lynn Stiles told me that I could be just as good as Brent Jones. Imagine how that made me feel when I had just been cut by the Eagles, picked up by the Rams, and my position coach was telling me that I could be as good as the best tight end in the game! It meant everything for my confidence to know that my coach believed in me. That was also why he made me work so hard. It was not going to be easy to be the best and that was just how Lynn liked it.

Both Lynn and my first NFL tight-end coach, Juan Castillo, took it upon themselves to teach me how to be a good blocker. Since I was not asked to do very much blocking at BYU, I had a lot to learn. Lynn introduced me to Rae Crowther—the brand of one of the best teaching sleds in football. The Crowther was a simple, two-man blocking sled that had to be hit just right or else it would spin around on itself. Lynn made it his mission in life to help me master the Crowther. We hit that sled all off-season long. We would continue hitting that sled every day during the season.

After a year of working with Lynn, I started to really get the feel of blocking the right way. I also started to enjoy it. Lynn was tough. He would lift weights in our weight room and try to keep up with the players. He was better in some ways. He would challenge us in towel holds. That was where we hung a towel over a chin-up bar and tried to see how long we could hang onto it with just our hands. After a minute of gripping that towel, our hands would burn like fire. Lynn could match even the best of us at that.

Dick Vermeil was one of the greatest surprises of my life. I was somewhat familiar with him after playing my first year in Philly. He was a legend there for having taken the Eagles to the Super Bowl in 1981. He was still featured on billboards all around the city for Blue Cross Blue Shield, who used him as a spokesman. But after hearing about the team mutiny, I had a lot of questions about Dick Vermeil.

The day I got to St. Louis, I met with the tight ends. I sat in on the meetings and had no clue what the plays were since the offense was so much different than the West Coast Offense I had learned. There were only three games left in the season, which was not going well for them at all. We finished the year 4–12, just about the worst in the League. I would not play in any of the remaining three games. I was added to the team for the following year. My role until then would be to help the team in practice.

When I went out to practice that first day with the Rams, I felt as though I didn't have anything to lose. By being picked up for the last three weeks, I was not worried about being cut. I planned on making plays in practice and trying as hard as I could to open some of the coaches' eyes to what I could do. When practice was running long that day, I asked Coach Vermeil if he thought he was a "tough guy" having practices that lasted so long. He bristled a little bit and just said, "Yep, I am a tough guy!"

That was the beginning of our close relationship. By the time I was released a year later, I had come to know and love Dick

Vermeil because he was a warrior as a coach and a great person in every other way.

Over the next three weeks, I was able to talk with Dick, here or there, several times. We talked about his time in Philly, and I asked him how much they paid him to still put his face on the billboards all those years later. Even though it was none of my business, he told me. We slowly started to get to know each other better. I learned to give him the respect that he deserved. I witnessed how much he loved the players he coached as I listened to him address the team over those last three weeks. There was not even a tiny particle of quit in him. Even though the season was a wreck, he was coaching as though we were heading to the Super Bowl.

I stayed in St. Louis all off-season to work in the weight room with two great strength coaches, Dana LeDuc and Chris Clausen. Dick was a frequent daily visitor to the weight room. I found out that he *was* tough and that he surrounded himself with tough people—both tough coaches and tough players. I also found out that he was a ball of enthusiasm. He brought boundless energy to each practice and each day of off-season workouts.

Dick Vermeil had a tradition of doing something that separated him from every other coach I've heard of. Each week he would invite a different group of around ten players and their wives or girlfriends to a barbeque at his home. He prepared the meat himself. It was an amazing cut of beef that tasted better than any meat I have had in restaurants. He and his wife, Carol, were in their element in these gatherings. They loved being with us and having us in their home. It was so cool to see and be a part of. They told us that they had hosted every single player who had ever played for them, going back to his days at UCLA. That was something else. I started to understand why Dick cried when he talked to the team. It was because he cared about us, and it was not just for show. It was the real thing. As we got closer to what would be a Super Bowl championship season, I grew to love him more and more.

I made friends with the third-string backup quarterback named Kurt Warner. He was a no-name, but not a nobody. I was surprised how well he threw the ball in practice. He had perfect timing and placement of the ball. Coach Lynn Stiles kept telling me that he was going to be something special if he ever got a chance to play.

Our starting quarterback that year was Trent Green. He grew up in St. Louis and had just signed with the Rams after tearing things up with the Washington Redskins. One of his coaches at Washington was Mike Martz. Coach Martz was hired by the Rams as the offensive coordinator. Trent and Mike had a great relationship. They knew each other very well and had a lot of confidence in each other.

During the preseason, Trent Green lit the League on fire. After a few games it was obvious that Trent was the leader of a very explosive team with such potent offensive weapons as Marshal Faulk, Isaac Bruce, Az Hakim, Tory Holt, and Ricky Proel. That offensive team earned the moniker, "The Greatest Show on Turf."

Trent suffered a season-ending knee injury when he was tackled by San Diego Chargers' safety Rodney Harrison. What happened after the game blew me away.

When we heard that Trent had torn his ACL and would miss the rest of the season, Kurt Warner grabbed a game ball and held it up in front of the team in the locker room. He announced that Trent was our leader but that he was down and would not be coming back. Then he said that he was going to lead the team and we would keep doing what Trent had started and we wouldn't miss a beat.

It was a display of humble confidence that was not fake but dramatic enough that I have rarely seen its equal. Kurt would go on to lead the Rams to the victory in the Super Bowl that season.

He led the team back to the Super Bowl the next year as well, where they were defeated by the New England Patriots. He was selected as the League MVP two times and would later lead the Arizona Cardinals to the Super Bowl in January 2009. Even though he didn't win the game, he cemented himself as one of the best quarterbacks in the history of the game.

Frank Gansz was our special teams coach and he was the greatest speaker that I had ever heard. I couldn't wait to get to the facility every morning so that I could hear Coach Gansz speak. He changed my life as a player because he taught me that life is serious business and it is worth fighting for. In his lessons to the team, he *sometimes* talked about football. He *always* taught us about life, war, and winning.

Frank never let a week go by without telling us that we would all be replaced as soon as the team could find a faster, younger, cheaper, or better player. He used that as motivation for us to give all we had on the practice field. I remember him likening the race to the moon between the United States and the Soviets as the same thing as football or business. We were in business to win. We were not in business to lose or to fail.

Frank was not a person who could be explained; he was a person who had to be listened to. I wish I had recorded every one of his stories. He was the best and most dynamic speaker who ever addressed a team. He spoke with an intensity that made us feel as though we were getting ready for war. His stories were almost always knit together with themes of war and the amazing job that our armed services do as they fight for us. He would research a story and describe a person in such detail that after an hour it seemed as though we all knew that person intimately. I often called home and told my parents and my brothers about the incredible stories and lessons that Frank taught. I wanted everyone I knew to hear what Frank had to say each day.

Dick's belief in bonding our team together with his love

carried over to the guys. Players bought into his style and his way of doing things. Early in that season, Mike Jones, a linebacker and one of the pillars of that team, stopped to talk with me in the locker room after one of our practices. Since I was one of the new guys, he knew that I could use some friends. And so he reached out to me in a way similar to the way Dick Vermeil reached out to every player he ever coached. Mike asked me if I wanted to join him and some of the other guys at his home for a fish fry. I thought it was cool that he would include me like that. So Michele and I drove over to his home and enjoyed every second of that fish fry and several more after that. We might have been the only white people at the party, but Mike made sure we fit in like family. We loved being included.

At the end of that season, Mike was the hero of the Super Bowl when he tackled Kevin Dyson of the Tennessee Titans at the one-yard line as time ran out, to preserve the win for the Rams. Everyone who saw the game witnessed not only one of the best linebackers in the game, but one of the greatest guys the NFL had ever known. He made St. Louis a better team. He made everyone around him a better person and a better player. He was part of the greatness that made the Rams a great team.

Coach Vermeil would cry almost every day. At first, I wondered what that was all about. Then I came to understand that he cried because he cared. He cared about the players and coaches first. But he also cared about the game of football. He respected the game and gave it all he had.

Later in that season, as we were tearing through the League on our way to the Super Bowl, I was released. It was after the ninth week of the season and right before Thanksgiving. Dick's secretary called me in on our day off and asked me to come and meet with Dick. I asked her if I was getting released, and she said yes. I called my agent, Don Yee, and let him know what was going on.

Don wasn't surprised. A week before, he had requested that

the Rams let me go. I was only being used as a backup, and the 49ers had some injuries at tight end, and Don also represented San Francisco head coach Steve Mariucci. Don was hoping the Rams would let me go and the 49ers would pick me up and I could get on the field. He advised me to let Dick know how much I thought of him and to leave a note with him. So that is what I did. Before driving to the team facility at Earth City right off of I-70 outside of St. Charles, I wrote a note to Dick Vermeil informing him how much respect I had for him. I even told him that I loved him.

Have you ever wondered what it is like to get cut by an NFL coach? When I walked into his office, he was not feeling happy at all. I could tell by the distressed look on his face. I wasn't happy, either, but I also understood the business of the NFL.

I was caught in the perfect storm. Two players were being added to the roster. Tight end Ernie Conwell had been on the PUP list. That is the Physically Unable to Perform (PUP) category, which allowed a player who was injured at the beginning of the season to take six to nine weeks to determine if they would be healthy enough to play that year. They had three weeks to practice and make that determination before they were either added to the team, put on injured reserve for the rest of the season, or let go.

Ernie had hurt his leg the year before and was making a remarkable comeback. He was also one of the NFL's finest. His work ethic was second to none, and he was a committed family man who would help any person at anytime for any reason. He was genuine, sincere, and loved by every person on the team. One of the surprising things about the NFL was how many terrific people both played and coached the game. Fans knew about the thugs because they were the ones in the news. But I thought the great majority of the fans would be surprised to know about the high quality of many of the individuals in the League. That might have been the best-kept secret of the NFL.

Dick told me that he did not want to release me. He thought about putting me on injured reserve just so I could be there for the next year. The more he thought about that, he said the more he knew that would not be the best thing for me. He wanted me to have a chance to play that year. I took out the card that I had written and handed it to him across his desk. He asked what it was, and I told him that I thought a lot of him and had said as much in the card. He stood up from the desk and walked to the other side of his office. He said how much he hated that part of his job, and he cried.

After he gathered himself again, he sat back down and we told each other good-bye. I am sure when people hear about his emotions they will wonder if he was faking it. I never once had the feeling that he was faking it. Not for a second. He was the genuine article. I loved Dick Vermeil and still do.

When a player is released in the NFL, he is placed on the waiver wire. Your name stays on that list for twenty-four hours. Every team has the same opportunity to check the waiver wire, see who has been released, and put a claim on the player they want to sign. The team with the worst current record is awarded the player.

As soon as I was released, the 49ers, the Eagles, and the Colts all put a claim on me. The Eagles and the 49ers had identical records, but the tie went to the Eagles because they had not had their bye-week yet. Assuming I would become a 49er, Steve Young had called me before the waiver wire time expired, and we had made an arrangement for me to live at his house in San Francisco for the rest of the year. The Eagles ended up claiming me when there were only five minutes left on the waiver wire. I boarded a plane within two hours and headed back to Philly.

The next day, while Michele was helping box up our belongings, Dick Vermeil called the house and talked with her. He made sure that she had everything taken care of and asked if there was anything else he could do for us. He told Michele that he was happy for me to be going into such an ideal situation with Andy Reid as the head coach. He told her that he was very sorry to let me go, but that he felt as though I would thrive in Andy's offense. He gave Michele his number and told her to call him at any time if she needed his help.

That was an incredible show of class. I am not aware of another coach going the extra mile like that. I was not at all bitter that the Rams let me go. I understood how things worked. I was the opposite of bitter. Because of how Coach Vermeil treated my family and me, I left the Rams with nothing but gratitude for the many opportunities they had given me.

Mike Martz was then the offensive coordinator for the Rams and he later became their head coach. He helped them win the Super Bowl that first year he was there, and he took them to the Super Bowl the next year when he was head coach. After I left Dick Vermeil's office, I went to the training room to get an exit physical. When I got there, I visited with Mike Martz, who had some very encouraging things to say.

As we stood there next to the taping tables in the training room, my heart was pounding because I was being cut. It was not a great feeling. I was being asked to leave the teammates whom I had fought and battled alongside. I was asked to leave the locker room that had become my home. Everything that I had worked for was over. In that strange vacuum of leaving what I had, and not knowing what was ahead, Coach Martz told me that I was the perfect tight end for the West Coast Offense. He told me that if I got in the right system that I would be a Pro Bowl tight end and that I would do it immediately. He said that he had confidence in me right then to catch a game-winning touchdown and that he didn't doubt for a second that I could do it.

When I later shared that conversation with some people, they couldn't understand why the Rams would cut me if that was how the coaches felt about it. I understood. It was business. It was difficult, but it was a necessary step in my career. I was grateful for the confidence that Coach Martz had in me. I drew on that confidence as I started life over again with the Eagles.

When I left the Rams and rejoined the Eagles, it was ironic that the last game of the season was against the Rams. It was in Philly. It was cool for me to see all of my old teammates. The Rams were on their way to the play-offs and had already secured home-field advantage. They did not need to win to help their play-off position. They took some of their starters out of the game near the end to prevent them from getting injured before the play-offs started.

In that game, I caught the go-ahead touchdown that helped us beat the Rams. It was a lot of fun. After scoring, I did the same shadow-boxing-type celebration that I used to do when I was a member of their team. It was called the "bob 'n weave" and was originated by Tory Holt. After the game, the whole Rams team gathered with me at midfield, and we exchanged hugs and hellos. Dick Vermeil gave me a giant hug. He said how excited he was for me that I was with the Eagles and in a system where I would be successful. It was the best way to end the year, with a victory over the team that had cut me, but without any malice or anger. It was great to see my old team, my friends, and the coaches with whom I had spent a year of my life.

One of the most important people I met in St. Louis was not a coach or a player, but he was just as important to me as any coach I ever had. His name was Phil Towle and he was the sports psychologist for the Rams. When the Rams were introducing me to their facilities, they gave me a tour of the place. When they walked me through the team offices, Phil was there visiting with one of the coaches and I was introduced to him.

I was surprised to know that the Rams had a sports psychologist on staff. I asked if I could use his services. The Rams told me that was fine with them. I asked if he had time that day. He said that he did, and we found an office upstairs in the facility and had a great talk. Phil was a great listener. I had a burning desire to become a great player but felt I was not reaching my full potential. He listened as I shared any frustrations that were weighing on my mind. Getting hurt and getting cut were not easy processes to go through. They carried with them a burden that was difficult to share with most people. From the first day, it was easy to talk to Phil about my weaknesses and frustrations as a player.

He asked what I wanted to do in my career. I told him that I wanted to go to the Super Bowl and that I wanted to be a Pro Bowl tight end. He always treated me like a Pro Bowl player. He never made me feel our conversations were a waste of his time. In fact, it was just the opposite. He remembered everything we ever discussed with detail, which proved to me he cared. His skill as a listener created trust in our relationship. Trust allowed us to continue. The very nature of a sports psychologist endures only if trust is total.

I visited with him a few times during the year that I played for the Rams. When I went back to the Eagles, I continued to call him when I felt as though I wanted to talk. He was instrumental in helping me clear my mind and focus only on the things that were important. He taught me to give mental credence only to the things that deserved it and to banish any negative thoughts from my brain. Phil was incredible. He had a gift; he could hear and listen. Adding him to my mix of coaches, friends, and confidants was a great thing. He was very instrumental in helping me to achieve the success I enjoyed on the field.

CHAPTER 17

BACK TO PHILADELPHIA, ANDY REID, DONOVAN MCNABB, AND TRAINING CAMP

Andy Reid is the best coach in the NFL, hands down. My opinion is biased, of course. He has proved his skill year after year. Even though he has not won the Super Bowl yet, he is still, in my mind, the best coach. In fact, I would not have continued playing in the NFL year after year if it weren't for Andy. Not just because he believed in what I could do as a player but because I believed in him as a coach.

After leaving St. Louis, I showed up at his office in Philly the next day. He said, "I know you wanted to go out with Steve Young and finish his career with him, but I need you here. I need you to help me turn this thing around!"

I told him that I would jump back into the West Coast playbook and do whatever it took to help the Eagles be successful. He followed up with his end of the bargain immediately. That Sunday we played the Colts and he inserted me directly into the game plan. In fact, I caught a touchdown late in that game, which was the first touchdown pass in Donovan McNabb's NFL career.

Andy made me the starting tight end for the next several years. He put together a unique team. There was a lot of competition at

Courtesy of the Philadelphia Eagles

Celebrating with Todd Pinkston (#87) after a touchdown to beat the New York Giants and win the NFC East Division.

each position, which only made each player raise his game to a higher level. But at the same time, we all played together well. It was a rare combination that isn't always found in the NFL, where many teams have fallen apart because they could not balance those two things—individual success and team success.

Andy was a successful coach because he was very organized and because he was supremely confident. When it came to organization, he was always ahead of the curve. He had things mapped out two weeks in advance and was never caught off guard by anything, not even injuries. He considered them a part of the game and was always prepared mentally and organizationally to deal with them.

The most dramatic display of his focus occurred after Donovan sustained a major injury against the Arizona Cardinals in a home game in Philly. While being sacked in the first series of that game, McNabb's leg was wickedly tangled underneath his body as he went down to the turf. He was in obvious pain, but he refused to leave the game. He was taped up by the trainers on the sideline. He had so much tape on his ankle, it was more or less a boot. Not only did he refuse to sit down and rest, but he also threw four touchdowns in our victory over the Cardinals. It was a legendary performance in my book because he played the rest of that game on a bone in his leg that turned out to have been shattered during the first series. I never doubted Donovan's toughness. He was a warrior.

We started the next week with our usual team meeting. Everyone expected Andy to address Donovan's broken leg. I thought for sure that he would encourage us to pick up the slack now that Donovan was out. But he didn't even mention the injury. He said that Koy Detmer was going to be our quarterback, that we were going to play the 49ers on Monday Night Football, and that we were going to win. With that statement, he ended the meeting. It was shocking that he did not spend two seconds dwelling on Donovan's injury, something that we couldn't change anyway.

Andy did not allow any room for us to be victims. He gave us no opportunity to use Donovan's injury, something as an excuse. His organization included his anticipation of injuries and his confidence saw that we would never lose focus because of them.

That very game, Koy Detmer dislocated his elbow and AJ Feeley took over as the quarterback in the second half. Now that we were on our third-string quarterback, I wondered how Andy would react in next week's team meeting. I shouldn't have been surprised that he did the same thing. He did not say one word about Koy getting hurt. He simply announced that AJ would be our starter and that we were going to keep winning games the same as before. After those two weeks of shocking back-to-back injuries, I knew what to expect from Andy forever. He would plow forward without giving credence to injuries or making excuses about anything.

The trajectory of my football career up to that point had been as up and down as the volatility of the stock market. It wasn't until I got with the Eagles again that things made a steady rise. Andy Reid and his staff were just what I needed as a person and a player. Donovan McNabb was a perfect quarterback for me and the skills that I brought to the table. The three Eagles quarterbacks were Donovan, Doug Pederson, and Koy Detmer. They embraced me as a friend and brother almost immediately. I had already been with Koy my rookie year, and we had remained close even when I went to the Rams. Those three guys were incredible people and provided strong leadership for a team that needed to go from the bottom of the League to the top.

Pat Shurmur was the tight-end coach during my second stint with Philly. Juan Castillo was still there on the coaching staff, but he had been moved to offensive-line coach. Pat was a young, on-the-rise offensive coach. I rejoined the Eagles a week before Thanksgiving, and Pat invited me to his house for Thanksgiving dinner. I enjoyed getting to know his wife, Jennifer, and their three kids, Allyson, Erica, and Kyle. They would later add another daughter, Claire, to their family.

Even though I got there in the middle of the season, Pat was incredible at working me into the system and teaching me the offense. It was a credit to Pat that he was able to get production out of me so quickly. The offensive verbiage was entirely different than that of the Rams. I had worked hard in St. Louis to memorize the playbook. Now I needed to forget all of it, instantly, and soak up the new plays and the new language of the West Coast offensive system. Learning a new playbook was always a huge challenge.

That first full year with the Eagles began with one of the best off-seasons I ever had. It seemed the whole team was in Philly for the workouts. All of the tight ends were there, and we threw with

Donovan almost every day. I began to get very comfortable with how hard he threw the ball. I also got to know him better and we became good friends. I learned just how talented he was on the field, and how funny he was all the time. I could feel that things were headed in the right direction.

When the off-season program was finished and all of the mini camps were concluded, the only thing we had left to do before the season was attack training camp. Nothing loomed larger than training camp. It was exceedingly tough the first year, but it got even harder every year after that. One of the reasons was that we knew what we were getting into. It would seem just the opposite—that because we already knew what to expect, it would be easier. Not so. Because we knew what was coming, we dreaded it for a whole year. In fact, as soon as training camp was over, players would remind each other that they would have to endure it again in just ten and a half months.

Training camp had some things in common with hiking Mount Everest. Sir Edmund Hillary and his friend Tenzing Norgay were the first climbers to reach the summit. In 1953 they overcame every obstacle to help each other stand where no boots had ever stood before. That unprecedented feat bonded them and they remained friends for the rest of their lives.

Getting to the top was only one of the challenges. Dealing with the freezing-cold elements and the extremely high altitude and carrying all of the gear required were just some of the others. In order for bodies to adjust to the altitude, base camp was set up, followed by a series of camps higher up the mountain. A climber had to acclimatize to base camp before it was safe to go farther up. A series of climbs up and down prepared them to make the final push to the top.

The difficulty of climbing Everest was in many ways analogous to preparing for a football season. Training camp was like setting up base camp on Everest. It helped establish the success or failure

Division Champs! Celebrating with the two best guys in the NFL,
Jeff Thomason (left) and Mike Bartrum (right).

of a team. And it was at training camp where a team learned how
to work together to have a strong season and hopefully a shot at
winning the Super Bowl at the end of a very long year. The importance of good team chemistry couldn't be overstated. The tight
ends for the Philadelphia Eagles always said, "Tight ends, tight
friends," and that was how we lived and played.

Mike Bartrum and Jeff Thomason were a miracle in my life.
The three of us were the tight ends for the Philadelphia Eagles for
several years. And through the fire of adversity and the challenges
that came with football, we forged a strong friendship.

Jeff came to the Eagles in a trade from the Green Bay Packers,
where he had spent seven years as a backup to successful Pro Bowl
tight ends Keith Jackson and Mark Chmura. Jeff grew up in
Southern California and had the blond hair and good looks one

would associate with a surfer growing up there. He played tight end for the Oregon Ducks in college.

Mike grew up in Pomeroy, Ohio. He was tall, dark, and had always had a mustache or goatee ever since he could grow one. He played tight end for the Marshall University Thundering Herd. As a pro, he played several years for the New England Patriots before joining the Eagles. Jeff and Mike even played against each other in Super Bowl XXXI. They were both extremely courteous and showed great concern for others, which was a testament and a tribute to their parents on how they were raised.

When Andy Reid put his plan in place to get the Eagles to the Super Bowl, among the players he brought in Jeff and Mike turned out to be key contributors. My good friend Luther Broughton and I were already there as tight ends. The addition of these two veteran players gave us a strong group at that position. Most teams kept only three tight ends; the Eagles kept all four of us together that first year.

Some of the media thought we were both too young and too old as a group to be effective. Luther kept one such article pinned up in his locker all year to remind him, and us, of the doubters. Nothing fires up an athlete like a doubter. Luther always pointed his finger to that article as a reminder that we needed to work hard and prove them wrong. When we experienced success as a group, he would likewise point to the article and smile. We wanted to prove that we could make plays and win games.

Most players could get *through* camp. But we were able to push each other and encourage each other in a way that helped us get better from camp and not just get through camp. Just getting through camp should never be a goal. Dominating through camp or excelling in camp, now that sounds more like what we should be shooting for. We will all have trials in life, and when surrounded by great teammates or great friends, it makes it possible to get through them well.

Andrew Geddes, Mike Geddes, Coach Andy Reid, and me the day before the NFC Championship game against the Tampa Bay Buccaneers, January 2003.

Coach Reid always preached that survival mode in training camp would not help you get any better. He said that survival mode would kill our team. What does survival mode mean? Camp is so hard that the natural response is to hunker down and just try to survive. It takes a greater vision of what you are doing to get better during each drill, each practice, and each day. It is harder to get better than it is just to survive, but with great people and great attitudes around you, camp is the difference between a play-off team and a team that is just going through the motions in anticipation of giving in to the rebuilding process.

It would be lofty to say that I always played with incredible vision and that I never fell into survival mode, but that would not be accurate. There were times when all I could do was fight to survive. Looking back on the experience has taught me that winning that fight is 90 percent of the battle. The fight that great players and great teams displayed was the desire to overcome any obstacle. It was having the appetite to take on any challenge or challenger, the passion to charge up any hill, the hunger to exceed any expectation, and the willingness to compete with all the energy of your soul.

It never got easy. After every hot and humid practice my muscles would cramp and ache. There is no pain quite like cramping muscles. It is a horrible feeling. Continuing to push beyond any previous threshold of pain amounted to self-inflicted torture. "Fatigue makes cowards of us all" is a true statement. Being weary causes a player to doubt his own skills. When you are in the depths of exhaustion is when confidence is questioned, when anxieties about injuries or getting cut are exaggerated. Being surrounded by great coaches and great teammates was what got you through.

Depressing conditions call for the most optimism. Wallowing in misery was never the answer to becoming great. I was trained and taught by my coaches to give more than the minimum. I was taught to give all that I had, and more, even when my body didn't feel like it—*especially* when my body didn't feel like it.

Going to training camp is like paying taxes. In order to enjoy good roads, schools, public safety, and our way of life, paying taxes is unavoidable. And to earn the right to be on the field making plays, training camp must be conquered. When you are in the middle of it, you get the feeling that you are in a long dark tunnel that will never end. But there is a light at the end that is barely visible at the beginning. After all of the agony, the real games hang out there as the light or the reward at the end of the tunnel. The thrill of playing in games, where you are tested man to man and team to team, in front of the whole world, is the prize. The reward is so great that all of the pain endured in training camp is worth it.

An interesting thing about training camp is that almost every player at some point wants to quit. Doesn't that seem strange? The best football players in the world who have trained and sacrificed for months and years are willing to give it all up in a second because camp is so hard. For some players, that feeling lasts only a short time, other players battle it longer. But make no mistake about it, training camp is hard enough that all who go through it must overcome the demon of doubt that creeps in and whispers that it would all be easier to just quit.

In my experience, the best remedy to fight this demon was work. Get to work. Forget yourself and your own pain. Stop the pity party. Know that no one is crying for you. Remember how hard you have trained and how much you have sacrificed to get here, and get to work. That was my mindset. If there was downtime before practice, I read an inspiring book or studied my playbook. I refused to allow toxic anxiety to creep in and erode my confidence or my love for the game.

Our love of the game was not something any of us had to consciously think about when we were young. We played for the love of the game. But as we got older and things got more difficult and more complicated, we needed to remember how fun it was to play football in our backyards as little kids. We needed to remember the feeling that we had when everything first clicked and we knew how much we loved it.

To be successful, we couldn't let it turn into *just* a job. It wasn't *just* work. Football is a game that requires everything a player has, and more, but it still has to be fun. Otherwise, a player is just going through the motions. Fans pay precious money to sit in their seats, and they can spot an imposter in about two seconds. And there is nothing worse for that fan than to watch a player giving only half an effort. That is not only laziness, but also an indication of lack of character. That is a principle for all of us, not just for athletes.

My job was football—catching passes, blocking, running,

jumping over people, winning games. Another person's job could be accounting, performing surgery, ironworking, homemaking, or doing anything else that pays the bills. Everyone should give an honest day's work at whatever he or she is doing.

The first day of training camp always started with a team meeting, which included all the coaches, players, trainers, doctors, public relations department, front office staff, and owner. That is when the head coach sets the direction for the season. The energy in that room, if bottled, could power all the cars in some small countries.

Hope springs eternal, and nowhere is it more apparent than in that room, at that time, with the opportunity to go after the summit of football's Everest. That mountain at that time was placed right in front of you. It felt so close. It didn't matter what happened last season; you have the same record—no wins and no losses—as the best and worst teams in the League. That meeting also marks the last time for about seven months that a player's body will be pain and injury free.

The first thing the next morning was the conditioning test. Each team conducts its own running tests to make sure that each player is ready for the season. In the case of the Philadelphia Eagles, we ran sixteen sprints called "half gassers." They were a sprint from one sideline to the other and back. Each sprint was to be completed in less than seventeen seconds. We were given forty seconds to rest between each rep. By the time all sixteen half gassers had been run, a player's legs felt like they were filled with concrete.

With that beginning, we were off to the races and wouldn't take another easy breath until the season was over.

Offensive and defensive meetings were held immediately following the run. The offensive plays for the first afternoon's practice were installed. A quick lunch was available, and then everyone got taped for the first practice.

Then something strange happened. The day turned into a blur reminiscent of Bill Murray's movie *Groundhog Day*. The same moment was lived over and over and over. Whatever a player was doing at the time seemed as though that was all he had ever done. Eating, getting taped, showering, meetings, practice—it just went on and on.

There were six weeks to make the team. There wasn't really anyplace to go to escape the pressure. The only way to make it was to have the drive to dominate. Some of the major challenges were winning the battle between the mind and a tired body, competing for a position, fighting to stay healthy enough to be on the practice field, learning the plays (and remembering them when fatigued), dealing with the heat and humidity, and wanting a spot badly enough to go get it. Everything was done with urgency.

Preparation for each practice started the night before. Plays were installed that were to be used the next day. That was when they had to be learned and concentration was required. Coaches used overhead projectors, video, white boards, anything they could to help teach us the plays. They wanted all of us to succeed. If a player messed up at practice, the head coach would not only yell at him, but the position coach would get yelled at as well. So believe me, the position coaches were motivated to see that every player did things correctly. The head coach didn't just care about the players who would be starting. His purpose was to get every person ready to play.

The cafeteria opened at 6:30 in the morning. The first breakfast at camp is outstanding. The eggs taste good, the French toast is just right, the cold cereal is fresh, and the fruit is juicy. Before long, the players' bodies were completely drained and sore enough that they didn't even feel like eating. At times during camp, eating became a chore. Nothing sounded or looked good.

Isn't it weird how at different times the clock seems to move faster or slower? In training camp during the day, the clock seems frozen, the minute hand moving like the hour hand. At training camp, during the night while you are sleeping, the clock goes faster than you can comprehend.

Training camp was a constant battle to maintain physical and emotional health. As much as each person needed to battle to keep his body healthy by getting the proper food, rest, and treatment in the training room, he also needed to battle staying focused mentally.

During training camp, different people were coming in and out of the locker room all the time and new recruits were constantly being evaluated. It was very different from college football. College teams can't recruit new players in the middle of the season, no matter how many injuries they have. In the business of the NFL, if someone was hurt or not playing well, that player was out, and a new player was brought in to see if he could take his place.

A disconcerting thing during my rookie year of training camp was watching our player personnel staff working out other tight ends during practices. It was a constant reminder to dominate on the field and never give them a reason to cut you loose. But I learned that a football player can't be successful if he spends his time stressing about other players who are trying out or worrying about what the coaches are thinking. Those were things I couldn't control. What I needed to do was stay focused on the work at hand. It took a few years before I wasn't bothered by other tight ends being worked out. It was all just part of the process for a team.

I learned through experience that I was best when I concentrated on each play, one at a time. If I could focus all of my thoughts and energy on one play, one minute, one rep at a time, I could get the job done. But there was a constant battle between the mental and the physical aspects of the game. Remembering all I needed to know while battling exhaustion was always the challenge. But the mental and physical battle "switch" was never turned off—whether at practice, mealtimes, in meetings, or sleeping—it was always on.

It is almost impossible to exaggerate the importance of a great leader and teammate during this time of testing and toil. Donovan McNabb was just such a person. He had the rare gift to make even drudgery fun. From the first day of training camp to the last practice, he would keep the team laughing with his constant jokes and unique ability to imitate the coaches.

He was like Bill Cosby when it came to comedic talent. He did a perfect impersonation of head coach Andy Reid. While walking out to practice, Donovan would have all of us busting up laughing with his imitations of Rod Dowhower, Brad Childress, or Marty Mornhinweg, who were our offensive coordinators through the years. I think he had more to do with our team loving Rod Dowhower than anyone else. Rod was an older coach who could easily have come off as an old curmudgeon. But thanks to Donovan, who got him to smile, we all loved Rod and couldn't say enough great things about him. Rod was the one who helped resurrect my career when he put me more and more into the game plan. He loved to call me "Big Boy!" That was something that Donovan used on me too. Donovan would imitate Rod's voice and say, "Hey, Big Boy, you gotta stick it!" Donovan's imitation was so accurate that the whole team would die laughing.

Imagine how much of a stress or pressure reliever he was to the team. When your body was beaten down and sore, the last thing anyone felt like doing was laughing. But then Donovan would come along with his impersonations or his jokes and before you knew it, you were laughing as if you were in the presence of a stand-up comic.

Andy Reid knew how important Donovan was to the team and so he never tried to smother his humor. Even when Andy had a strong feeling that Donovan had the whole team rolling at his own expense because he was impersonating him, he would just give a wry smile and acknowledge that the joke was on him. He would rather have a loose team whose members could let their personalities show than be the dictator who would not stand for such humiliation. Both of these leaders, Andy and Donovan, used their talents and strengths to forge one of the winningest combinations of coach and player over that decade in the NFL.

Since Donovan is still playing, his record is still being written. But my own record of him has been written in stone. He was an incredible teammate, and I can't thank him enough for what he did for me, for my family, and for my career. His loyal friendship, his determined leadership, and his inspired play are bright evidences that he is one of the most talented people I have ever met. I will also say that his parents are some of the best people I have ever known. They treated me like a son, and I will love them forever. In my case, I was on my way to having an ordinary career in the NFL, but I had the good fortune to run into an exceptional quarterback, a solid coach, and a host of determined and selfless teammates.

Practice in training camp started early for all of the skill positions. The daily schedule had practice posted for an 8:45 start. That really mandated to be out there fifteen minutes early, catching balls, getting loose, or working with your coaches on areas where you could improve. The QBs, snappers, and kickers needed to be out there to work on the timing of the kicking game.

It was a common saying among players that the three letters *NFL* stood for "Not for long." We were all fully aware that any one of us could be cut and sent packing at any time. That being the case, all the players on any team believed in the idea of "The more you can do . . ." That referred to the benefits of being flexible, understanding other positions, and mastering several skills. A player needed to make himself so valuable that the team would not get rid of him. With that in mind, I learned how to become a deep snapper for punts and field goals. I also learned how to become a holder for field-goal attempts. Because of an injury to Mike Bartrum, our snapper, and another injury to Koy Detmer, our holder, I was able to apply those skills in regular season games. I found that doing them in practice was one thing, but doing them in a game gave me a whole new appreciation for the talent players in those positions had.

The first punt I snapped for was from our own one-yard line. Our punter, Sean Landeta, was standing so close to me that when I looked at him from my snapping position, he looked as though he was in the shotgun formation. His heels were only an inch away from the back line of the end zone.

The Titans knew that Bartrum was out of the game and so their rush plan was to buck the center. I was the center that got bucked. The only thing that I can remember after snapping the ball was looking up at the sky. It's a good thing that Sean had the fastest snap-to-punt-time in the NFL because he was able to get off a rocket of a punt. It was no wonder to me that his pro career (NFL and USFL) would last an amazing twenty-five years.

Though some people thought snapping was the easiest job in the NFL, I knew from limited experience that snappers were some of the most important players on a team. Mike Bartrum built a reputation as the best snapper in the NFL over his fourteen-year career.

Holding for field-goal attempts required the same amount of practice and sound technique. Many games have been won or lost on a botched snap. Tony Romo, the QB for the Dallas Cowboys, fumbled a snap on a field-goal attempt that would have won a play-off game against the Seahawks. The one game that I got to hold for a Dave Akers' field goal was a Monday Night Football game against the 49ers in San Francisco.

In the same Cardinals game where Donovan broke his leg, I received a laceration to my buttocks. It was wickedly painful—

one of the most painful injuries I have ever had. While I was getting sewn up at halftime, Donovan took a look in the office where I was getting stitched. I asked how he was feeling, and he said, "Better than you."

He said he was going to tape his foot up again and keep playing. That inspired me to keep playing with the five stitches holding me together.

In relief of Donovan, Koy Detmer was tearing things up until his elbow was dislocated as he fell to the ground. AJ Feeley came in to replace Koy at QB, and I replaced Koy as holder. The first time I got to hold was on the extra-point try after AJ had thrown me a touchdown pass. I thought it was so much fun to hold.

But later in the game, I was to hold for a long field-goal attempt by Akers. It seemed as though the time between the snap and the kick would never end, and my heart was pounding. I was more than relieved when Dave booted the ball through the uprights, something he did more accurately than any other kicker but one for a few years. Dave and I had a tradition of sitting next to each other on all our flights. We sat on the same row for seven years. He had a difficult start to his career by making quick exits from several teams before the Eagles finally gave him the support he was hoping for. The Eagles were rewarded with one of the best place kickers in the game. He set the record for the longest string of successful kicks in the play-offs at nineteen. It will be a long time, if ever, before that record is broken.

Entering the Eagles' practice field at Lehigh University had two constants. One was the heat and the other was Eagle Joe.

First the heat. It wouldn't be training camp without the heat and humidity. Growing up in Utah, I learned how to deal with the dry heat of the desert in summer as I hiked with my family and Scout troop all over the state. As long as water was available I was fine. Even super-hot dry heat was manageable with some water.

The climate at Lehigh University in the Bethlehem-Allentown

area an hour north of Philly was not quite as hot and muggy as Taiwan, until you put on your shoulder pads and a helmet. Once they were on and practice got going, it was no different than the sweltering heat and stifling mugginess of Southeast Asia. Just walking to the practice fields triggered a major sweat.

I had to get used to sweat pouring off my nose and landing all over the ball each time I would bend down to get ready to snap. I know Koy wasn't too happy to catch the snap when my big sweat drops would splash all over his face. And that was just warm-ups. Let the sweat fest begin.

The other constant at Eagles training camp was the presence of Eagle Joe. Joe Brown was one of the most faithful Eagles fans of all time. For thirty years he had spent his vacation time watching camp. Buddy Ryan found out about Eagle Joe and gave him a field pass to stand inside the ropes with the players. That tradition had lasted through several head coaches and continued with Andy Reid.

Every summer Eagle Joe stood like a sentinel at the edge of the practice field to greet each player for every practice. He knew everyone's name on the team and where we played in college. He commonly asked us questions about our families. He was always courteous. He was always friendly. He always carried a camera and wore the same clothes—an Eagles ball cap, T-shirt, shorts, and tennis shoes.

Andy Reid made sure that he was decked out in the latest Eagles gear. The players regarded him with the same respect that he extended to us. When his vacation was over, the players always made it a big deal to thank Eagle Joe for coming to camp again. I recently learned that Eagle Joe has become legally blind and unable to drive himself to training camp. In what was one of his greatest acts of kindness as the Eagles owner, Jeffrey Lurie began sending a limo to pick up Eagle Joe for practice and take him back home at night. The traditions of sweltering heat and Eagle Joe's attendance at training camp will continue indefinitely.

CHAPTER 18

TRAINING CAMP GOES ON

Playing football in the heat caused me to sweat so much that it was not uncommon for me to lose up to ten pounds of water weight during one practice. I had to force-feed myself through training camp or else I would have gone from a tight end to a wide receiver.

Rick Burkholder, the head trainer, kept a watchful eye on each player and made sure we were drinking as much Gatorade and water as possible. He required us to drink in meetings, drink at meals, drink during practice, and drink at night. Drink, drink, drink.

Rick even had some of the guys who perspired the most go through a sweat study, which was paid for by Gatorade. I was one of the guinea pigs. They tested me before and after each practice to find out how much weight I was losing and putting back on before the next practice. My urine was tested for exact pH information to know whether I was dehydrated or not. My blood was tested by pricking a finger. Then a hematocrit centrifuge was used as another way to check for dehydration.

One of the most interesting tests was performed by using a

space-age thermometer. It was covered in a white plastic capsule and looked just like a big pill. After I had swallowed this "pill," the trainers were able to take my precise core temperature by waving a scanner, similar to those used at the checkout counter at the grocery store, behind my lower back during practice. They needed to be only about six inches away from my back to get the reading. The pill stayed in my system for two days worth of practices. When they first told me about it, I thought it was funny to be scanned, just like a gallon of milk.

It worked so smoothly that I rarely knew they were checking my temperature. If the scanner indicated that I was warming up too much, Rick would slip an ice-cold, wet, towel-like hat onto my head to cool me down. It was amazing how fast my body core temperature would cool off when that was done.

This sweat study was done for two straight training camps. They concluded that I perspired a little more than average and that my sweat was very salty. They encouraged me to add salt to my meals. That was it. Keep drinking fluids and add salt.

My tendency to cramp up pretty quickly made the first several years of training camp excruciating for me. When practice was over, the muscles in my legs felt as though they were twisting into knots. While sleeping at night, I would be awakened by violent cramps that would seize my hamstrings, quads, calves, or feet. I have never had a heart attack but something tells me it must be a similar feeling.

Drinking more fluid was not the only solution. It wasn't until I started using a supplement called Stim-O-Stam that the cramps finally went away. Thank heavens for Stim-O-Stam. It brought great relief to my cramping muscles.

Just thinking about how painful it was to go through an episode of muscle cramps reminds me of injuries. No player wanted to be injured. Foolish thoughts came to my mind as a high-school football player in the middle of two-a-days. We called it "hell week" back then. I laugh when I think about how short it was compared to two and a half weeks in college and six weeks in the NFL.

Bryan Rowley was the best player at Orem High School. We had been best friends since grade school at Hillcrest Elementary. We used to drive to practice together and joke about getting into a minor car wreck that would slightly injure us, just enough to miss some of the practices during two-a-days. What a weak mind I had back then. I have learned through the years that the pain of training camp would pass. It seemed as though it would last forever and a day, but it would eventually end. The wisdom gained from life experience helped me push through the difficulty.

Instead of entertaining the childish fantasy of getting into a car wreck just to miss a practice, my mind got tougher through the years. It has taken focus and effort, great coaches, and strong teammates to help me endure it, and I have found we get better at the things we work at. Mental toughness is no different.

Lest anyone think that creating an injury or even faking an injury is a legitimate way out of training camp, let me just say that it would have been a team-wrecking and devastating idea. That did not happen among players who were focused on making the team better. No player ever got respect from his teammates by faking an injury. Team players work their guts out to make the team, get better, and fight through small injuries themselves.

Coaches do not cut down reps because of injuries. They do not shorten practice because of the absence of a player. What I am saying is that if you miss a practice, then your teammates, the other tight ends, have to do more of the work. They are already tired, but now they have been put in a position where their already difficult workload is increased. Not cool.

Jeff Thomason and Mike Bartrum made a career out of being tough and practicing even when their bodies were screaming to take a day off. If they did miss a practice, it was because Rick

Burkholder pulled their pads away from them and forced them to rest a torn muscle or an injury. He would do it for the good of the team.

Even then, they didn't want to miss practice because all of us knew that "You can't make the club in the tub." That meant that if a player were spending too much time sitting in the training room soaking his bruises and sorrows in the Jacuzzi, he would not make the football team. And it would be very difficult to gain the respect of his teammates. There was a fine line between being hurt and being injured. And there wasn't anyone to tell a player where that line was. They just had to know it or figure it out really quick. There was also a fine line between earning respect and losing the confidence of teammates. Most of those fine lines were undefined. They were simply rules etched deep in our hearts as young football players. It is impossible to spell them out perfectly. Players just needed to *know.*

As soon as we did have an injury that required us to miss practice, we knew that we could be cut or replaced in the lineup, and that helped speed up the recovery process mightily. That helped us work even harder to get our treatment, and to rehab whatever was hurting, so that we could return to the field, return to our teammates, and return to our profession. That was how we took care of our family. That was the means. That was the vehicle.

Training camp was a battle zone. It was a perfect example of a place where you needed to surround yourself with greatness. You needed great teammates who could inspire you to work hard even when you felt like dragging—guys who could pick you up when you were down. Jeff and Mike did that on a daily basis, through their words, their example, their friendship, their comic relief, their ability to fight through pain, their toughness, their humility and their unselfishness.

One play at a training camp practice will always remind me of Jeff and Mike. Jeff ran a route that we had run a million times.

The play was "22 Texas Y out." It required a tight end to run ten yards straight downfield, stick his left foot in the ground, and break straight out to the right. The fullback would start from the backfield and run for the flat, into the area vacated by the tight end, but after four yards he would plant his right foot in the ground and sprint for a spot directly over the center, six yards beyond the line of scrimmage.

It was a sweet red-zone play because it put the middle linebacker and the outside linebacker in a quick bind. They would have to instantly decide if they were going to pass off defending the crossing fullback and the tight end, or if they were going to defend them man-to-man.

On that occasion, Jeff ran a nice route and Donovan threw the ball on the money. When Jeff reached for the ball, it jammed his left pinky finger, causing him to drop the ball and resulting in a boutonniere deformity that he will have for the rest of his life. *Boutonnière* is a French word meaning "buttonhole," and a hand with a boutonniere deformity looks as though one of the fingers is curled down toward the palm more than normal. It is caused by a tear in the tendon sheet that resembles a buttonhole and is a common football injury.

Andy Reid blew up. He shouted at Jeff that he had just run the worst route that he had ever seen. Jeff smiled through the pain and even laughed behind his face mask as he held his finger, which was killing him. He knew Andy well enough from Green Bay to know that sometimes a coach needs to let off some steam. Andy knew that Jeff could take it.

Standing behind the line of scrimmage, Mike and I were dying with laughter at how funny it was that Jeff had jammed his finger only to get yelled at by Andy. We were in the throes of two-a-days. At that point, anything funny was made funnier by the sheer physical and mental exhaustion we were all experiencing.

But here was Jeff, feeling miserable about dropping the pass, in pain from his messed up finger, and we were all laughing together, basically sharing Jeff's misery. The three of us still refer to that play and that explosion from Coach Reid as the stress reliever that brought the biggest smile to our faces in the most difficult time. Jeff worked on that finger with the trainers for the rest of training camp so he could still catch the football. He continued to rehab it for the rest of his career.

Because of frequent injuries, we needed the best possible doctors and trainers around us. It was critical also that we were able to trust them, but it took some practice to learn to rely on a paid representative of the club. As young players, we knew that our situation was not very stable. We knew that being hurt was only one step away from heading home. We were worried that the advice given to us by the team trainer might serve the team's interest better than our own.

For the most part, the team doctors and trainers were incredible. They knew how tough it was to stay healthy, and they did a great job giving us the resources that we needed to stay well, or if we were hurt, to get better. Their commitment to their jobs was just as strong as ours. They would arrive at the training room before any player, and they would also be there long after the players would leave each night. They did this day after long day for the whole season. It was a grueling grind for a player, and just as grueling for the trainers. They were part physical therapist, psychiatrist, sport psychologist, friend, motivator, liaison with the coach, and comedian all wrapped into one. They earned every penny of their paychecks. *Every* penny.

Any player with an ounce of gratitude had great love for his trainers. I felt that way about all of the trainers that I had in the NFL—from James Collins, my first trainer with the Eagles, to the St. Louis Rams' talented trainer, Jim Anderson, to the Eagles' trainers Rick Burkholder, Eric Sugarman, and Chris Paduzzi. Each dedicated his life to making sure we could perform on the field.

Their commitment was total. No hour was too early for them to open the training room. If an injury required staying well into the evening, they did it. Trainers did their work out of the spotlight. If training camp was long for the players, it was just as long for the trainers.

I could trust my life with George Curtis, the trainer when I was in college at BYU. He always had time for any of the athletes and even opened his own home when necessary to take care of his players. It didn't matter if you were an All-American or a walk-on, he treated you the same.

Football is a wicked and demanding sport. And, as mentioned before, it was a common saying that your feet and legs were your "money makers" because they made it possible to make plays. Without your feet and legs being healthy, you would do very little on the football field. I have seen some of the nastiest blisters known to man on my teammates' feet in the training room. The worst part about an oozing, painful, and bloody blister was that you still needed to practice on it and you still needed to make plays with it. No matter how hideous the blister or severe the injury, there was no one crying for you at training camp. Everyone at camp was hurting in one way or another. The key was to get tough or get gone.

It was a rare day during training camp when you left the practice field with dry feet. The hot summer combined with the stifling humidity made it so you were sweating as you walked out to the practice field. It took only a few minutes of drills until you would be sweating profusely. Gravity allows sweat to find its way from your head, through your shoulder pads and uniform, down through your socks, and into your shoes. If you have ever been hiking through a stream, you have felt the water squish out of your shoes with each step. Training camp was no different. Running each step of a pass route produced the same squish of water, forcing itself out of any shoelace hole, mesh fabric, or even the tiny stitching holes in the leather.

After being marinated for three hours, your feet were pickled inside of your shoes and socks. The cycle of soaking, drying off for meals and meetings, and then soaking again, was never-ending. Your feet were under constant duress. The reason you could run so fast on grass was because of the seven or more cleats on the bottom of your shoes. Those cleats not only dug into the turf for better traction, but they also dug into the bottoms of your feet with every cut and change of direction that you made. I would work all off-season to keep my feet in "cleat shape" or else they would dissolve and blister once this pickling process began.

Because the mantra at training camp was drink, drink, drink, a trip to the bathroom during the night was often required. Your feet were so sore that walking across the floor felt as though you were walking barefoot on a hot summer afternoon across an asphalt parking lot strewn with broken glass and rusty nails. Each throbbing step was an assault on your willingness to fight for a job. Sore feet, aching muscles, and cramps and charley horses that hit your toes, calves, quads, hamstrings, or your lower back in the middle of the night were all evidence that you were living the "good life" of an NFL football player at training camp.

In extreme cases, players went to the hospital for help. One of my teammates on the St. Louis Rams suffered a classic attack. We were in the cafeteria after our afternoon practice at Macomb, Illinois. He was carrying his tray to the table when he experienced a massive cramp that involved every major muscle group of his body. He had no choice but to flop down right there on the floor between the tables. He screamed in agony as he tried to massage the cramps in his quads. Being at training camp was disconcerting enough, but to hear his screams was a violent reminder of what we were all going through. In his attempts to squeeze the cramps away, he created more cramping in other parts of his body.

Within seconds, he was reduced to what appeared to be an epileptic seizure.

Several of us ran to his side in an effort to calm his muscles down. We massaged his legs, arms, and shoulders. He was lying on his back. We had two guys on each leg, two on each arm, and one person was working on his neck and shoulders. His fingers had cramped to the point that he couldn't straighten them. It was a scary sight.

A doctor was called, who decided to get an IV of saline solution into his body. He worked for several minutes just trying to get a needle into his veins, but they had collapsed due to dehydration. An ambulance was called and we continued to massage him. It seemed as though it took forever for the ambulance to get there, and the other players and I who were working on him started cramping ourselves. The ordeal was relentless as his muscles continued to stage an epic revolt against training camp.

The EMTs (emergency medical technicians) finally took him away and they were able to get some IV liquids into his body. He stayed in the hospital overnight where they continued to pump fluids into him. He didn't get discharged until just prior to practice in the morning. It wasn't too shocking for us to see him in the locker room right before we took the field for practice because training camp left no time and no room for sympathy. If you whined, they gave you some cheese and said, "Here is some cheese to go with that whine!" Training camp was not for the faint of heart.

At least cramping was something that would go away with the addition of salt and liquid into your system. Some of the injuries that lasted for weeks were the ones to your fingers, shoulders, and neck. There was also constant wear and tear on your hands. As a tight end you blocked a defensive end or linebacker one play and caught a laser thrown by Donovan McNabb on the next. Your hands needed to be strong enough to block a locomotive and soft enough to catch a touch pass. Without fail, something would happen to one of your fingers during practice, just as it had to Jeff Thomason's. It was bad when it happened, but worse when you needed to keep blocking and catching with it. By the end of training camp, your body was hamburger. Here is how bad it would get. It was a welcomed favor if someone opened a Gatorade bottle for you. Your hands were hammered enough that this was a very generous thing to do for a teammate.

The mental battle at training camp was just as brutal as the physical one. Your focus was to make the team and stay healthy. In your attempts to make the team, you saw good players getting cut all the time, players who you knew were good enough to help you win games. The NFL was a business and you were reminded of that every day when good players got cut for business reasons. Sometimes they were making too much money for their position and were cut to give your team more money to spend on other positions.

Each team had a "grim reaper" who was assigned to tell players that they were getting cut and needed to turn in their playbooks. You were never certain when it was your turn. You had your own gut feelings sometimes, but you never knew for sure. The "grim reaper" certainly was not a favorite among the players. We didn't like seeing him come close to us during camp. We didn't sit with him in the cafeteria. We tried not to have any contact with him whatsoever. It wasn't anything personal against him; we just didn't like his job.

All the coaches told the players not to worry about what anyone else was doing. They tried instead to keep us focused on doing our jobs to the best of our ability. They also warned about "counting numbers," which was counting how many players there were at your position and trying to analyze how many players at that position the team was going to keep on the roster. Counting numbers also meant that you focused on how many reps each player was getting or not getting. If you tried to do the math, that meant you were counting numbers and so the effort you were giving on the field was not focused as much as it needed to be. Even the coaches were not always sure which players were going to be kept. Those decisions were made by the owner, the president, the head coach, the special teams coach. The coaches were right. Counting numbers took our focus off that which was most important—performance.

But in reality, it was difficult to avoid when you saw coaches, trainers, and other staff personnel discussing your abilities right in front of you during drills. When that happened, it couldn't help but rattle your nerves. It did worry me early on. But by the time I was a veteran, it didn't bother me as much. It said a lot about the toughness and maturity of a player if he was able to dominate at what he was doing with so much specific analyzing of his play going on at the same time. I learned that it didn't matter if the player was a rookie or a ten-year vet. Growing up and being mature was a conscious decision. It had nothing to do with age.

Tony Stewart and L. J. Smith were rookie tight ends who came in with a level of mature wisdom that was great to see. They came to the Eagles as "old" rookies. I never got the sense that they were starstruck by the other players or that they were intimidated or flustered by being analyzed. They were tough, hard working, hungry guys. They practiced hard and they played hard. They were good pros. It was fun to play next to them.

As of this writing, both are still active players. Tony plays for the Oakland Raiders and L. J. plays for the Baltimore Ravens.

There were light moments in training camp as well. Those usually resulted from the simple things that players did, which would not have been funny to outsiders. Take for instance something that Mike Bartrum and I would yell during stretching exercises after practice. When the Eagles stretched as a team, we were led by Mike Wolf, the strength and conditioning coach. One of the first stretches he would designate was, "Drop to the right knee, grab the left toe!" As soon as he would call this out, Mike Bartrum and I would holler in unison, "Grab your partner, do-si-do!" It always got a chuckle.

I missed the first eight games of the 2005 season due to having Lis Franc surgery on my left foot. Not only did it keep me out of the Super Bowl, but it also kept me out of the first half of the next season. I missed practicing with my teammates and playing in the games. After returning to practice, for the first time all year, I joined Mike in belting out our usual, "Grab your partner, do-si-do!" as loud as we could. As we were walking into the locker room, one of my favorite guys, Sheldon Brown, a cornerback from South Carolina, said how much he loved hearing those words again and expressed how much he had missed hearing them over the two months I was rehabbing and not with the team. One of the things I miss being away from the game is the little things that happen on a team that help create the unique team chemistry it takes to win games.

Coach Reid never tolerated hazing. He did not want rookies to worry about anything other than performing their best. Each year there would be reports on the news from all around the country about hazing incidents in high school. They ranged from silly to life-threatening. I thought Andy took the perfect approach. That kind of stuff would not be tolerated. It would spiral out of control into bullying and intimidation faster than you could say, "Boo!"

The only thing that Coach Reid condoned was the tradition that required rookies to buy some food for the veterans for road trips. Each rookie would get some food for the other players at their specific position. Most rookies would buy fried chicken from Popeye's, which included red beans and rice.

Reno Mahe, one of my favorite teammates, who had also played for BYU, took this tradition to a whole new level. Not only would he buy meals for the other running backs for road trips, but he would serve them as though he were a waiter at the practice facility before the bus left. The first time it happened, the running backs thought it might be a one-time deal. But Reno did it the whole year. He even continued doing it the following year when there were no rookie running backs on the team.

Reno's willingness to serve others had a good effect on our team. It was a rare quality and ability that he possessed. He brought this same attitude to the games and practices. He would do anything for another player to help that player perform better. He was always willing to take an additional rep so a teammate could get a breather.

The best example was during the games when he brought his enthusiasm to each play. If I made a catch, Reno would jump all over me, slapping my helmet and pumping me up to make other plays. He never stopped encouraging everyone. Every team should be lucky enough to have someone like Reno Mahe on the squad.

Justin Ena was another BYU player who made the team with the Eagles as one of our special teams aces. To dominate on special teams in the NFL meant that you were as tough as or tougher than anyone who walked with two legs. Justin was one of those battering-ram-type guys for our team. He never feared running into a wedge on kickoff coverage. The wedge was a group of three or four blockers, usually offensive lineman, who loved to mow down the first would-be tacklers they could see. Justin could blow up a wedge like a bowling ball hitting pins for a strike. He was a warrior in every sense of the word.

He was also one of the most loyal guys I ever played with. He would never say anything bad about his coaches, even if he just got chewed out for doing something wrong. He knew how to be a team player and a coachable player at the same time. When Justin, Reno, and I would eat lunch together in the facility, the guys often referred to us as "the Mormon Mafia." We had a blast playing together, working together, and giving everything we had to help the Eagles win.

The people I came to appreciate most in my years in the NFL were people such as Jeff Thomason, Mike Bartrum, Dave Akers, Reno Mahe, and Justin Ena. They each made an unusual effort to make a positive contribution to the team. They did it by going out of their way to help others, keeping a friendly disposition, not taking offense, and not taking themselves too seriously. When they made a mistake, they apologized and moved on with a smile. They were humble and genuine.

I think of them whenever I am tempted to think that I stand alone on top of the world. All of us need to appreciate the people around us who build us up, who support us, who do nice things for us, who give us honest feedback even when it hurts, and make it possible for us to succeed. Such people are part of the greatness around us.

CHAPTER 19

THE PRO BOWL

Pat Shurmur took it upon himself to turn me into an all-around tight end. When I entered the League, I could catch the ball and run routes very well. But by NFL standards, I was not a good blocker. After working my first year with Juan Castillo and my second and third years with Lynn Stiles, I started to become a better blocker. The hard work continued with Pat. He was an outstanding center for Michigan State when he played in college. He knew how to teach me how to block and was patient with me as I steadily got better and better.

If I needed help understanding anything or preparing for the game, he was available at any time of the day or night. I went into the office every Tuesday, which was our day off, and spent about an hour watching film with Pat and breaking down our opponent. It was above and beyond the call of duty for Pat to take that kind of time for me. He helped me see things in our opponents that I was able to attack on game day. I remember scouting the New Orleans Saints defense with Pat, and he pointed out how they sometimes overreacted to play action from the quarterback. We talked about selling the run a little more than usual in an attempt to get behind the strong safety.

It could not have worked better when we played them that Sunday. I caught a touchdown pass on a play that was the direct result of meeting with Pat on Tuesday. He was a pivotal and necessary person in my development to become an all-around good player. By now I was the full-time starter and was no longer taken out of the game on running situations. Jeff Thomason and I, as the tight ends, could handle any situation.

Pat and the rest of our coaching staff were very loyal. They were loyal to the organization, which included the owner, and, most importantly, they were loyal to the head coach. Pat was especially loyal to Andy Reid. He consistently told the tight ends in meetings how much he appreciated the commitment that Andy had made to the coaches and their families. Pat told us how rare it was that Andy always did more for the coaches' families than anyone else in the business. Andy made sure that the coaches had regular time off to be with their families.

In February of 2009, Pat was named as the offensive coordinator for the St. Louis Rams. The new head coach was Steve Spagnuolo, another one of Coach Reid's former coaches. Up to that point, two of Coach Reid's protégés, Steve Spagnuolo and John Harbaugh, were head coaches in the NFL and several others were working as coordinators.

That first year back with the Eagles was a magical year. The combination of Andy, Pat, and Donovan proved to be a successful combination for me. Donovan threw me a lot of footballs and my catches started piling up through the year. Our big-play running back Duce Staley tore the Lis Franc ligament in his foot and required surgery, which put him out for the rest of the season. Duce caught a lot of balls out of the backfield, and losing him meant that the rest of us needed to step up and take on more of the load. Donovan looked to me as one of the answers.

Courtesy of the Philadelphia Eagles

The NFC Championship game against the Tampa Bay Buccaneers was the last football game at Veterans Stadium.

I had tremendous confidence catching the ball and it seemed to grow with each game. My teammates Charles Johnson, Alex Van Dyke, Torrance Small, Jeff Thomason, Mike Bartrum, David Akers, and Luther Broughton all had much to do with that. They would tell me during practice that I could catch anything. They pumped me up and inspired me. Not only did we work very hard as a team with fast-tempo practices, but we had a lot of fun.

Practices were fun. Games were fun. Donovan was the key contributor to that. He made sure we were loose and playing with a smile all the time. He would get after us if we ever got tight.

I received a lot of attention from the press that season about the chance of being selected to the Pro Bowl. The hype started early on and continued right up until the end of the year. Donovan encouraged me to keep playing at a high level.

The night before we played the Cleveland Browns, one of the Eagles' media directors, Rich Berg, informed me that if I had a good game, there was a great chance of being selected. Rich was selected as the person to help with all of my media requests and promotional activities that year. He was a good friend and a longtime employee of the organization.

The next day, Donovan threw it to me five times for one hundred yards. It pretty much secured my selection to the Pro Bowl. Even though it was not official, it felt better than I could have imagined. We also secured our spot in the play-offs, although there were still three weeks left in the season.

Because we had a bye the next week, I went home to Utah. While I was there, I got a phone call from Andy Reid. He congratulated me on being named the starting tight end in the Pro Bowl. He was happy for me. My success helped vindicate his faith in me as a player. When he brought me back to the Eagles, there were some detractors who didn't think I would ever become an every-down player. I have endless gratitude to Andy for sticking with me and giving me a chance to prove that I could play. I called Donovan and thanked him also for being the person and the player he was and for helping make it possible for me to be selected for the Pro Bowl. He was runner-up for the NFL MVP that year and we would enjoy the Pro Bowl together.

That year, in 2001, we finished with a record of 11–5. In the play-offs we beat the Tampa Bay Buccaneers and the Chicago Bears to get to the NFC Championship game against my old team, the St. Louis Rams. They had won the Super Bowl two years earlier, and they were the team to beat. The game went down to the last second and we ended up losing a heartbreaker. The pain of getting that close to the Super Bowl and losing was something that ripped my heart in half. It had taken an incredible team effort to get that far, and there were no guarantees that we would get back again. Walking off the field in St. Louis, with confetti falling on the Rams, was a painful experience. Up to that point in my life, it was the most painful and heartbreaking loss I had ever experienced.

Coach Martz, the head coach of the Rams, and all of my former teammates congratulated me for a fine season and a great game, but time was the only thing that was going to heal my pain. After getting that close, I had a burning desire to be on the other side of the falling confetti. I wanted to have it fall on my shoulders. I wanted it to fall on the Eagles. I wanted to go to the Super Bowl.

Our return trip to Philly was bitter. Not only was it freezing cold standing outside the buses waiting to go home, but our hearts were frozen as well. It is tough to describe the bitterness of getting that close to the Super Bowl, so close that we could taste it, and then being denied.

The next day we had our exit physicals. It was a strange situation in pro football to finish the year because it is much different than college. In college the year ended with a football banquet where everyone had a chance to say good-bye and the season was officially wrapped up. There was closure. In the pros, the last day was abrupt. A short team meeting where the head coach addressed us was followed by a few minutes where the guys could say what was on their minds. Then doctors and trainers examined us and listed and documented any injuries. Anything requiring surgery was scheduled. After the exams we cleaned out our lockers and left. That was it. Game over. Season over. Good-bye.

Since I would be going to the Pro Bowl I still needed to stay in game shape. I anxiously awaited the chance to meet all of the other players selected to the Pro Bowl. Thanks to playing on a great team, I played in three Pro Bowls in a row in the years 2000, 2001, and 2002. Along with being a tight end, I also doubled as a snapper for punts and field goals. The Pro Bowl was the All-Star game for the NFL, and the League chose the beautiful island of

Picture day at the Pro Bowl in Hawaii, 2000. From left to right: Hugh Douglas, Jeremiah Trotter, Troy Vincent, me, and Donovan McNabb (kneeling).

Oahu, Hawaii, with its warm weather as the location for the game each year.

Selection to the Pro Bowl was decided by votes from three groups of people—the coaches, players, and fans. Played the week after the Super Bowl, it was a wonderful reward at the end of a long season. There are so many great things about the Pro Bowl, but the best part was getting to know the players from the other teams. It made playing the regular season games from that time forward that much more enjoyable. Once you got to know the guys on the other teams, it changed the dynamics of the League. You weren't playing against a bunch of people that you knew only from TV; you were playing against your friends. It made the League much smaller. Making the Pro Bowl also got a player a higher level of respect from the other players. The honor was never taken for granted.

Given the festive nature of the event, the contest was not as competitive as a regular game. There were also special rules in the Pro Bowl prohibiting certain things, such as blitzing on defense. It was too complicated to learn a whole new system of offense or defense in one week, including all of the calls at the line of scrimmage—audibles and checks. So the game was simplified for obvious and necessary reasons.

One of the changes involved the snappers. They never got bucked. I was not aware of that rule when I snapped for my first Pro Bowl. When I got down to snap, I looked at the mountain of a man who stood in front of me. It was noseguard Ted Washington. At 6'6" 375 pounds, he was one of the biggest guys to ever wear an NFL uniform. I was obliterated by his shadow.

After snapping the ball I braced myself for the impending collision. But, strangely, it never came. I wasn't even touched. What a relief. My career could have been severely messed with had Ted been allowed to drop the hammer. He could have squashed me like a grape. As soon as the play was over, I told him thanks for not turning me into a pancake. He was cool about it because he smiled. He knew the literal impact his size and strength had on people.

The Pro Bowl players, coaches, and staff took over the entire hotel at the Marriott Ihilani on the west side of Oahu. My kids loved swimming at the pool. Donovan would jump in the water with them and pretend he was a shark coming to get them. They all screamed in delight as the big shark made the sound from the movie *Jaws,* "duh-Nuh, duh-Nuh, duh-Nuh!"

I recognized while swimming with my kids that my dream of playing in the Pro Bowl was a reality. I was there because of the rock-solid support of my family, the coaching staff that not only gave me a chance to play but also created ways to get me the ball, and a quarterback who resurrected both my career and the

*At the Pro Bowl in Hawaii, 2003, with my kids, Jake, Emily, and Sarah.
Donovan pretended to be a shark and chased my kids all over the pool.*

Philadelphia Eagles franchise at the same time. I had fought to earn the right to be in that water as a Pro Bowler. It was a struggle and a fight, but it was possible because of all the people around me. No swimming pool ever felt better.

After the Pro Bowl was over, demands on my time quadrupled. The challenge I had was managing the requests for my time while still devoting my energy to my off-season duties. Every player, whether a Pro Bowler or not, has to do the same thing. The more focused we can be with our training and preparation for each season, the better we will play on the field. But we also need to give back along the way.

The experiences I had speaking to schools, teams, church groups, and companies taught me that I learned more from them than I was able to teach them. One such experience taught me a lesson on class that I have cherished.

What Is Class?

*Class never runs scared. It is sure-footed and confident
in the knowledge that you can meet life head-on and
handle whatever comes along.*

*Jacob had it. Esau didn't. Symbolically, we can look to
Jacob's wrestling match with the angel. Those who have
class have wrestled with their own personal "angel" and
won a victory that marks them thereafter.*

*Class never makes excuses. It takes its lumps and learns
from past mistakes.*

*Class is considerate of others. It knows that good man-
ners are nothing more than a series of petty sacrifices.*

*Class bespeaks an aristocracy that has nothing to do
with ancestors or money. The most affluent blueblood can
be totally without class while the descendant of a Welsh
miner may ooze class from every pore.*

Class never tries to build itself up by tearing others down.

*Class is already up and need not strive to look better
by making others look worse.*

*Class can "walk with kings and keep its virtue, and
talk with crowds and keep the common touch." Everyone
is comfortable with the person who has class—because he
is comfortable with himself.*

*If you have class, you don't need much of anything else.
If you don't have it, no matter what else you have—it
doesn't make much difference.*[7]

I first saw this great definition of class in a favorite book of
quotes called *The Edge* by Howard Ferguson. He was a wrestling
coach in Ohio for whom I have great admiration. My brothers
gave me his book in 1991 for my birthday. Howard Ferguson died
in 1989, but his legend and legacy live on.

I learned a great lesson in class at a Best Buddies talent show at
BYU. My friend Andy (Buzz) Robinson invited me to speak at

their talent show to honor the members of the local Best Buddies program. It is a program designed to enhance the lives of people with intellectual disabilities by providing opportunities for one-to-one friendships and integrated employment. The aim is to change people's lives, one friendship at a time.

This was the first Best Buddies talent show that I had been invited to so I didn't really know what I was getting myself into. When I arrived, I was greeted by Andy, who shared with me the particulars of the program. I was introduced to another guest, Donny Osmond, who had also been invited to participate. I had previously never met him. He was nice. He was gracious. He shared with me the enthusiasm that he had for the Best Buddies program. I was a little surprised that he wasn't taller. TV makes everyone look larger than life.

The participants performed on a stage in a theater room in one of the buildings at BYU. There were probably 150 participants, their buddies, families, and friends. It was a fairly intimate group. When I was asked to speak, I shared my gratitude for a program that I felt was doing great things for people who loved it and needed it. The warmth and kindness displayed by all of the people there created a feel-good atmosphere. The faces of the participants were lit up with joy as they looked at me on the stage. Any celebrity status that I had was neutralized. It felt as though we were all on the same team. There was a feeling of love and service and family. The love and concern for these special-needs people was real.

When I finished speaking, I returned to my seat at the back of the theater. Most of the talents shared were in song, and most of the performances weren't polished. What made it fun and inspiring was to observe the earnest efforts of the participants. This was their time to be stars. With all of these stars sharing their prepared numbers, it was easy to get lost in the event. Even keeping track of time didn't matter. All of us in the audience that day were surrounded by greatness.

One of the boys who performed appeared to have Down syndrome, and he was to sing "Any Dream Will Do," from the musical *Joseph and the Amazing Technicolor Dreamcoat*. The most famous "Joseph" ever to take the stage was sitting two rows in front of me, and I was wondering what Donny Osmond was thinking about this performance when the music coming from the stage suddenly stopped. Halfway into the first verse, the young man had frozen. He stood there with his eyes growing bigger but no sound coming from his mouth. Everyone was hoping he would be able to remember the words and continue singing, but he was stuck.

It was an awkward moment, but Donny Osmond did not even hesitate. Without a word and without any fanfare, Donny jogged down the aisle, bounced up onstage, and with the grace of a professional musician who had grown up on similar stages, put his arm around this young man and began singing the song. With that help, the young man remembered his words and found the courage to begin singing again.

The lump in my throat was almost too big for me to continue breathing. I could hardly see the stage since giant tears blurred my vision. I didn't want to move. Now *I* was the one frozen—frozen with a pounding heart, witnessing an example of class whose equal would be difficult to find. Every person in that theater seemed to experience a feeling of brotherhood. Tears ran unashamedly down our faces.

It was a joy to listen to this duet, made up of one voice hitting a perfect pitch and another voice perfectly hitting the strings of our hearts. How could it be any better? My answer came immediately. At a certain point in the song, the background singers chimed in, "Ahhh ahhhh, ahhh ahhhh!" Now the entire audience became the background singers. It was incredible. If you have not heard this song before, now is a good time to jump on the Internet and find it so that you can better enjoy the power of what I have tried to describe.

Later in the program, another performer, this time a young woman, froze while singing the hymn "I Know That My Redeemer Lives." Again, without hesitation and without fear of others thinking he was trying to be cool, Donny sprang to his feet, jogged down to the stage, put his arm around the young woman, and helped her sing until she had the courage to remember the words and finish a duet that produced the same teary eyes and lump-in-the-throat effects as before.

Donny demonstrated what class is all about. He gave—with his heart, his voice, and his quick actions—what he had prepared to give through a whole lifetime of work. I have stood in football huddles with some of the biggest men on the planet. If you have ever stood next to one of these modern-day Goliaths, you can appreciate the peculiar sense of smallness that you feel standing in their shadow.

For me, Donny was a giant that day. It had nothing to do with his physical stature but everything to do with the size of his heart, his compassion, and his character. His spontaneous, unself-conscious example motivated me to worry less about myself in such circumstances and inspired me to have the courage and class to openly care about and love other persons. What a powerful lesson of greatness. We were all humbled by the actions of a giant.

CHAPTER 20

9/11: THE DAY THAT PUT FOOTBALL IN PERSPECTIVE

Philadelphia is very close to New York City; by car, it is just over an hour away. Philly is also close to Washington, D.C., only two hours away. When the events of 9/11 began happening, I felt as though we were part of the war zone. It was one of the most unforgettable days of my life.

But for me, the closeness of it all started two months previously in a once-in-a-lifetime experience on Wall Street.

One of the Philadelphia Eagles' business sponsors, Sovereign Bank, made its leap from the NASDAQ to the NYSE in July of 2001. In order to get as much publicity as possible, they wanted a Philadelphia Eagles player to help them ring the closing bell on Wall Street. When they called to ask if I would like to be the player, I jumped at the chance.

Joining them meant giving up three days of cherished, summertime, pre-training camp time with my family in Utah. Instead of going with me, Michele suggested I take my mom. Mom was working for a company that teaches trading principles, and she followed Wall Street on a daily basis. She tried to defer to

Michele, but Michele and I finally convinced her she needed to be the one to make the trip.

We were given first-class airfare to New York City. It was the first time Mom had flown first class, and I was thrilled to share the experience with her. We enjoyed the additional leg room and the extra amenities of first class as we made the journey to visit one of the most important financial institutions in the world.

When we arrived in New York, we went straight to our hotel, which was the Marriott at the World Trade Center. The twin towers were constructed in 1971, the same year that I was born. We had dinner that night in the fabulous Windows on the World Restaurant. It took up the two top floors, 106 and 107 of the North Tower, and was world-famous for both its menu and its view.

While waiting to be seated, we looked out one of the windows, very, very far down to the street below. We talked about how crazy it was that eight years before, some crazed lunatics had tried to blow up the building we were standing in.

As we looked down, we wondered aloud where these buildings would go if they were knocked down? This was a steel giant, scraping the sky—literally a city in the air. There was no room below for a building this big to fall. The notion of the building collapsing was so uncomfortable to imagine that we quickly dropped the topic.

After a fantastic dinner—with views of the summer sun setting over Manhattan, which could only be seen from there or through the window of an airplane—we decided to visit the observation deck of the South Tower. We descended the North Tower, changed elevators, and went back to the top of the South Tower. We walked out onto the observation deck and looked at the glowing lights of the city shining in the night. The enormous size and height of those buildings was breathtaking.

The next morning we were joined by Bob Lang of the

Philadelphia Eagles public relations department. Rob Alberino and Rich Gentile were the football highlight gurus of the Eagles Television Network, and they were to film the whole adventure.

Larry Harmer just happened to be in town on business, and he joined us as well. Jay Sidhu, the president and CEO of Sovereign Bank, and Dick Mohn, the chairman, were gracious hosts and seemed genuinely happy to have my mom and me there with them.

Before ringing the bell, we attended a small reception with Dick Grasso, the CEO of the New York Stock Exchange. We were instructed on bell ringing and clapping at the appropriate time. And Dick, who is a big football fan, and I tossed a football back and forth.

After we rang the bell, we took a tour of the wooden trading floor, which was a beehive of commotion. We shook hands with many of the floor traders and found some were Eagles fans, along with Jets fans, and a whole bunch of Giants fans. Some of the floor traders asked me how I was able to handle the stress of playing in the NFL, and I asked them how they were able to handle the stress and madness of working on the trading floor every day. It was cool to get a glimpse of how things operated, and I appreciated how hard they worked, how early they had to leave for work, and how late they got home. It was a reminder that life is not easy. Work is a gift. We should appreciate the jobs that make it possible to take care of our families.

Fast forward two short months. The day off for NFL football players is Tuesday. Most players still go in to their facilities to lift, run, get treatment, and watch a little film. It is a great day that is so needed. The human body was not designed to smash into other human bodies at full velocity. The day of rest and recovery is what allowed us to make it through each week and, ultimately, the season.

September 11, 2001, found me sitting at my kitchen table in

Marlton, New Jersey, reading from the Bible. For me, reading the scriptures provides a feeling of peace, security, and a connection with God. I had been taught by my parents from my childhood to read the scriptures every day as a way to maintain that connection and closeness to my Father in Heaven. That has been some of the greatest instruction I have ever been given.

The peace and great feelings that I was enjoying from reading in the Bible were about to be shattered. I received a call from one of the best people on the planet. My father-in-law, Doug Fellows, was on the phone with the news that a plane had just crashed into the World Trade Center. He thought it was a small plane and did not think too much of it. He said that he was watching the report of the accident on TV and that he could see a small fire. He encouraged me to turn on the TV when our conversation was over to see what was going on.

I thought about my recent visit to the World Trade Center and hoped that the damage was as small as possible. As soon as I got upstairs to my bedroom and turned on the TV, I realized that this was a much larger fire than it first appeared to be. After standing at the top of those buildings, I had a better appreciation of their mind-boggling enormity.

Michele and I both watched the coverage for a minute, hoping that the people in those buildings were able to get away from the fire and get down and out of the tower.

I quickly called my mom, who had just become aware of the plane crash, and while watching the coverage, we talked about our recent trip. We recalled the height of the building and listened intently to each new piece of information, wondering about the size of the fire, the chances of people getting down, the possible loss of life, the important papers flying out of the windows, the chaos that must be taking place, the close quarters for rescue personnel, and the dizzying heights at which the fire was taking place.

The more we watched, the more we realized that there must

have been a sizeable loss of life. Just as all Americans, we were heartsick over the incident. After a few minutes of conversation, we decided to hang up so that we could pay closer attention to the TV reports.

A short time later, while still watching the telecast, another plane came into view in the background of the live TV feed. It was an eerie sight that seemed out of place. Before I could make sense of why it was there, I noticed it was heading for the towers. In a terrifying instant, it slammed into the other tower with a hellacious fireball. The peace I felt while reading the Bible could not have been more opposite than the desperate feeling of helplessness that I felt watching this horror unfold. It took my breath away. I was crying and angry at the same time. We were under attack. Enemies of freedom had committed an act of war against our country. Terrorists had brought their hatred to life by inflicting death on innocent people. Just as everyone else who was watching, Michele and I could not believe what we were seeing. We decided to drive to our girls' school and pick them up. This was war. We were under siege.

I called my mom again and we shared our feelings of panic and rage. We thought about the people working on the upper floors, above where the planes hit. How could they possibly get out? Would the elevators be working? Would the stairways be intact? Would helicopters be able to land on top and help people out? Would they be able to put the fire out? How would the firefighters get up there fast enough? The memory of looking out the windows of the restaurant came back. I felt true panic for the people that were there because I could feel how high up they were. I could not get that image out of my mind.

My brother Dave called on the other line and we talked about my recent trip to the WTC and the madness that was being played out in front of our eyes. This was Pearl Harbor all over again. This was war. Who was doing this? How did they get the planes? What would the fire do to those buildings?

As Dave and I talked, something happened to one of the towers. It looked like a part of it sloughed off. I told him that part of the building just fell down. We quickly realized that it wasn't a *part* of the building, but the whole building, that had just collapsed and come crashing down. Then it hit us. That building would have been full of people trying to escape and firefighters and emergency personnel trying to get people out of there. The chaos and terror were impossible to imagine.

The rest of the day was a blur of emotion and confusion. When the Pentagon was hit, the scope of the tragedy expanded even more. New York was not the only area of attack. The bad news would not stop. Another plane went down in Pennsylvania. What else was going to happen? Where else would we be hit? Who was doing this?

I thought there would be a call that night from the Eagles or from the NFL saying that Sunday's games would be postponed. The call never came.

Our team arrived at our facility on Wednesday and went to work as usual. We had all of our regular meetings. We had practice at the usual time. We talked about the terrorist attacks with each other and with our coaches, but we were definitely in the traditional football mode of having blinders on and staying focused on the job at hand. We were getting ready to play the Tampa Bay Buccaneers that week.

When we took the practice field, the skies were noticeably vacant and quiet. It was unusual not to have a single plane in the sky since our facility is very close to the Philadelphia airport. I remember how distracted we were by one military plane that flew over the city. We all turned our heads to watch it pass over the field. I didn't know how we were going to play a game that week when most of us wanted to head up to New York and tear through the rubble to find our neighbors and countrymen who could have still been trapped.

Football meant nothing on this day.

We showed up to work on Thursday and things were somewhat different. As players, we'd had a little time to let this attack settle in. We were all following the events on TV as closely as we could. There were people in our neighborhoods, members of church congregations, and even spouses of people who worked in the Eagles facility who worked in Manhattan. We were very close to where all four planes had gone down.

Terrorist attacks in other countries that had filled our nightly news programs were now a living reality in our home, the United States of America. Our home had been attacked. Our citizens had been killed.

When we showed up for work on Thursday, as a team, we felt we needed to do something to support the rescue effort that was being made and the state of mourning that had settled in. The schedule was still regular, with no changes. That was not acceptable.

We decided to hold a players-only meeting. Troy Vincent, one of our team leaders and player representatives in the players union, took charge of the meeting. Troy was one of the best defensive backs in the NFL. After a standout career at Wisconsin and being an early-round draft pick, he became one of the fiercest DBs in the league. He grew up in Trenton, New Jersey, and told me that he learned how to fight with his fists very early. He played the position of cornerback with the confidence and skill of a heavyweight boxer. He was a rock on the field and in the locker room. Just to show you what others think of Troy, he has been voted NFL Man of the Year and also selected as president of the NFL Players Association.

When he addressed the players-only team meeting, Troy wanted to know how we felt about playing the game that coming Sunday. Many of us had major reservations about playing while the country was still scrambling to find loved ones. By not playing, players would lose part of their salaries, but Troy and some other team leaders offered to put together a fund for any rookie who felt he could not make the financial sacrifice to boycott the game. Donovan McNabb and Brian Dawkins were two of the guys who spearheaded the effort. That is leadership. Troy said he thought not playing the game would be a symbol of something that was morally right.

Wow! Where did that kind of leadership, on and off the field, come from? The Philadelphia Eagles were blessed with this tough person and player from Trenton. I don't know how Troy ever learned everything that he knows, but I do know that he is a great leader, a great teammate, and a great friend.

That day, football was only a sport. It was still only a luxury. It was not a necessity.

We took a team vote and it was unanimous that the Philadelphia Eagles would not play on Sunday. We voted to boycott the game in favor of paying respect to the nation. When we walked out of that meeting, we were one.

Do you remember the feeling we shared as a country during that time? We came together as Americans. We were united. I wish it could always be that way.

Troy phoned Gene Upshaw, the executive director of the Players Association, to inform him of our decision. Gene said that he understood and agreed with us, and that he would call the League office to work with them. Troy let Gene know that there was nothing to work out. We had made our decision, and it was the right decision. Troy told him, "Our decision is final."

We got the word from the League office that Commissioner Paul Tagliabue was going to make an announcement, and our whole team gathered in the cafeteria to watch the live broadcast on ESPN.

In addressing the press, the commissioner spoke with inspiring confidence and strength. There was no trace of hesitancy in his voice. Most people are not artists, but they can recognize the beauty and masterpiece of Michelangelo's Sistine Chapel. The inspiring leadership of the commissioner of the NFL could similarly be recognized by anyone who heard him speak. Here is part of what he said:

> We in the National Football League have decided that our priorities for this weekend are to pause, grieve, and reflect. It is a time to tend to families and neighbors and all those wounded by these horrific acts of terrorism.
>
> We understand those individuals in sports who want to play this weekend. We also can empathize with those who want to take the weekend off and resume their personal lives and professional careers next week. We strongly believe that the latter course of action is the right decision for the NFL.
>
> On Sunday, September 23, the NFL, its players, and coaches will return stronger than ever and resume our playing schedule.
>
> A decision on whether to reschedule this weekend's games or play a 15-game regular season schedule is under consideration and will be announced as soon as possible.

The commissioner's dynamic presence and his straightforward announcement left no room for equivocation. He stood before the cameras with strength and a toughness that inspired the American people and me and my teammates. The previous commissioner, Pete Rozelle, had gone on record as saying he had one major regret during his tenure and that was not canceling the games following the assassination of President John F. Kennedy. Commissioner Tagliabue had heard Pete Rozelle repeatedly refer to that regret, and it helped him make the tough decision to reschedule the games, which turned out to be the right decision.

Jeffrey Lurie, the Eagles owner, and head coach Andy Reid immediately called another team meeting that included the coaches and players. We all needed some way to express our grief and make some sense out of the heinous thing that had occurred, and Jeffrey helped by predicting that the awful events would unify our nation's citizens. Then Andy talked about grief and love. He said, "There must be a time to grieve for loved ones lost. We can't forget them. We have to remember them. Love is what must replace our grief." Both men helped put the tragedy in perspective and each demonstrated his great leadership.

Andy gave us the rest of the week off so that we could be with our families. My family spent that time playing in the parks in Mount Laurel, New Jersey, and visiting with friends in their homes. The shock of the event did not wear off. I hope it never does.

Our next game was against the Seahawks in Seattle. We prepared that week with our blinders on. When it was time to practice, we did what football players are trained to do—we focused on our jobs and nothing else. We prepared for the game against Seattle by channeling the rage triggered in us by the attacks.

Football started to mean something again.

As we sat on the long flight to Seattle, I remember looking down on the nation I love and thinking of my fellow Americans who had died in the crashes of those four hijacked planes. I thought of how horrifying it must have been for them to look out the windows as they were heading into buildings or into the ground, waiting for the inevitable impact, knowing they were about to die. I could only imagine the shock and grief experienced by the victims' loved ones.

I have a few framed quotations hanging on the wall of my home office. One is by Todd Beamer, the American hero who died with many other heroes on Flight 93, which went down in Pennsylvania. I love him even though I have never met him. When I think about the legacy that he left his family, I can't help but cry with solemn pride and gratitude for his example of courage. Taped to a photo of my family, in blue letters, are the words spoken by Todd just before he and others took back control of the plane, preventing the terrorists from crashing it into the White House or some other target. After his farewell cell phone call to his wife, she heard Todd say, "LET'S ROLL!"

Another quote that I have displayed is from Winston Churchill. It is in small black letters, and it declares a strength and a determination that not only moved a nation to fight for freedom and win, but it moves me to action today. It reads: "Do not despair, do not yield to violence and tyranny, march straight forward and die if need be—unconquered!" I am surrounded by greatness in my office.

We were told there would be a special pregame presentation in Seattle. We had already taken note of some of the NCAA football games played that week and particularly the crowds chanting, "U-S-A!" with full emotion. Just walking out onto the field before the game, my emotions were at a full boil and goose bumps covered my skin.

Itula Mili was a Seattle Seahawk. We played football together at BYU, where we were tight ends at the same time during our sophomore, junior, and senior seasons. We became very close during those years, and we both felt fortunate to be playing in the NFL. Aside from the game itself, seeing Itula again was what I looked forward to most on our trip to Seattle. We chatted on the field before the game about the horrible events of 9/11. The NFL made sure that this game would be special. Commissioner Tagliabue's promise to return stronger than ever was kept. Just before the kickoff, players from both teams stood along the perimeter of the field, and with the help of uniformed policemen, firemen, and members of the armed services, we held the borders of one of those gigantic American flags. Directly across the flag from where I was standing was Itula Mili, and I looked at him through tear-filled, blurry eyes. The huge crowd started chanting, "U-S-A! U-S-A!" It was such an emotional and powerful moment.

Courtesy of the Philadelphia Eagles

Me, Itula Mili (#89), and Justin Ena (#95).

Football meant everything that day.

John Harbaugh, our special teams coach at the time and current head coach of the Baltimore Ravens, said of that patriotic demonstration: "We all felt a part of something really grand. How great it was to be an American and to participate in something so wonderful. . . . I mean, I get chills just still thinking about it, the crowd chanting, 'U-S-A, U-S-A!'"

Aeneas Williams, one of the great leaders in the League and among the best defensive backs of the NFL, playing for the St. Louis Rams, shared his feelings of playing on that incredible day. He said, "When we were in that arena, we were competing, but we were still one. It's all of a sudden, now someone has messed with the family. We're gonna play this game, we're gonna enjoy and we're gonna compete, but we're upset now, but we're upset collectively."

My prevalent feeling that day was that even members of the

opposing team and I were family, and I know they felt that way about me. I could see it in their faces, and you could feel it in the way everyone treated each other. The pre- and post-game exchanges between players meant more. We were all more grateful to see each other.

Football was a symbol for America and it was a means of bringing the nation together that day and in the days that followed.

There are other unforgettable football images from that time. One is of a warrior, Chris Gizzi, a linebacker for the Green Bay Packers and a former player for the Air Force Academy, carrying the American flag out onto the field for Monday Night Football. When he led his team out of the tunnel, he sprinted onto the grass at Lambeau Field, in a free country, and held the colors high in the air for the whole world to see. We had played against each other in college, and I had great respect for him as a competitor. What a sight to see such a truly fitting member of the NFL represent our league by carrying the flag for all of us.

Another image is that of Joe Andruzzi, of the New England Patriots, taking the field for the coin toss with his brothers, who are firefighters in New York City and who had all helped extinguish the fires caused by the terrorist attacks on 9/11.

Most NFL players are careful when walking through a group of rowdy fans. After 9/11, that caution seemed unnecessary. I felt like hugging everyone who cheered for us. Americans were unified.

During that awful time in American history, football became more than just a game; it became a symbol of the war between freedom and terrorism. As crazy as it seems, that is a war that will go on forever. And I, along with many other Americans, hope we will never lose our focus, that we won't ever forget the way we felt about our country after those attacks, and that we will always have the courage and determination to stand up for what is right.

CHAPTER 21

NFC CHAMPIONSHIPS

In the 2002 season we went 12–4, but we lost Donovan for the last six games of the regular season. It was a devastating blow to our team. It has already been discussed how Andy handled the situation. Donovan kept himself in great shape while he was injured, a testament to his desire to be a world champion. AJ Feeley helped us win five of our six games down the stretch before the play-offs started. Our defense crushed opponents week after week. We earned a bye and home-field advantage throughout the play-offs.

Donovan came back for the first play-off game, against the Atlanta Falcons. On the first play of the game, he scrambled for a first down. It was a statement to everyone that he was back. Our team played inspired football. We beat the Falcons, and Veterans Stadium went crazy. We only had one game standing between us and the Super Bowl.

Our opponent was the Tampa Bay Buccaneers, who had never won a game when the temperature at the start of the game was below forty degrees. To add to their troubles, we felt as though we had their number. We could not have been more excited to play them. We were also happy to know that the temperature at game time would be below freezing. One more thing—it was to be the last game played in the Vet. After thirty years of Eagles football and Phillies baseball, Veterans Stadium was being torn down immediately following the game. I felt like we had everything on our side to give us an edge going into that game.

The game turned out to be the most heartbreaking loss I had ever been a part of. The Bucs came into Philly and played with more precision and passion then we did, and they left with a win and the right to play in the Super Bowl. The pain from some losses never goes away. Such is the case with that one.

The next season started with an echoing thud. Even though we were returning with a strong team and expectations that were sky high, we suffered humiliating losses to Tampa Bay and New England. To make matters worse, they were the first two games played in our new stadium, Lincoln Financial Field. Not very many teams can rebound from a 0–2 start.

Andy Reid did not change anything after those two deflating losses. Most coaches would have lost their minds. They would have dumped their strategy out with the trash and remade themselves. Not Andy. He was consistent and steady. We rebounded and played with a determination befitting one of the League's best teams for the rest of the year. We fought our way back into the play-offs and earned home-field advantage throughout.

Our son Jefferson was born during the bye week before we played the Packers. Michele was very uncomfortable in the last few weeks before delivery. She thought he was going to be big because her ribs were hurting worse each day, but we had no idea how big. Jeff weighed eleven pounds five ounces! He was a giant. I had never held a newborn baby as big as Jeff. As he grew, we found out that his heart was just as big as his body.

We played the Green Bay Packers and beat them in a thrilling finish. With time running out, on fourth down with twenty-six yards to go for a first down, Donovan threw a deep pass down the middle of the field for our wide receiver Freddie Mitchell. Freddie caught it for an unbelievable first down. We continued to drive down the field, and David Akers kicked the game-winning field goal. Brian Dawkins sealed the victory by intercepting a pass thrown by Brett Favre. We headed to our third NFC Championship game in a row.

One of the things that made Andy successful as a coach was his creation of a players' committee, made up of one person from each position. The committee would meet at the beginning of each week for a few minutes before all the team meetings started. Andy used the meeting to introduce any messages he wanted to convey to the team. He would also share the schedule for the week and bring up any issues he thought needed to be addressed. The players would also have a chance to bring up any issues or problems that the guys had. Sometimes the meetings lasted only two or three minutes and sometimes they lasted a half an hour. Andy would take whatever time it took to resolve any problems. It was also a way for grievances to be aired and given an audience with the head coach.

The most notable players' committee meeting took place the day before the 2003 NFC Championship game between the Eagles and the Carolina Panthers. The day started with our special teams meeting. John Harbaugh was our special teams coach for several years. The special teams coach had the rare forum to speak to the entire team nearly every day. The offensive and defensive coordinators didn't even get to do that. Some coaches wilted under that kind of pressure. Not John Harbaugh. Instead of wilting, he always spoke with a confidence that inspired our team to fight to be our best. It was not surprising to me at all when he was made the head coach of the Baltimore Ravens and took them to the AFC Championship in just his first year. He was a head coach long before he was ever made a head coach because he believed it, acted like it, spoke like it, coached like it, and had the toughness that it took to be successful.

When his special teams meeting was over, we all headed to the team meeting room where Coach Reid would address us. At that point, two of our players inexplicably got into a fight. As a team, we were stunned because we had a team chemistry that was second to none. Fights at practice every once in a while were viewed almost as a part of the game, but this was altogether different. As players we were not aware of a problem that had been festering between two of our guys. The pressure of the moment caused them to act contrary to what we were all about.

It turned out that one of the players was on the practice squad and he had been jealous of another player who was on the active roster. Unknown to me and the rest of the team, the practice squad player had been taking verbal swipes at the other player the whole year. They were small, cutting remarks that were either under his breath or quiet enough that no one else heard. Those types of social infections needed to be lanced or they would develop into the major distraction that this one turned into.

As the team was walking into the team meeting room, one last comment from the practice squad player was enough to bring the issue to a head. The player told the practice squad player that he had had enough and that if anything else was said, he would take care of business. Another smart remark was made, and the situation immediately escalated into a fight. The player broke the nose of the practice squad player with a head butt and following punches. It happened so fast that most of us didn't know that it had happened even though we were standing only a few feet away.

After the team meeting, Andy was informed of the fight, and he called a players' committee meeting. We sat with Andy for close to an hour as we discussed what we thought would be the most effective solution. Andy was very patient with all of our comments. We were patient with each other even though the discussion was emotionally charged. It was charged because it was a big game and because we were trying to determine what to do with two of our own. They were our friends and teammates. It was complicated.

The final outcome was a fine for both players. They were both to publicly apologize to each other and the team during the walk-through practice for the distraction they had caused. Difficult situations such as that were more the exception than the norm. Andy showed great restraint and a willingness to let the players' committee become part of the solution. He had great confidence in us as players and men.

It pains me to write this, but we lost that game for the third year in a row. Donovan was knocked out of the game with an injury to his ribs. We never recovered and the Panthers went on to beat us, ending our season one game short.

An interesting thing happened after each of those three NFC Championship game losses. In the post-game TV interviews, Coach Reid displayed no quit. Instead, he spoke passionately and energetically about the future of our team. Where I was hurting and wondering if we would ever make it back, Coach Reid was resolute. He was firm and full of confidence that we would not only get back but that we would win the Super Bowl. I was blown away by his unwavering belief in our team. That was one of the indicators of his greatness. He never lost the fire to get our team to the top.

In 2004, the Eagles made a dramatic move by adding Terrell Owens to the offense and Jevon Kearse to the defense. Both players were high-priced free agents who were playing at the top of their game. Terrell was one of the League's best receivers. We played in the Pro Bowl together for three years in a row, and he had let me know how much he wanted to play for the Eagles because Donovan was our quarterback. Jevon came from the Tennessee Titans and was the League's most athletic defensive end. They both made significant contributions to our team. Terrell raised the level of intensity for every one of our practices. Even though he had been a lightning rod at times when he played for the 49ers, he seemed to fit in with everyone in Philly. We all got along very well.

We played excellent football through the regular season and again sealed up home field advantage throughout the play-offs. We beat the Minnesota Vikings in the first play-off game to earn our fourth NFC Championship game appearance in a row. After losing three in a row, I didn't think it was possible to lose another one.

The night before the biggest game of my career, there was a gigantic snowstorm and the temperature in Philadelphia was below freezing. In fact, it was the coldest game of my life. The field was covered and then cleared of every snowflake before we started pregame warm-ups. We were playing against the Atlanta Falcons and the feeling on our team was one of confidence.

It was just prior to this game that I had the unforgettable national anthem experience described in chapter 15.

We played as a team and we played with the fire and devotion required to win an NFC Championship. Our whole team was united with one purpose. The Eagles had a motto for that season. It was: ONE TEAM, ONE CITY, ONE DREAM. That game was the epitome of that motto. We were one.

Donovan threw two touchdown passes to me in that game. The credit for my first touchdown reception goes to my tight-end coach, Tom Melvin.

Tom Melvin replaced Pat Shurmur as the tight-end coach for the Philadelphia Eagles when Pat was made quarterbacks coach. Tom had been the offensive quality control coach for three years. Tom was similar to Pat in his loyalty to Coach Reid. He was actually the first player Coach Reid ever coached when they were together at San Francisco State University. Tom was a member of the offensive line for that team and they had been close ever since.

Tom had dedicated himself to a few years of incredibly long hours as the offensive quality-control coach. As such he was the one who stayed up all night preparing cards for the practices. In order for the practice team defense to be lined up in the correct spots, cards had to be made for every play in practice. The coach made those cards after he had already sat through all the other players' and coaches' meetings. It meant crazy, long hours every day, and Tom basically lived in his office for a couple of years. He actually slept there on a cot that he brought from home.

His dedication to Andy and the Eagles was total. He was a true players' coach and was always open to our input as tight ends. If we felt we needed a certain drill in practice, Tom was more than willing to work with us. He would devote whatever time we needed to get better. In the several years that I knew him, he never once even intimated that we were wasting his time. He was available 24/7 to us. He always stayed after practice to work with the younger tight ends on any part of their game that needed extra work.

Tom started the off-season that year by having all the tight ends do a sideline reception drill every day. We enjoyed the drill because it was fun to catch the ball on the sideline and tap our toes in bounds before falling out of bounds. We worked that drill to death. It just so happened that because Tom focused on that discipline I was able to make a play when called upon. My body and my subconscious had been prepared to come through when it mattered most.

Donovan threw me a play-action pass when we were near the goal line in position to score. After the play action, he rolled out to the right and threw a pass for the corner of the end zone. The wind blew Donovan's pass farther than he intended it to go. I ran to catch it before it sailed out of bounds. I reached up and caught it just in the nick of time. I tapped my toes on the sideline with no more than a centimeter to spare. The official was right on top

Courtesy of the Philadelphia Eagles

*I was so grateful to play tight end for the Eagles. I wish everyone could
feel the thrill of catching a touchdown in the NFL.*

of the play and ruled it a touchdown! Jim Mora, the head coach of
the Falcons, challenged the call. The officials reviewed it, and the
call stood. Touchdown! It was my favorite catch of my life because
it combined focused, dedicated training with the moment of the
NFC Championship. Tom had conditioned my eyes, hands, and
feet to make the play when it counted.

The game continued to go our way. We had the chance to
wrap up a victory with one more touchdown. With two minutes
remaining in the game, we were again on the Falcon's goal line.
Another play-action pass was called and I was again the primary
receiver. After the play action, Donovan again rolled to the right.
I was wide open, but this time, instead of leading me with the
ball, he threw it slightly behind me and I had to slow up to make
the catch. I had planted my left foot to get the leverage to turn
and make the grab, and just at the moment the ball hit my hands,

the cleats on my left foot got tangled in the turf, twisting my foot in an awkward way. The result was something that made it feel as though my foot had exploded.

While clutching the football in my arms and falling to the ground, it seemed as though time stood still. I felt what I can only describe as a release of pressure in my left foot that was similar to when I broke my ankle at BYU. It was again as though a sniper's bullet found its mark, and its mark was my foot. I immediately knew that it was broken. I knew that my season was over. I knew that we were going to the Super Bowl, and I knew that I would not be able to play. A few of my teammates had torn their Lis Franc ligaments over the last few years, and now I had done the same thing.

It would have been even more devastating had it not been for the blessing that my dad and my brothers Dave and Todd had given me in their hotel room just prior to the game. Because of a torn tricep on my right arm from the Vikings game the week before, I asked them to give me a blessing. While I was falling to the ground holding on to the ball, the memory of that blessing flashed through my mind. Instantly I experienced a feeling of peace. I can't describe it any better than that. That sense of well-being was more powerful than the game. It transcended the moment and the emotion.

Because I couldn't stand, I sat on my butt and celebrated the play. The fans were going bananas. After losing three consecutive NFC Championship games, we were *finally* going to the Super Bowl. The eruption was Vesuvius-like. When my teammate L. J. Smith lifted me up, I told him that my foot was broken. I tried to line up for the extra point, but I could not even crouch down into my position. I had to call a time out and limp to the sideline.

Upon reaching the sideline, I told Coach Reid that I had just broken my foot. The doctors confirmed my impression when they removed my cleat and sock and nearly pulled my big toe off my foot in the process. It hurt like crazy for them to manipulate my foot. They wanted to get an X-ray right then, but I would not miss the rest of the game for anything. I stayed on the sideline with my team, standing on the outside part of my foot.

When the game was over, our team stormed the field. I was being interviewed by a local news station when my wife, Michele, ran onto the field and jumped on top of me. She did not yet know that my foot was broken. She was as excited as I had ever seen her. She was smiling and laughing and yelling all at the same time.

When I shouted above the noise of the crowd that I had just broken my foot, she didn't believe me.

It was the worst news I could deliver. I wished that it weren't true, that I was fine and healthy, but I wasn't. My brothers were right there as well, and I could see the perplexed disappointment in their faces. As much as I hated to say it, I assured them that it was true. I wanted to celebrate with them. We had all worked for so many years to get to the Super Bowl. They had been with me every step of the way. I couldn't believe I was telling them that I would not be playing, but it was true.

X-rays taken after the game confirmed the ligament tear. Mark Meyerson, the foot doctor from Johns Hopkins in Baltimore, was at the game. He was the foremost surgeon in the United States when it came to repairing the Lis Franc injury, named for a physician in Napoleon's army, Jacque Lis Franc. When cavalry men fell from their horses in battle, their foot would sometimes become stuck in the stirrup, resulting in a violent dislocation of the forefoot. The only remedy back then was to amputate the foot. Since that time, the main ligament that holds the foot together has been called the Lis Franc, and so is the surgery that repairs it.

While the city of Philadelphia was in the middle of total celebration and my teammates and coaches were on cloud nine, my family was huddled in one of the doctor's offices of the training room getting the bad news from Rick Burkholder and Dr. Myerson.

Surgery was scheduled for Wednesday at Johns Hopkins. My season was over, and possibly my career.

As a family, we prayed. That was what we knew. That was what we relied upon in both good times and bad. That prayer was a strength to me.

The following Sunday, as our team flew to Jacksonville for Super Bowl XXXIX, I was on the plane with two screws through my left foot holding it together. I was elated that I had helped our team get to the Super Bowl, but I was equally disappointed at not being able to practice and play in the game with them.

Then it hit me, a day or two before the game, but when it did, I finally realized what I had always known. *My family is my Super Bowl!* It was just that simple. I had dreamed about playing in that game since I was three or four years old. I had worked for it my whole career. Humiliating losses and heart-pounding victories had all paved the way to the Super Bowl. And now that I was there, instead of crying about what I didn't have, I rejoiced that my Super Bowl would be with me forever! It wasn't just a one-day thing. Families are forever. My family surrounded me with their greatness every day. My wife, Michele, loved me, and I loved her, and that lifted both of us together. My parents' love for me had carried me along and allowed me to overcome the small hurdles and challenges while growing up. They loved me even when I didn't deserve it. Through good times and bad, we were a family. My children were better than any touchdown that I would have ever caught in the Super Bowl. They are my Super Bowl: Emily, Sarah, Jacob, Jefferson, Maxwell, Tanner, and Todd!

CHAPTER 22

COACHES AND PLAYERS

Andy knew when to crack a joke or when to crack the whip. When some coaches might have been intimidated by strong personalities such as our defensive end Hugh Douglas, Andy embraced them. He always encouraged Hugh to let his personality show. Hugh was *the* comedian for our team. He got us all laughing before the games with his singing and crazy, off-the-wall rants, and then he backed it up every game by playing out of his mind. Without fail, Hugh would sing, "Bombs over Baghdad," and "If You Ain't from My 'Hood, You Can Get from 'Round Here!" as he walked around the locker room. His effectiveness as a player dramatically increased because Andy gave him plenty of room to use his gifts. He lifted the whole team with his personality and skill.

David Culley was the Eagles receivers coach and one of my favorite guys on the staff. He was the epitome of positive. I don't think I ever saw him down for one second. He was similar to Pat, Tom, and the other coaches in that he was dedicated and loyal to Andy. Coach Culley was fun for the whole team to be around because he could smile even when times were tough. He brought an attitude of gratitude to work every single day. It didn't matter if it was the off-season, the beginning of training camp, or the Super Bowl. He was consistently happy.

At the end of my career, Andy was trying to make the decision whether to keep me the starting tight end or to install L. J. Smith as the new starter at that position. Every veteran player eventually reaches that point in his career. It was a part of life that was not unique to football players. Dick Vermeil preached that all of our jobs and positions were on loan and since that was the case, we should play with all the enthusiasm and passion that we had. None of us knew how long we would be playing in the League.

Coach Culley made it a point to visit with me in the locker room one day during a mini camp when the coaches were trying to make that decision with regard to me.

He tracked me down like a hound dog and set me straight. He told me that we would not be any good without me in the lineup. He told me how much he appreciated my work ethic and that I battled every day as a player. He reminded me that he had full confidence in my abilities as a tight end and a team leader and so did most of the other coaches on the staff. He told me not to worry or hang my head for one instant because I was still going to be every bit as included in the strategy and game plan.

His message could not have been more reassuring. It was a conversation that I will long remember as a symbol of his greatness. He went out of his way to deliver that message, and I was a better person and player because of it.

Good teams always have strong team chemistry. One play in a game against the Minnesota Vikings in November of 2001 highlights some of the team chemistry that we had. In that game, we started clicking as an offense, scoring touchdowns from all over the field. Late in the game, we had a sizeable lead and all three tight ends were in the game—Jeff Thomason, Mike Bartrum, and I. We were on the five-yard line and Andy called "64 U

Corner," which called for me to run block for a full second while we did a play action in the backfield. Then I was to release to the corner of the end zone and Donovan would throw it my way for a TD. In the huddle, Jeff Thomason looked at me and said, "Let's give this to Bartrum!"

In this particular set, with three tight ends in the game, Bartrum was supposed to be on the back side of the play as a third or fourth option, running a slow crossing route at the back of the end zone.

I said, "Okay," but just as soon as we agreed to do this, Jeff wondered if that would hurt my chances to get back to the Pro Bowl. He said that I needed the stats to get back to Hawaii. He was always looking out for people other than himself. But with so little time until the snap, Jeff and I quickly agreed to switch it up so that Bartrum would take my spot and would now be on the front side of the call and be the primary receiver.

The play worked perfectly. Donovan threw a beautiful touchdown pass to Mike and we all celebrated like crazy by jumping on top of each other before the extra point. It was such a fun moment to share with these great friends on the NFL stage in the old Vet. Not one person in the stands had any clue of what switches we had made in assignments. The announcers had no idea of the change, either. But as usually is the case, the team knew what was going on. We all smiled that Bartrum, one of the unsung heroes of the team, got some recognition for being the kind of person that other people wanted to pull for.

As the offense came off the field, Coach Reid looked at me with his big grin and said, "That was classy; good job!" He could have wigged out because we changed the play or he could have felt that we pulled a fast one on him. But he knew exactly what was going on, and he loved it.

I was happy that Mike and Jeff were so fired up. It was one of the great moments in my career. All smiles. Jeff started saying that

he wanted to give me all of his TDs for the rest of the season because I did that. He meant that if he were ever the primary receiver in a red-zone situation, he would change positions with me
so that I could score the TD.

When I got to the locker room after the game, Tom Melvin,
who would become our tight-end coach the following year, said,
"Good job, that was big-time!" Pat Shurmur, our outstanding
tight-end coach said that was the kind of thing that made him
very proud to be my coach. He was happy for all three of us.
Every coach feels the pressure, weight, and stress of that job. It was
awesome to see in Pat's face that he was proud of the guys he was
coaching. His expression of acknowledgement made it worth it.
Team chemistry is manifest in many different ways. That was one
small example of the kind of thing that happened all the time on
our team.

Jeff Thomason, true to his word, forced me to change positions with him the next week when we were playing the Dallas
Cowboys. In the huddle, Donovan called Jeff's play. It was "pass
97 U Corner halfback flat." Jeff immediately grabbed me and told
me to line up in his spot and take the touchdown. There was no
time to argue since the clock was winding down and we were all
walking to the line of scrimmage. Just as the week before, a touchdown was given as a gift from one teammate to another.

Andy, perhaps feeling as though this switching of positions
was becoming routine, just smiled at us as we walked back to the
sideline. He knew he had a team. He knew he had a bunch of unselfish guys who cared about each other more than they cared
about themselves.

Jeff Thomason and Mike Bartrum were examples of two great
guys in the NFL. I think one of the least-known facts about the
NFL is how many great people there are who are part of the game.
With the number of negative stories on the news about some of the
bad actions of football players, it is easy to make the assumption

that the NFL is full of thugs. There were a few guys who acted in ways that were completely different than they were taught and coached. But the great majority of players were awesome.

One example of quiet greatness that illustrates the point is James Thrash, a receiver for the Eagles. We began our careers together, but he was cut before we even got to training camp that first year. But he made the team with the Redskins and played in Washington for the first four years of his career. The Eagles signed him as a free agent to help us get to the Super Bowl. We got to three NFC Championship games with him but sadly never got to the Super Bowl.

James and I were roommates every weekend for the game. If it was a home game, we stayed at the Airport Marriott in Philly. If it was on the road, we were roommates there as well. I got to know James at practice, in games, and as my roommate. He was a warrior on the field and a gentleman off the field. He treated everyone he ever met with kindness and class. He was a great family man in every way. He loved his wife and children and spoke of them with fondness. James was a good person and one whom the NFL was happy to have represent them. He did everything right. He was an incredibly hard working and upstanding person.

James was also an unselfish teammate who would do anything the coaches ever asked him to do. He had a great attitude that he brought to work every day. He was a lot of fun as a teammate and a lot of fun to be around each day for the seven months of the season. When people would ask me if there are any good people in the NFL, I would tell them not only good but great. James Thrash was a classic example of that.

Jermane Mayberry was another such person I played with in Philadelphia. He was an offensive lineman and one of the biggest people I have ever known. At 6'4" and 325 pounds he was a first-round draft pick for the Eagles in 1996.

Jermane was inserted into the lineup as a tackle but did not dominate as a tackle, partly because of a problem with his eyesight. He suffered from amblyopia, which was an underdeveloped optic nerve in his left eye. He was sometimes booed as a player because some of the Philly fans thought he was a bust. He never lashed out as a result of the slings and arrows that went his way. He only kept his nose to the grindstone in an effort to get better.

When he was moved to right guard, he flourished for the Eagles. He was a dominant player and earned a trip to the Pro Bowl in 2003 as the game's best right guard. He donated a great deal of his own money to help start a vision testing program for the Eagles Youth Partnership, the charitable wing of the Eagles organization. The Eagles took a huge motor home and turned it into an "eyemobile" that provided more than ten thousand low-income students with free eye exams in the Philly area.

Jermane was a team favorite because he was genuine and gracious. If every player in the NFL were as good a person as Jermane Mayberry, the NFL would be the greatest force for good on the planet. When school kids or other people would ask me who I thought was the best guy in the NFL, Jermane was my answer. He was a solid player, a great friend, an incredible teammate, and just a wonderful person.

As one of the leaders on our team, Troy Vincent embodied toughness, wisdom, and professionalism. Perhaps the story that says the most about Troy Vincent happened when we left training camp to attend the funeral of Korey Stringer, our Pro Bowl teammate with the Minnesota Vikings. Korey died during practice in a tragic accident related to the heat. Andy Reid gave permission for Troy Vincent, Hugh Douglas, Damon Moore, and me to miss a day of practice to attend the service, represent the Eagles and the NFL, and support his family in their hour of grief.

While we were at the airport in Bethlehem, Pennsylvania, Hugh Douglas, one of the funniest personalities ever to play in the NFL, asked me about the scriptures that I was reading. My scriptures contain the standard works of my faith, The Church of Jesus Christ of Latter-day Saints, which include the Holy Bible (King James version), the Book of Mormon, the Doctrine and Covenants, and the Pearl of Great Price, all bound into one volume. That made a pretty thick book, larger in size than what Hugh was accustomed to seeing. He hefted the book and said, "Whoa, Chad, what's up with your Bible, bro?"

After I explained what books were included and where they came from, his curiosity was satisfied and he responded with, "Cool." Troy also responded to my answer to Hugh about the contents of my book. His response was profound. He looked at me and said, "I don't know everything about those books, but I know enough to say that I will never put God in a box and say that He can't do something."

That was a leader. I was so impressed with that comment. It showed great faith on Troy's part. Each NFL team is comprised of players from all backgrounds, all walks of life, all different religious affiliations and, in order to form a strong bond of team chemistry, they need to come together. As one of our team leaders, Troy Vincent earned the respect of every teammate because he worked his tail off on the field and showed the wisdom of Solomon off the field. His presence in the locker room and on the field had enough gravitational pull that he held people accountable for their work. His approach didn't always make people comfortable, but it almost always assured success.

CHAPTER 23

THE PRESIDENT OF
THE UNITED STATES

After beating the Carolina Panthers at home, the Eagles were 5–0 and life was good. When you were undefeated in Philly, things were good. Very good. In my opinion, Philadelphia is the number-one sports town in America. Philly fans love their teams like no other, and when those teams are performing well they make a great fuss over their players wherever they go, even if, as I discovered, the president of the United States is nearby.

After the win over Carolina, Michele and I heard that President Bush was going to be speaking at a location within a mile of our home. We both thought it would be fun to hear him, so Michele called and got some tickets. On Monday, October 18, we went to the Marlton, New Jersey, town hall to hear President Bush's stump speech. We waited in a long line to get in. We did not have any special tickets. We were not VIP or special guests of any kind. We were just there as citizens. The building where the rally was to be held was relatively small, holding only a couple thousand people.

Outside the city building were thousands of Bush supporters who were there without tickets and came just to see the president fly in and out on his helicopter, Marine One. Michele and I went through the metal detectors and were cleared to enter the building, but before we could find a place to sit, a group of people gathered around me asking for my autograph. Pretty soon there were a lot of autograph seekers. Like I said, Philly is a major sports town, and being a part of an undefeated Eagles team puts you in the spotlight.

As I continued to sign autographs, a woman popped up out of nowhere and said, "Hi, I am with the White House. Who are you?"

I wondered what she was thinking and guessed that she was concerned about the confusion in light of the fact that the president would be arriving very shortly. I told her that I played for the Eagles and since we were undefeated, a lot of people were really excited and wanted my autograph. She asked if we had seats and then asked if we wanted to sit in the front. We took her offer and sat on the second row, right in the middle.

It was an impressive moment when President Bush entered the room. People were fired up to see him, and his entrance created quite a stir. Music was playing, and he was flanked by his Secret Service detail. Michele and I had never been that close to the commander in chief, and it was a lot of fun.

After the president finished speaking, he left the stage and began shaking hands with the people in the first row. We were hoping to reach from the second row to shake his hand as he passed in front of us.

But before he reached where we were standing, the same woman from the White House who had given us our seats came up to us. She told us with great urgency to follow her. We did what she asked and left the place where people were clamoring to be. We followed her through the crowd, around the side of the stage, and into a hallway on the back of the building. The hallway led to a door to the outside on the rear of the building.

When we exited the building, the first thing we saw was a large group of Secret Service agents standing there waiting for the president. Just behind them sat Marine One, the large green helicopter that had brought the president to the rally. All the people who had come to see the president fly in were on the other side of the building and shielded from our view. We could see no other people besides the Secret Service agents and sharpshooters stationed in the fields surrounding the building.

The woman from the White House told us that we were going to meet the president. We both started to smile and chuckle a little bit. It was happening pretty fast and we were very excited. Within one minute, the president came out and conferred briefly with his Secret Service detail. Then he turned to us and said, "Big Chad Lewis, how are you?"

For Michele and me, all the butterflies that we had went away almost as soon as President Bush shook our hands. He had a genuine smile and a warmth about him that was easy to be around. He was fun and easy to talk to. He made us feel as though we were old friends. There was no stammering or searching for words that we had sometimes seen when he was on TV. He seemed relaxed and in no hurry to board his helicopter and leave. He was more than comfortable talking with us.

He asked about the Eagles and Andy Reid and wondered how things were working out with Terrell Owens now on the team. He also asked where we had grown up and what schools we'd gone to. When I told him that Michele played volleyball at BYU and that is where we met, he took an interest in that and mentioned he had just had the Women's National Volleyball Team in his office the day before. He was a sports fan, having been one of the owners of the Major League Baseball team, the Texas Rangers.

We asked him about the series of televised debates that he had just completed against Senator Kerry. He said he had been nervous, and that when he looked into the audience, he saw that his wife and daughter were nervous, too, and that made him even more nervous. He confided that he felt things hadn't really gone that well for him in the first two debates but that the last debate was fun because it was with the people. He said he enjoyed that format the best and felt he had been able to get his message across.

After about five minutes, we thought that he needed to be heading out and so we thanked him for his time and attention. He was still in no hurry to leave. In parting, I told him that we were grateful for the great leadership and service he had provided our country after 9/11 and that we were praying for him. He looked at me with an added level of seriousness and said, "Thank you. That means more to me than anything else, that the citizens of this country would pray for their president."

After that, we shook hands, said good-bye, and he was off. Within a minute or two he was flying a low circle over the people who had come to see him, and Michele and I were standing there on the side of the building wondering about the awesome experience we had just had. We were amazed that he had taken time to visit with us like that.

We did not have a camera and we did not get any of it documented. It was enough to have had the chance to meet and talk with him. It would have been sweet to have taken some photos, but we were not about to cry over that. We marveled that he had treated us so cordially and had been so gracious.

We drove home with perma-grins on our faces, asking ourselves if that had really happened. We called our families and told them all about the meeting. We got the same response from them. They all just giggled and laughed at the unexpected and great encounter we had enjoyed.

That was followed up by another incredible event the next week. We flew to Cleveland and played the Browns. We played very well and beat them. I caught a touchdown pass in the game and was feeling pretty good after the win. Dave Akers, the Eagles' most prolific kicker, and I sat next to each other on the plane as we had for years. While we were talking about the win and getting ready to take off, I got a call from the White House on my cell phone. The person asked me if I wanted to introduce President Bush at one of his last stump speeches in Bucks County, north of Philadelphia. I was blown away. How many times had I received a call from the White House? That was the first.

I told the caller that I would get back with him because I wanted to ask Andy Reid if that was okay with him. The reason I felt obligated to get Coach Reid's approval was because of the policy he announced at the beginning of training camp each year—that players stay away from two topics in the locker room: religion and politics. We were together, he always said, for one purpose, to win the Super Bowl, and he warned us how those two topics could divide a team faster than anything. He demanded from us that we respect each other's beliefs and give each other space. We needed to be a team and have great chemistry if we were going to accomplish our goal of becoming world champs.

If Coach Reid had said that he did not want me to introduce President Bush, I would have followed his wish. On our flights, position coaches routinely visited with their players on the plane. Tom Melvin, our tight-end coach, stopped by to talk with me about the game. I told him about the phone call from the White House and asked him if he would talk to Andy about it. I didn't try to sell it to him; I figured Andy would either say yes or no.

Tom came back in a few minutes with a big smile on his face and said, "Andy said, 'Since it's the president, I'll relent!'"

I could hear Coach Reid's wry sense of humor in his words. He had been a great friend to me and he was having fun with me by answering that way. I was thrilled to have the clearance from him to do that.

When we landed, I called the White House to inform them that I would be happy to introduce the president. It would be on

Thursday, after practice, in Bucks County. I could invite anyone from the team who wanted to come. During the week, I let everyone know that they were invited to come with me, whether they were Republican or Democrat, or even if they didn't care about the political process one way or another. If they wanted to meet the president of the United States they were more than welcome.

Andy allowed those of us who were going to skip out of post practice meetings a few minutes early. We did not have any special police escort up to the event. Heading up I-95 North in rush hour was very slow going, even on a good day. But since there would be a lot of traffic for that event, we knew that it would be extra crowded.

Butch Buchanico, the Eagles' longtime director of security, agreed to drive me up there. Mike Dougherty, or "Doc" as he was known, was the Eagles' video director and my good friend, and he was going to go with us as well. Mike had been with the Eagles since the Dick Vermeil days. Not only was he the video coordinator for Dick Vermeil, but Mike had been struck by lightning on his video tower when foul weather rolled through training camp. It turned out that Dick did not want to stop practice; he was way too tough for that, and so he kept things going regardless of the weather. It almost cost Doc his life.

When Mike was struck, he thought it was lights out for him. His face was burned a little and his camera was hammered. It was a close call. After that, Dick changed his philosophy on bad weather. Doc would hold a lightning meter with him in the tower and when the danger level reached a certain point, he would let Dick know, and the team would run off the field. Doc was out of the spotlight and under the radar on the team, but players loved him because he was such a genuinely great guy. We all felt the Eagles were lucky to have him, and Doc felt as though he lived a charmed life to work for the Eagles. It was a match made in heaven.

As we hopped into the truck, Butch flipped on some portable flashing lights, like Starsky and Hutch, and we headed out of the Nova Care facility, heading for Bucks County. Eight other players agreed to come with us. Reno Mahe, Jeff Thomason, Corey Simon, Paul Grasmanis, Dirk Johnson, Hank Fraley, Dave Akers, and Mike Bartrum made a caravan of four SUVs and we all headed up together.

The drive up was one I will never forget. The beautiful fall leaves of the Northeast looked like they were on fire. The sun was hitting the hardwood trees that lined the highway without any objection from clouds. They seemed to light the way up to Bucks County with bright oranges, reds, yellows, and greens. It was breathtaking. The singular beauty of that day was a sight that burned itself onto the hard drive memory of my brain.

Thanks to the flashing lights on Butch's vehicle, we navigated the traffic very well. But as we came within ten miles of our exit, we ran into a line of cars that were stopped on the road. It was gridlock. Our flashing lights would do nothing to penetrate that. Within a minute or two of sitting still in traffic, another caravan, this time of highway patrol cars, went flying past us down the shoulder of the road. After they passed, we jumped in right behind them on the shoulder.

We followed them for about a mile before the patrol car just in front of us stopped; the trooper got out and came back to our car with an incredulous look on his face. We rolled down the window, and he asked us what we thought we were doing following a line of squad cars. Butch responded with all the confidence of an NFL security director and told the state trooper that I was going to introduce the president and that I needed to be up there ASAP. He had no doubt or uncertainty in his voice. The state trooper nodded and told us to stay on his tail the rest of the way. It was classic Butch, and it was a classic moment, on a classic day.

We got to the venue, which was in an open field, without any more slowdowns and met with the Secret Service, who inspected our cars and ran each of us through a security check before they let us into a roped-off area. We were met there by Michele and my two girls, Emily and Sarah, as well as Vai Sikahema, who was there with NBC10 News, and his wife, Keala. Some of the other players' wives were there as well.

After standing in a VIP section for about an hour with Senator Rick Santorum, Senator Arlen Spector, my teammates and some of their wives, and others, someone escorted me behind the stage to wait for the president to arrive.

The stage was made up of hay bales stacked high enough so that I could not see the crowd from where I was standing. There was music playing and it got louder as the president got closer. When it was dark, his motorcade rolled up the road with lights flashing, and then they drove straight across the field right to where I was standing. I was told to get on the stage and start my introduction.

I took about two minutes to introduce him. It was a spirited group that had been standing there in the fields waiting for him for a long time. They were all pumped to see him and hear from him. After introducing him, I turned and told him that I loved him and gave him a hug. I left the stage and walked back to my family and teammates for the rest of his speech. As soon as the president was finished, our little group was escorted behind the hay-bale stage so that we could meet with him. Our wives were told that since there were so many players, they would not be able to join us. That was the only bummer of the night. I took my daughters Emily and Sarah along with me because it was a once-in-a-lifetime moment that I wanted them to have.

President Bush met with all of us and we exchanged hellos and wished him luck. We had signed a football and Doc presented it to him for us. We got together and took a photo, which hangs in my office today. I love looking at that picture and seeing my teammates with smiles on their faces. Those were good times as we marched toward the Super Bowl. We had a great team and a great year and that picture is a sweet reminder to me of the feeling we had. I especially liked the brightness of the president's face. He wore the genuine smile of a great man.

Afterwards we got to visit with President Bush, and he thanked me once again for introducing him. Dave Akers told him that we were all praying for him and he stopped in his tracks and told us how much that meant to him personally, that we would pray for him. I am glad there was a photographer there that time and that I have a photo of the occasion. I was also glad that I got to share it with my family and my teammates.

The concluding chapter of this story about President Bush happened when we were in Jacksonville preparing for the Super Bowl. I received another call from the White House on my cell phone. Since I was injured and could not play, I was not required to be in all of the team meetings and I was in my room. The person was a member of the president's staff and was calling to ask if Michele and I would like to attend a state dinner at the White House on Valentine's Day. I didn't have to ask for permission that time and immediately responded that Michele and I would be honored to accept the invitation. I was informed that it was black tie and formal. No problem.

I was told that same morning by the Eagles' owner, Jeffrey Lurie, that the NFL commissioner, Paul Tagliabue, was going to spend a week in China promoting the game and visiting our sponsors as well as government officials. Jeffrey wanted to know if I would like to be his guest for that week and go on the trip. It was so disappointing not being able to play in the Super Bowl, but things were quickly adding up that took some of the short-term sting away.

For the first day in Jacksonville I was on the crutches that were issued to me by the hospital. I asked the hotel where our team was

This is the scooter I was given at the Super Bowl in Jacksonville, Florida. The whole team signed it.

staying for the use of a wheelchair, and they were more than willing to accommodate me. Instead of sitting in the wheelchair, I stood in front of it with my left knee on the seat and used my right leg to push it backwards like a scooter.

It worked well for a day until I called a scooter store and asked if I could borrow a motorized cart for the week. They said they would be there in an hour or two with a scooter. Sure enough, they came through like champs. They let me use an electric scooter that turned out to be such a big help. It was all black with a leather seat. It had turn signals, rearview mirrors, a horn, and a basket. I was amazed how mobile it was. I could drive into any restaurant and not bump into a chair. It could weave into tight corners and it had some get up and go, too. The whole team signed the cart, and Tammy Reid wanted to buy it from the store and auction it off for charity. The scooter store didn't want to let it go. After the Super Bowl, they put it in the showroom of their store and said they would keep it there forever.

As an injured player, it was doubtful that I would be allowed on the sideline for the game. Initially, I was told that I would be in the box for the game, that I posed a risk because I could not run away from danger. I talked with Andy and let him know that I would stay out of the way and that I would never be a problem. He made it possible for me to be on the sideline. I was so glad to be there with my teammates. The game did not go like we wanted it to go, but it was one of my life's dreams to be in the Super Bowl. Even though I couldn't play, I felt as though I had contributed to us being there, especially with the touchdowns in the NFC Championship game.

When we got back to Philly after the game, I had my end-of-the-year meeting with Coach Reid. My contract was up, which meant that I was not going to be back the following year. That also meant that I was not allowed to work out at the facility or use the training room to rehab my leg. The meeting gave me the chance to say thanks to Coach Reid, not just for the Super Bowl, but for the chance to play for him all of those years and for his friendship with me and my family. I let him know how much he meant to my career and to my life. There wasn't any better coach in the NFL for me. He was awesome and I told him so.

We packed up our home and called a moving company to move all of our stuff to Utah. Since I was hopping around on one leg, we called my mom and she came out and helped us for a few days. She watched our kids as we drove down to the White House for the Valentine's dinner.

Michele said that she felt as though she were going to prom all over again. She got a sweet dress for the occasion. It was silver, full length, modest, and beautiful. She looked like a million bucks. She had her hair done, I was in a tux, and we were ready for a memorable night. We were given directions on how to get into the White House. Isn't that weird? We were driving right to the White House!

When we got there we went through some major security checkpoints. A steel barrier that was about a foot thick blocked the way at the entrance. After our ID was approved, the gate was lowered so we could enter the grounds.

I dropped Michele off at the door and parked the car. Since my foot was broken and I was not to put any weight on it for four months, I was using a small scooter that I kneeled on with my bad foot. We had to go through another security check, similar to that at an airport, and then we waited in a little sitting room as more people came. While I was signing the guest book, someone to the left of me asked how I had broken my foot. Without looking up, I answered I broke it in the NFC Championship game against the Falcons. When I did look up, I saw Lynn Swann standing there with a big smile. I introduced myself and Michele and told him that he was my hero when I was in grade school. He was so gracious. I loved Lynn Swann. We met his wife, Charena, and we also met Willie Mays, the "Say Hey Kid" himself, and his wife. That night was getting better by the second.

Once we were all signed in, we went down a hallway to go up some stairs. Because of my injury and scooter, we actually got to take the "President's Elevator." In any other house it would be the elevator, but since we were in the White House, it was called the President's Elevator. We entered a foyer area where they were serving hors d'oeuvres and drinks, which included orange juice, water, and several different wines. Michele said she had two glasses of orange juice and only one hors d'oeuvre. She would have had more, but since no one else was, she didn't want to act as though we were starving.

We had been standing in the foyer for five minutes when President and Mrs. Bush came in and greeted everyone. They walked around and shook hands with each person there. We were visiting with the Goodnights from North Carolina for the first part of the evening. They were gracious and very friendly to us. They had been invited to these events before and did not go, but Mrs. Goodnight said this was one event that she was not going to miss. Michele and I felt the same way.

Secretary Bodman, the secretary of energy, introduced himself to us. His wife, Diane, knew that I was a tight end for the Eagles and said she was sorry that I had not been able to play in the Super Bowl. Michele was impressed that she knew more about me than her husband did. Then President Bush came up, shook hands with the Goodnights, then turned and said, "Chadly, how are you? Is your foot healing up OK?" I loved it because only my offensive coordinator Rod Dowhower has ever called me "Chadly." The president asked about my roll-a-bout scooter, and within a couple minutes he was on to greeting other guests. There I was, in the White House, wearing a tuxedo, standing next to the girl of my dreams, talking with the president of the United States. It was sweet.

Just then the secretary of health and human services, Michael Leavitt, and his wife, Jackie, walked past us with two other couples heading to meet Roger Staubach and his wife. Michele reached out her hand and introduced herself to Secretary Leavitt. Michael Leavitt used to be the governor of Utah, where I had the chance to meet him a couple of times. He turned to me and we immediately started talking about Cedar City, where he was from. He knew my Grandpa Belden Lewis, who had built the Leavitts' family home and the church house where the Leavitts worshiped. He was also childhood friends with my uncles Alan and Evan. He told some funny stories about growing up. If there was any nervousness about being there, he put an end to it with his friendly manner and great personality.

Secretary Leavitt informed us that couples normally did not

sit together at state dinners; it was customary for couples to sit at different tables with other guests. If he had previously put us at ease, all of that changed with Michele when she heard that we would not be sitting together. She got a little anxious. He told her not to be nervous but to just follow the lead of the cabinet member at the table and she would know what to do.

When Michele inquired if she should call him "Mr. Secretary" or "Governor," he responded, "Mike is just fine."

Michele asked, "What if I see Dr. Rice?"

And he said, "It would be appropriate to call her 'Secretary Rice.'" He spoke with a warm smile and an inviting manner. He had always represented himself in public and on camera with class. He was no different with us.

As we were talking with the Leavitts, Mrs. Bush walked up and introduced herself. Michele and I had always admired her. She always seemed to be above politics, and after seeing her on TV and watching the dignified way in which she carried herself, it was something else to speak with her. She wore a red dress, and her genuine smile, blue-blue eyes, honest face, and gracious personality made it a pleasure to meet her.

She quickly perceived that we knew the Leavitts because he was our governor in Utah. While we were visiting, a couple from Detroit stopped and said hello to the First Lady. They mentioned a conference they had just been to in Detroit where Mrs. Bush had met with six hundred of the local high-school coaches. She told us that she felt America was forgetting about teenage boys in our society. She said that next to their parents, boys looked up to their coaches, and so she was making a push for coaches to realize what an influence they could have on those youth.

My mind immediately went to my football coaches. I thought of Lee Salmans, Tom Rabb, LaVell Edwards, Ray Rhoades, Dick Vermeil, and Andy Reid. She was right. I have had the most impressive string of coaches of any player in the history of the game.

Secretary Leavitt then told how he had grown up with five brothers and had four sons of his own. He said he had basically been around fourteen- and fifteen-year-old boys his entire life and thought her agenda was great. Mrs. Bush was incredible. She looked everyone in the eye and was polite and genuine. She didn't leave anyone out of the conversation but looked around at each person and made sure that she connected with them. What a beautiful person.

Soon after Mrs. Bush left our little group, we met Roger Staubach and his wife, Marianne. They were the real deal. I say that because they looked at each other with a love in their eyes that spoke volumes about who they were together. It was a look that would be nearly impossible to fake. It seemed to me that he recognized that he did not get to where he was by himself. I asked them about their history, and they said they met in the second grade. It figured; they sure acted comfortable with each other. He told us he was in the real-estate business, developing sites all over the country. I was impressed with him because of all he had accomplished since finishing football. He was still contributing to society in more ways than just his fame as a football player. Standing next to him and talking with him was inspiring.

By now everyone was being escorted into the Red Room, a small room just off the foyer. There was a camera set up for every couple to get a picture with the president and Mrs. Bush. When it was our turn, Michele stood next to President Bush and I hopped on one leg and stood by Mrs. Bush. I was worried that I would lose my balance and fall on her. That picture hangs in my office as well, and it is another great reminder of the way we were treated by some wonderful people. The Bushes were a great example to me of class and kindness.

We were one of the last couples to get our picture taken. We then entered the Blue Room, where tables were beautifully set for dinner. We were given cards with our names and table numbers on them. Michele had table number three. As we were looking for our tables, President Bush walked up behind Michele and tapped her on her shoulder and said, "Michele, you're at my table. Follow me."

We looked at each other and wondered if that was really happening. Michele sat at the table with President Bush, the secretary of energy's wife, Dr. Benjamin Carsen (the most celebrated pediatric neurosurgeon in the world, from Detroit), the British ambassador, Roger Staubach, Charena Swann, Willie Mays, and the wife of the ambassador from Japan.

Before the president sat down, and while I was still trying to maneuver to my seat with my scooter, the president used his knife to tap on a glass at his table. While everyone else in the room was seated, I just stood there by the wall next to the window that looked out on the south lawn and toward the Washington Monument. I wondered how thick the glass must be and if it was bulletproof.

The president thanked everyone for being there and then asked us to join him in a prayer. I loved his prayer. It was a humble expression of gratitude to our Father in Heaven for the circumstances of the evening. The thing Michele and I remember most about his prayer was that he fervently asked the Lord for a blessing on our troops, wherever they served, and that he prayed for the expansion of freedom around the world. Because of the ease with which he prayed and his expressions of gratitude, it was evident to me that prayer was a part of his life. It was touching to hear *him* praying for *us*.

When I finally made it to my table, I couldn't believe the table setting. There were more plates than I had ever seen, and I wondered who else had eaten from them. I sat next to Pat Ryan, who was the chairman of the Aon Corporation and part owner of the Chicago Bears. He had lost 175 of his New York City employees during the September 11 terrorist attacks. Would it be possible for us to ever forget that? I hoped not. In our conversation he informed me that he had been at BYU two years before to accept an award given by the school for his ethical contribution to business. He smiled easily, asked me about the Eagles and BYU, and made me feel comfortable. He had an engaging personality, and I could have talked with him all night.

John Goodnight was also at our table, as well as the secretary of energy, Samuel Bodman. Secretary Bodman was the head of our round table. Following the instructions of Secretary Leavitt, I just watched and took my cues from him. Also seated at my table were Rusty Powell, the director for the National Gallery of the Arts; Allan Hubbard, the economic advisor to the president; Dr. Carsen's wife, Candy; Stephanie Johanns, the wife of the secretary of agriculture; and Mary Margaret, the wife of the late Jack Valenti. It was not hard to recognize that I was sitting with a table of very important people.

The food was as elegant as the ornate place settings. We started with some fancy oyster soup that was very tasty. The menu called it Oysters and Pearls (oyster stew garnished with Ossetia caviar). We were served a filet of beef that had a small potato under the meat. The rest of the official menu read: Tenderloin of Buffalo; Hudson River Foie Gras; Asparagus, Carrots, and Grilled Vegetable Bundles; Butterhead, Red Oak, and Arugula Salad; Raspberry Crème Brulee, Chocolate Flourless Cake, and Vanilla Sugared Beignet. Each person at the table had a menu and before the evening was over, we autographed each other's. I thought that was cool. I don't remember who provided the marker, but someone did, and we all signed them. That made for a nice keepsake. I wondered if they did that for each state dinner.

I mostly just listened to the conversation at my table but also chatted with Pat Ryan.

I later enjoyed hearing about the conversation at Michele's table. She had fun sitting with the president and the other guests.

He had done his homework on her because he introduced her to the table by asking about her volleyball career. Then he asked her how many children she had. The table gasped when she responded with four. They would have really gasped if they knew we would later have three more children.

President Bush and Roger Staubach shared their favorite Willie Mays stories with the table. Michele said Willie just smiled. He was quiet and he didn't say much all night. President Bush commented on the wish of so many young people that they might become the president of the United States. He said that as a young boy he wished he could be Willie Mays. I wanted to be Lynn Swann. It's great to have a wish, and it is great to have hope. We live in a beautiful country where children's dreams can come true.

The conversation at Michele's table turned to the funeral of President Ronald Reagan. President Bush was trying to describe the funeral procession, only he couldn't think of the word. The only word that came to his mind was *parade*. Michele said that she spoke up and said exactly what she pictured her mom, Geneva Fellows, would have said: "I'm sure President Reagan wouldn't mind if you called it a parade."

He responded with, "You're right, he wouldn't. He was a great man. Of course you know that, being from Utah."

Michele said, "Actually, I grew up in Las Vegas back when it was Republican."

President Bush smiled and laughed. He knew how to treat people. His halting way when speaking was often ridiculed by others, but I thought he was comfortable in his own skin and whatever mistakes he might have made were more endearing than something to be laughed at.

When dinner was over, the president just stood up, helped the two ladies by his side out of their chairs, then walked over and helped Mrs. Bush out of her seat and out of the room. We all followed them into the hall heading toward the East Room.

We stopped in the hallway for a few minutes, and the next thing I knew, President Bush and Lynn Swann were at my side and we were talking about Philadelphia. Our conversation flowed to the topic of a glitch with one of the voting machines in Philly during the election, and the president chuckled about that. The machine malfunction had awarded votes to the Democratic ticket before the polls were even open, but President Bush found some humor in that. His good humor was another great quality I observed in our commander in chief.

After a few minutes of visiting, we went into the East Room for some entertainment. Herbie Hancock was the celebrated guest and was asked to play some jazz piano pieces. He had just won a Grammy Award the night before and was going to record a song with my favorite musician, Paul Simon, the next day. He played four numbers on the piano and then wished everyone a Happy Valentine's Day and sat down.

President Bush then stood up and told us that the evening was a gift to him from Laura. The dinner, the guests, and the music had all been planned by her. He said he was pleased that we could be there with him to celebrate Valentine's Day, thanked us for a great evening, and wished us all well. Then he and Mrs. Bush headed out of the room. It was only 9:15 P.M. I shouldn't have been surprised; I had heard he was known for going to bed early. I remembered something my brother Dave used to say, "Early to bed and early to rise makes a man a stud."

As soon as the president and First Lady left the room, Mrs. Leavitt came over to Michele and thanked her for the way that we had represented BYU and the state of Utah. Michele was very impressed with that and later commented that Mrs. Leavitt could have easily just kept that to herself. But she went out of her way to say something nice to someone else. The room was emptying and it took extra effort for Mrs. Leavitt to do that. That was class.

We stayed in the East Room for a few minutes and visited

*Surrounded by greatness! Lynn Swann and Roger Staubach
in the White House, February 2005.*

some more with the Staubachs and the Swanns. We finally made
our way to the President's Elevator. As we were riding down,
Lynn's wife asked the man operating the elevator if he was going
to give us a tour of the place. He responded that he was not about
to upset the president and our only ride was down to the first
floor. I thought it was fun that she tried. She wasn't stuffy, and she
just wanted to have a little fun with the guy. I was also glad that
the Swanns and the Staubachs were just as happy to be there as we
were. We were impressed to be with one of the greatest Cowboys
and one of the greatest Steelers of all time.

On the ground floor we visited the library and took some
photos together. Roger, Lynn, and I posed for a picture that I will
be proud to pass on to our kids. All night I felt as though I was
surrounded by greatness and was grateful for that unusual opportunity. I was with people who treated others with class and respect.
I was inspired to be nicer to other people. I wanted to be as

gracious as President and Mrs. Bush, Secretary Leavitt, Roger Staubach, and Lynn Swann. That is the beauty of being surrounded by great people: they make you want to be a kinder and better person.

We were eventually ushered out of the library by the White House staff and into the Vermeil Room (pronounced vur-may), or the Gold Room, where portraits of some of the First Ladies, including Nancy Reagan, are on display.

After saying our good-byes to the Staubachs and Swanns, we got in our car and headed home. Neither of us had felt comfortable eating large portions of our dinner, and we were still hungry, so we stopped and got some Chinese takeout. What a great Valentine's Day for us!

I think we will remember it for a very long time.

CHAPTER 24

THE NFL IN CHINA

While participating in my first Pro Bowl in Hawaii, I was introduced by some NFL representatives to a sports marketing firm from Asia. They wanted to know about the possibility of my doing a player tour the following May. It sounded like a lot of fun, and Michele and I planned the trip. We went on a ten-day media and goodwill campaign and visited the countries of Taiwan, Thailand, and Singapore. We were accompanied by Anna Pettiti from NFL headquarters in New York City. A three-man crew from NFL Films also joined us to document the trip.

We stayed in Taiwan for four days. It was so much fun for me to travel through the area where I had served as a missionary so many years before. I struggled to remember the Chinese that I used to speak with so much fluency and was surprised how much of the vocabulary had disappeared from my brain. I knew what I wanted to say, but my tongue had forgotten how to say it. Anna put together our schedule, which was packed from early in the morning until late at night with interviews on the radio, on TV, and with the print media. We visited schools and parks in the Taipei area for filming and explaining the game of football. The trip was put together in connection with ESPN Star out of Singapore, which helped fund the promotional tour.

Michele was surprised by all the traffic in Taiwan. I had told her how crowded it was, but it still took visiting the island herself before she could totally comprehend just how congested it really is.

The highlight of the trip for me was a day-long visit in the town of Taichung, where I had spent the majority of my mission. It had changed so much since I had been there that I hardly recognized it. There were new buildings everywhere. We attended a professional baseball game, and I was invited to throw out the first pitch. I had driven by that field numerous times as a missionary and it was sweet to finally go inside. Not only did I go inside, but I hung out with the players and was able to speak with them in their language. We talked about football and they all thought it was a great sport to watch. I grew up playing baseball when I was young and I felt right at home on the mound.

We also did a Mother's Day pep rally-type appearance on a stage outside a new shopping mall in Taichung. It was fun to address so many people in Chinese. When I was a missionary I would have loved to speak to so many people at one time. They were an energetic crowd. I threw out footballs and T-shirts and we all enjoyed a festive atmosphere. When the pep rally was finished we joined the local Taiwan media group for lunch inside the shopping mall. I don't think I have ever been in such a crowded building.

After the several media appointments that day I was given the night off to do whatever we wanted. I met with the LDS congregation where I had once lived. We held a meeting known as a "fireside get together" where Michele and I shared some stories and bore our testimonies of the Savior. The meeting was conducted by Steve Hsiung, who was a missionary with me in the early 90s. He was now serving as the bishop, or lay leader, of the congregation. He had been born and raised in Taiwan and had been a fun and energetic missionary. It was great to see him again.

When the meeting was over, I offered to answer questions from those in attendance. That was the best part. A woman seated in the back of the room, who I instantly recognized, stood up and said, "You keep talking about Feng Yuan as an area that you loved when you were a missionary here. I feel bad to say this, but I live in Feng Yuan, and I don't remember you!"

That caused everyone to giggle, but it was understandable. I looked a lot different than when I served as a missionary. I had put on fifty pounds and I didn't wear my Clark Kent glasses anymore. I looked at her and said, "Well, I remember you. You are Sister Wu, and you were married to the branch president when I lived in Feng Yuan. You had a one-year-old baby boy, and we visited your family at your house a bunch of times."

She stared at me with a perplexed look on her face. She wondered how in the world this big tall guy from America could know so much stuff about her when she couldn't remember him at all. The same thing happened with another family in the audience. The Lu family asked a question and I responded by telling them about their family and how I had visited them several times as well. They were stunned, just as Sister Wu had been.

I had brought some photos with me of some of them when I was a missionary and had known them many years earlier. As we looked at them together, they laughed out loud when they saw what I looked like before. They all said the same thing, "You have become so fat!"

It was a great evening spent with wonderful friends. I really enjoyed seeing them again. I told them that I was surrounded by their greatness and they were a big reason why I was fortunate enough to play in the NFL. I am so grateful that I was given that experience to tell them thank you for treating me so well when I was nineteen years old.

I was hoping to see my old friend called Gypsy. He was a young man in Taiwan who was a few years older than I. He had suffered some kind of injury or illness that impaired his speech but was a great friend to the missionaries, even though he could barely be understood. When I had known him, he spent his days traveling all over the island of Taiwan, living like a gypsy and trying to help the missionaries, which must have been how he got that name. He popped up in random places, and I saw him numerous times during my two years—sometimes at church and other times on the streets or in train stations. He would ask people for food, and to my knowledge, that was how he survived. I didn't know if he was still alive.

I was shocked with happiness when I got to Taichung and saw him standing in the hallway at the church. He just happened to be walking through. I took a picture with Gypsy and told him that I had been a missionary years before and I had fed him many times. I don't know what kind of understanding he had, but it was a highlight for me to see him again. I felt it was not just a coincidence that he happened to be walking through the hallway the same time I visited the church for the first time in over a decade.

From Taiwan we set off for Singapore, where we visited ESPN Star headquarters and filmed several interviews that they would show throughout the year. We also visited an American school called the Eagles. They had a football team and we conducted a football clinic at their school. I was surprised to discover the large number of expatriate families who were working there for big oil companies and technology companies. The school was as nice as the best college campus in the United States. It was immaculate with computers on every desk in the classrooms. What a great opportunity for those people to live in Singapore for a few years.

We also visited the US embassy in Singapore. Ambassador Frank Lavin invited us to play football with the Marine detail on the grass field out in front of the embassy. There were four

Standing with NFL Commissioner Paul Tagliabue in Beijing, China,
during the city finals of the NFL Flag Football tournament.

Marines who played catch with me for a few minutes in the hot sun. I was so impressed with the Marines. If I were ever in trouble somewhere in the world, I would want them to come find me. These men were clean-cut and sharp, as fit as linebackers, and as polite as they could be.

After leaving Singapore, we visited Thailand for three days. Bangkok was almost as crowded as Taiwan. I wanted to speak Chinese with everyone we encountered, but they just looked at me as though I was crazy. The people spoke Thai, not Chinese. I learned a few phrases of Thai, and the people were all very gracious when I tried to speak with them. Most of them could speak English fairly well.

I enjoyed the numerous interviews I gave where I shared my passion for the game of football. We put on a big flag-football

On the Great Wall of China, surrounded by ten teams from around the world who were competing in the NFL Flag Football World Championships.

clinic for some of the local flag-football teams that were a part of the NFL Flag Football League.

I met a kid named Stang who was really a bright and enthusiastic young person. He was a lot of fun because he knew the game of football as well as any fan in America. He had his own Donovan McNabb Eagles jersey and was anxious to share with me everything he knew about the game. It was a kick, being in Thailand, talking with a kid who was as crazy about the game as I was. Even though we had a language barrier, we talked like brothers and understood each other perfectly.

One of the things I love about sports is that they are universal. It doesn't matter what language is spoken, sports fly under the radar of life's problems and complications. Sports are one of the greatest and most simple unifiers. That's why the Olympics is so popular around the world and why increasing numbers of people outside America are drawn to our uniquely American games of football and basketball.

Since that initial Pacific Rim tour, I have represented the NFL several times in China. Gordon Smeaton and Michael Stokes of the NFL's International Division have coordinated their efforts so that I could help promote the game with the biggest potential audience on the planet. They initially asked me to help with some highlight packages at NFL Films in Chinese. I filmed them during the play-offs of 2003 at the Eagles facilities. Because we lost the NFC Championship game that year to the Carolina Panthers, I would not be going to the Super Bowl. Since I was available, I was asked to call the Super Bowl in Chinese between the Panthers and the Patriots as the color analyst. That was a great opportunity.

Even though football terms were not a part of my speaking jargon as a missionary, I knew I could brush up enough to have some fun with the broadcast. I had never before called a football game even in English. I couldn't believe that I was going to be doing the game in Chinese on CCTV that had a potential audience of 1.3 billion people. I talked with Darryl Johnston the day before the game. He played fullback for the Dallas Cowboys when they won three Super Bowl championships in the 90s and was going to call the game for an international feed to the United Kingdom. When he learned what I was going to be doing, he laughed that I was going to be covering the game for more people than any other media analyst at the Super Bowl.

Watching the game was bittersweet since I wanted to be playing and had a lot of work to do at the same time. I prepared a chart full of Chinese terms that I kept in front of me the whole game. I could refer to that chart at anytime to help me describe the action. But when I was excited, I would revert to my missionary vocabulary. I would say things such as, "I testify that Tom Brady can throw a true pass!" I would much rather have been playing in the game, but it was also a great experience for me to work with the CCTV team of broadcasters.

That experience dovetailed into my next trip to the Far East. The following year the Eagles were in the Super Bowl. Because of my injury, I was not able to play, but just being there with the team was the realization of a lifelong dream. Before the game, the owner of the Eagles, Jeffrey Lurie, visited with me about Commissioner Tagliabue's interest in traveling to China and invited me to go with him. I was pumped at the opportunity. I met the commissioner on the sideline before the game and told him I would love to do a media tour with him to China. He was a lot taller than I expected. It was fun to visit with him on the sideline of the biggest stage in the world. He told me to plan on a trip that May.

The trip to China with Commissioner Tagliabue was eye-opening in every way. We started with a couple of days in Shanghai. Words could not express how happy I was to finally be in China. I had thought about visiting China ever since I received my mission call in July of 1990. To be there was a dream come true. To be there with the commissioner of the NFL was even better. I would never have thought as a missionary in Taiwan that I would return to the Chinese people as a traveling companion with Paul Tagliabue. He was generous with the Chinese people. I have seen many people who could not speak the language get frustrated and impatient very quickly with the language barrier. I never saw the commissioner even hint that he was frustrated. He was gracious toward each person he met. It didn't matter if we were visiting with the school principal, the janitor, the hotel bellman, the mayor of Beijing, or any of the expatriate businessmen that we met; he treated them all the same, with class.

We visited a middle school and spoke to the students outside of their classrooms on the ball field. The commissioner and I gave them a short message about the game and then I held a football clinic and enjoyed teaching them how to throw and catch. At the time, the NFL had begun a long-term effort to build interest in the game at the grassroots level by creating flag-football leagues at the middle-school level. One hundred twenty-five schools from the north of China to the south were a part of that plan. The kids loved to play, and the schools that didn't have the flag-football program wanted to be a part of it as well.

We also spoke to the American Chamber of Commerce in Shanghai. I shared my love for the game of football as well as my love for the Chinese people. It was humbling for me to visit with a room full of successful expatriate businessmen and women because fresh on my mind was the tremendous influence two other expatriate businessmen had had on my life.

I was referring to Kent Watson from PricewaterhouseCoopers and Tim Stratford from the US Embassy in Beijing. I explained that I had been dramatically influenced for good under the guidance of those two people. They had busy lives full of promise, promotion, and lucrative contracts. They had put all of that on hold to serve as mission presidents to a bunch of nineteen-year-old missionaries. Not only did they put their careers on hold, but they put their shoulders to the wheel in their efforts to work and to teach us to work. They changed my life in every way. In fact, I told my audience that I never would have been able to play football in college or the NFL if it hadn't been for their direct influence on my life and work ethic.

I shared with the American Chamber of Commerce group that they could be just as influential in the lives of others if they would look around for ways that they could serve. They could be of service by surrounding others with their greatness and the unique gifts they had to offer. I expressed my belief that given their special talents and abilities they could bless the lives of people by consciously looking at their schedules and making time to reach out to others.

Commissioner Tagliabue shared with them his passion for the game. He also brought an honesty and transparency to his job that knocked my socks off. After speaking briefly, he offered to answer any questions. He fielded everything. Nothing was too off-agenda for him to respond. The response that most surprised me was his answer to a question about the use of steroids and other perform-ance enhancing drugs that were marring the integrity of the game. It was his opinion that the use of human growth hormones was the biggest offense in sports. He acknowledged that it was a huge problem in the NFL and that as the commissioner he was very much concerned about it.

He informed the group that there was not yet a blood test, a hair follicle test, a urine test, or any other test that could detect human growth hormone. He said as soon as the scientists were successful in developing a means of detecting usage, he would im-plement testing without delay.

I had no idea that the commissioner was so knowledgeable about the widespread abuse of the drug. I took heart that he not only knew about it but that he was as active as he was about find-ing a way to test for it. He did not hide anything. He admitted that athletes abused PEDs (performance enhancing drugs), and he stressed the need to eliminate their use because it would ruin the game. From that moment on I had even more respect for him. He was an honest man and I knew that he could be trusted.

We traveled to Beijing for another few days and our schedule was packed with important meetings. At each meeting, the com-missioner had me sit right next to him and he would introduce me to the group as one of the NFL's finest players. How did that make me feel to be introduced by the commissioner in that way? It was humbling, of course, but being with him made me proud of the association I had with the NFL and more grateful for the won-derful opportunity it had been for me to play in the League.

We also addressed the graduate students at Beijing Culture

Playing catch with a football on the Great Wall of China.
The size and scope of the Great Wall is truly awe-inspiring.

University and described for them what it was like to be participants in the most popular sport in America.

We met with the mayor of Beijing, and I gave him a long-sleeve Philadelphia Eagles shirt that I autographed in Chinese. We also met with Li Zhaoxing, China's foreign minister. He spoke wonderful English and read us some poetry that he loved. Commissioner Tagliabue was perfectly at home speaking with any of those people. It was obvious by their reactions that they were duly impressed with him. We attended the Beijing City finals for the NFL flag-football tournament. We were both gratified to see the kids of China having fun playing a game that we both loved.

At the tournament I was introduced to Willie Yang, who was the president of Reebok in China. He was an accomplished individual who reminded me of the commissioner. He asked me how

I was able to speak Chinese and I told him it was because I had been a Mormon missionary in Taiwan many years before. He spoke fluent English, Chinese, and Spanish. I thought it unusual that he would speak Spanish, and he then told me the story of his life.

He was born in Taiwan, where his mother was a surgeon in the Taiwan Army. When he was a young boy, two Mormon missionaries met his mother and taught her the gospel of Jesus Christ. She believed and converted to aligning her life with the teachings of the Savior. His family was then required to move to Argentina, where he lived for the next several years and where he learned to speak fluent Spanish. He said the Mormon missionaries ran into his family again and taught and fellowshipped them. He thought it was incredible that whether he was in Taiwan, Argentina, or China he would run into the Mormon missionaries, who always treated him with love and kindness.

I smiled at Willie and pointed to my friend who was standing with me on that football field in Beijing. It was Rob Lamb, my former missionary companion in Taiwan. He became an attorney and had built a strong Chinese practice and was accompanying me since my wife was pregnant and unable to travel. I told Willie that there he was in Beijing, and he was still surrounded by Mormon missionaries. We had fun talking and making friends. He was one of the most outstanding people I met in China. He shared a love for his country and his people that brought it to life for me. I better understood how the Chinese wanted to be recognized for their gifts to the world just the same as every other people. I was in the presence of greatness, standing there with Willie.

Each day began with a breakfast at Commissioner Tagliabue's hotel where he would hold court with the whole NFL group by telling stories of the great players of the past—players such as Byron "Whizzer" White, Alan Page, Walter Payton, and Roger

Staubach. He loved all of those players and brought their memories to life in the way that he spoke of them.

We usually finished the evening with another group dinner. Again, the commissioner would make the dinner more enjoyable by sharing his memories and the lessons of life that he learned from others. He said that he had learned one of the greatest lessons from his father. When Paul was young, his father would tell him, "Don't be a jackass; use your brains and not your back." That was one of the reasons why he went into the law profession. He played basketball at Georgetown and was quite an athlete in his day.

At a dinner to celebrate his and his wife, Chan's, fortieth wedding anniversary, he told of a unique lesson that he recently learned and that had changed his mind about something. He was invited by Arthur Blank, owner of the Atlanta Falcons, to attend a retreat at a location in Montana. Although it was difficult for him to get away for a couple of days during the middle of the season, he made a commitment to Mr. Blank and he made sure that he fulfilled it. Before he got there, he discovered that Stephen Covey would be the featured speaker at the retreat. As soon as he learned that, he said he felt like canceling. He told us he had seen Stephen's books for sale in every airport around the world and felt their popularity was probably due more to hype and marketing than substance. He wondered if he would be able to able to handle a couple of days sequestered with the author.

What I learned from the commissioner that night was that he is as humble as he is accomplished. He confessed to us that being with Stephen Covey in person had dramatically changed his perception of him. He couldn't say enough about how much he had enjoyed being exposed to Covey's approach to life and his philosophy of relationships and behavior. In fact, he said, he wished he could have spent more than just those few days with him.

He encouraged every one of us to buy Stephen's book, *The 7*

Habits of Highly Effective Families. Then he shared with us some of the lessons he had learned from the author—the importance of taking one night a week to be with our families and to focus love and attention on each member. He talked about some other principles he had learned and said how grateful he was to have had the opportunity to change his mind about Stephen Covey.

That was a lesson and a revelation to me about humility. The commissioner, who is one of the smartest men I've ever met, was open to learning something new. He was not too proud to acknowledge he had been wrong. And he was even more willing to share the lessons that he learned. It was awesome to sit with him that night and see greatness in action. I got the book as soon as I got home.

Pete Abitante was the assistant to the commissioner and was with us on the tour. I sat next to him a number of times, and he told me about his appreciation for Paul Tagliabue. Pete was a longtime employee and executive of the NFL and after having such a close relationship with the commissioner could not have been more loyal to him. He shared some of the experiences the two had had together, which only reinforced my admiration for Paul Tagliabue. It was an incredible opportunity for me to see the leaders of the NFL and realize that I was in great hands as a player because of their integrity and proficiency. They were professional in every way.

I wished that every NFL player could have had the same opportunity to spend time with Commissioner Tagliabue and Pete Abitante and Gordon Smeaton so that they could see why the NFL was so successful. Sure, part of the reason was because of what we did on the field, but it was revealing to see the caliber of people who ran things in the front office. I had the opposite experience of Dorothy in *The Wizard of Oz*. When she finally got to see the wizard, she found out that he was a little man behind the big curtain and the big fake voice. When the curtain was pulled

Attending an NFL dinner in Beijing, China, with Commissioner Paul Tagliabue and Jeffrey Lurie, owner of the Philadelphia Eagles.

back on the talented people who ran the NFL, I found them to be larger than life and way better than I expected.

While we were in Beijing we attended an economic forum put on by *Fortune* magazine. Commissioner Tagliabue thought it would be fun if I introduced him in Chinese. That is what I did. I introduced myself in English and asked all the foreigners (non-Chinese speakers) to put on their translator headphones. Then I introduced the commissioner to the group. Clyde Drexler was in the audience and he looked at me the way most Chinese people looked at me when I spoke to them in their language—with wide eyes and a big smile. When I sat down, Clyde asked me how in the world I had learned to speak Chinese. I told him of my experience in Taiwan, all the while staring at him with wide eyes and a big smile because I had admired him for many years as "Clyde the Glide." I loved how he played the game of basketball.

Ma Guo Li, the founder of CCTV-5, the sports station in China, was also in the audience. He told me that I did a great job and that I had made only one small mistake at the end. Ma was put in charge of the Beijing Olympic Broadcast Company and was in charge of everything put on TV during the Beijing Olympics. We had met a year earlier, when I was color man for the Super Bowl and he was in Houston in charge of the delegation from CCTV. It was fun to see him again, and I appreciated his mini Chinese lesson. He gave me a nice compliment and at the same time made sure that my head didn't get any bigger.

As part of the economic forum, we had dinner with the president of China, Hu Jintao, at the Great Hall of the People in Tiananmen Square. It was quite an experience to be in the heart of the People's Republic of China headquarters. Just three months before, I had eaten dinner with the President of the United States in the White House. The dinner at the Great Hall was not as intimate as at the White House. I was one of about a thousand people in attendance. But the experience was not lost on me that I had the unique good fortune to have dinner with the two biggest leaders in the world.

On the flight back to America, I sat next to Commissioner Tagliabue, and we talked most of the way. It was awesome to finish the week we had spent together with more conversation about football, China, and the love we both have for the game. He was the real deal. I told him how impressed I was by how patient he had been with everyone and that the same was true for his wife, Chan. She was from Georgia, and I thought they were a perfect team and great ambassadors for the NFL.

The commissioner retired a year later and invited me to share some comments at his retirement party, which was attended by many of the owners and most of the NFL staff from New York City. I was grateful for the invitation, and I looked forward to sharing with the audience what I had learned from some of my experiences with the commissioner. As a player I had a perspective that was different and unique from all of the executives who would be there.

There was so much air traffic that my plane had to land in Syracuse for an hour and refuel before we could land at Newark. I was disappointed because I thought I would miss the entire event. When I finally got to Newark, Pete Abitante called to tell me that the evening was almost over and that I had missed it. I jumped in a cab and told the driver that I hoped to get downtown pretty fast. He smiled and said that it would take a lot longer than I hoped it would, but as we drove we did not encounter any traffic at all. We flew through streets that were usually choked with cars and trucks.

Pete called again when we were almost there and said the program was running long and I still might be able to make it. I threw my suit on right there in the backseat of the cab and was ready as soon as I arrived at the hotel.

I got up to the ballroom just as the evening was wrapping up and all of the guests were standing in an ovation to the commissioner. I was walking in as people were starting to walk out. But as soon as the commissioner saw me, he grabbed the microphone and invited everyone back into the ballroom for a special presentation. He introduced me to the group with more superlatives than I deserved and gave me the floor at his party.

I was glad that I hadn't missed the chance to share with the people just how much I thought of him. They needed to know what the players thought about him. They needed to know that he was the best in the business and that he had an uncommon common touch with people all over the world. I described our experience in China and his patience with the people and the language. I kept it brief, although I would have liked to have taken a lot longer. I was so grateful to have been included and to have had the chance to thank him for being such an outstanding commissioner for the NFL for so many years.

I continued to represent the NFL in China over the next several years. Many doors were opened to me through my association with the NFL and the ability to speak Chinese. One trip was for the US embassy Fourth of July party that was held for Chinese government officials and guests. Ambassador Clark Randt asked me make some remarks at the party, along with him. It was an NFL-themed party, with pennants from each team decorating the ballroom. There were football highlight videos playing on big screens throughout the room. It was a special way to celebrate the Fourth of July.

I took my daughter Emily with me, who was only ten at the time. On the morning of the Fourth, while the rest of our family was running in a little Freedom Festival 5K in Provo, Utah, Emily and I held our own Freedom 5K. We ran from our hotel down to Tiananmen Square and back. Emily and I missed the fireworks, the picnics, but most of all being with the rest of the family on such a special day. She was very homesick the whole time we were there, but it was a great experience for both of us. I am glad that she felt what it means to be homesick.

Benjamin Watson, the great tight end for the New England Patriots, was also in Beijing for that trip. He noticed that Emily was feeling pretty homesick and he asked her about it. He told her that it can be intimidating to be the minority or the only one of a color or ethnic background. He was awesome. I was so glad that he talked to her and taught her such a valuable lesson about feeling empathy for others. She learned firsthand what it meant to be away from home and to be the minority.

On another visit, Michele and our baby boy Maxwell made the trip with me when I was asked to introduce the Beijing Olympic mascots to the world at the International Olympics press conference. It was held at the Red Theater in Beijing. The trip was noteworthy because everywhere we went the Chinese people thought Max was so cute. They would say, "Hao ke, ai, Da yanjing xiao bizi!" which means, "Very cute, big eyes, little nose!" We heard that so many times that week that it became the theme of the trip. We visited the Great Wall of China, the most impressive human accomplishment that I had ever seen, and all the Chinese tourists repeated the same phrase, "Big eyes, little nose!" Max had his face touched by hundreds of friendly Chinese people and his photo taken with as many.

CHAPTER 25

LIFE AFTER FOOTBALL

After retiring from football I entered the work force in Utah as the general manager of Century Steel, a rebar supply company with headquarters in Las Vegas, Nevada. Michele's brother Steve was the CFO for the company.

The company had discussed the idea of opening an office in Utah as they expanded throughout the West. When Steve first visited with me about the idea of my working for him, I thought he was crazy. I didn't know anything about the steel industry or working with steel workers. The only thing I knew about steel was that the Pittsburgh Steelers had one tough defense.

But I met with Todd Leany, who was the president of the company, and we started to get acquainted. I had a lot of learning to do before I would be comfortable running a division in Utah. I spent four months touring one of the steel mills in Southern California, personally interviewing as many people from the company and the industry as I possibly could, and doing my share of praying about it. I asked the estimators, detailers, accountants, and secretaries what they thought of Todd and what they thought of Century Steel. The response was unanimously positive.

I was impressed by how positively Todd was viewed by all of his employees. I was also impressed that he kept his ego in check. One of the first questions that I asked him was how he dealt with workers or competitors who were either union or nonunion who wanted to get tough with him about his decisions. He looked at me with a puzzled look and responded by saying that he didn't get into any of that stuff. He said that he just tried to treat people the way he wanted to be treated and he never worried about tough-guy retaliation or acts of intimidation that often made the news in Philly. I knew Todd Leany was the kind of person that I wanted to work with because of his integrity, competence, and his kindness.

We opened an office in Salt Lake City and set up meetings with the estimators at each of the big construction companies in Utah that might use rebar in their projects. It was quite an education. I stood in front of those people knowing full well that they knew I was a novice. I didn't try to hide anything about the fact that I was learning about the industry as fast as I could, but I answered their questions as well as I could and told them I would get back to them when I didn't know the answers. It was exciting and frightening at the same time. The learning curve was very steep. I relied on Todd for much of my training.

He told me to pursue a placing company in Utah that we could team up with and acquire. I visited with Frank Sutera, who had the best reputation in the state for placing steel, doing it on time and under budget. Frank's oldest boy, Casey, played defensive line for the University of Utah, but Frank had no idea who I was or anything about my career in the NFL. I liked it that way.

I always found it refreshing to talk with people who knew nothing of my football career. The first thing that impressed me about Frank was the love that he had for his crew. He couldn't talk about his workers without telling me how great they were and that they worked harder than anyone in the business. It was as though he was telling me about his family or his closest friends. I had played team sports my entire life, and I was talking with the greatest team player that I had ever met. He was saying all of the things that I liked hearing from my own teammates. He was a tough guy but he was not so tough that he would hide his true feelings for his guys. That was impressive.

The smartest and best move that I made in the steel business was teaming up with Todd Leany and Frank Sutera. Frank brought his company, Lakeside Rebar, and rolled it into Century Steel. Lakeside Rebar had the strongest reputation in the business, and it was a major leap of faith for Frank and all of his guys to join forces with us. That meant that they would lose the name of their company that they had worked so hard to define. I had great respect for their decision.

Frank and I began immediately spending all of the workday together. I needed his wisdom and I trusted his experience in everything I did. He had a crew of forty union ironworkers that he had gone to battle with over the years. He made sure that I got to know every one of them. When we shared the news of our acquisition, Frank made sure that I was there to look each of his guys in the eye and discuss the advantages. When we made any decision for the company that affected the guys, Frank had me visit with them face-to-face. I loved that about Frank. He cared about the individual members of the team. He cared. He loved them. They were his family, and they were becoming my family as well.

We worked on several important jobs together. When there were shortages in a load, someone had to get the new rebar fabricated, loaded on a truck, and hauled to the job site immediately. When no one else was available, I drove a load of rebar in the back of my truck to Boise, Idaho. One of our jobs with Layton Construction was the Boise State football stadium press box expansion. It was a large project with numerous challenges that needed to be met. Frank and I worked in tandem to answer all of the questions and to see the project to completion. We leaned on Curtis Van Norman and Danny Prince, guys from the Las Vegas office, to get all of the problems solved. It was not easy starting a new company, but with Frank's constant help and direction we were succeeding.

I gained enormous respect for the crew. They worked like craftsmen—in the rain, snow, heat, and freezing temperatures of Utah. We had jobs in the tops of the mountains making hotels and water tanks. Sometimes our jobs would get shut down because of the snow, but the guys were always there to work through it. I had played football in some of the coldest weather imaginable, but I had the luxury of heated seats, hot air blowers on the sideline, and hot cider if we were so inclined.

Our rod busters (ironworkers) stood out in the wicked mountain elements all day long, tying steel as fast as they could. They also had to carry the heavy rods from wherever the truck unloaded them to the place of installation. I was amazed, watching their agility as they scrambled up steep inclines and over rough ground. Their feet were as coordinated and nimble as cats. Their hands were tougher than leather and their hearts were what made this country great. I could not have been more impressed than I was working with people who made up the foundation of the United States of America.

After I had spent a year and a half with Century Steel, the company was acquired by Pacific Coast Steel, a subsidiary of Gerdau Ameristeel, which was the largest steel provider in the world. It was going to take Century Steel from a large, privately held, family-owned business to a large, publicly traded company. Michele and I deliberated and made the firm decision to move on from the steel industry and let the steel professionals take over. I was compensated by getting our Utah office off the ground.

Todd Leany said that he was sad to see me go. I was sad to go.

I would miss my association with him and the rest of the guys. But I was grateful for the amazing opportunity that he gave me to run the business in Utah. I was also glad to turn the keys of the operation over to Frank, who knew every nook and cranny of the business. Besides the advice of trusted people, the book *Good to Great* by Jim Collins was the best resource I had. I recommended it to anyone and everyone because the principles in it had been so sound, instructive, and extremely helpful to me as I tried to learn the business.

When I left Century Steel or PCH, I really missed my association with Frank. He and I had been bound at the hip for a year of my life. He was one of the greatest men I had ever met. He had heart. He had love. He had compassion. He had unyielding toughness. He had a desire to be the best by performing, not by pretending. Frank was a self-made success story. I would not have been successful if it were not for Frank. Every day that I went to work, I benefitted from his greatness.

One of the desires I had following my football career was to "give back" something in payment for the success I had enjoyed. I think every successful athlete, businessman, or professional ought to find some way to return part of his good fortune to society. Aside from speaking at schools and church groups and helping my friends such as Steve Young who run their own charities, I chose two main avenues to give back.

The first was a commitment to help the American Indian Services provide scholarships for willing participants who had good grades and paid for half of their tuition. I had been more than casually interested in Native Americans since I was in fifth grade. My teacher, Dennis Knuckles, read us many books about the history of the West; among them were *Sitting Bull, Crazy Horse, Custer's Last Stand,* and *Tonka,* which was a story about a cavalry horse that survived the Battle of the Little Bighorn. I developed early on an admiration of and a love for Native Americans, especially Crazy

Horse. I admired their ingenuity, their resourcefulness, their intelligence, their respect for the land, and their history.

When I walked on to the BYU football team, there was a Native American named Nathan Clah who walked on at the same time. Nathan was from Shiprock, New Mexico, and played quarterback. We became fast friends. After our freshman year, Nathan left school for two years to serve an LDS mission. While serving his mission, he was hit in the head by a group of thugs. His cheekbone was broken and it required a titanium plate to hold his head together, which of course precluded him from playing any more football.

He came home for a couple of weeks to recuperate, and I visited with him at that time and learned he held no malice whatsoever for the guys who did that to him. After recovering, he was able to finish his mission. When he returned home, he got married and had a child. Then Nathan's life was tragically cut short by leukemia. Nathan was a great friend, and I wanted to help Indian students like him have a chance at an education.

I knew that Steve Young used to visit with the Native Americans on their reservations in Arizona, Utah, and New Mexico. When he decided to put more emphasis on his own charity, I was invited by Dale Tingey, who ran American Indian Services, to visit the reservations and speak with the young students about the importance of getting an education. I would tell them that gaining an education was the key to making a better life for themselves and their families. I came to believe that an education was one of the greatest gifts that one person could give to another.

I have since visited with Native American students from all over the Navajo, Hopi, and Zuni reservations. I have been able to conduct football clinics with them in many cities and I have seen their great desire to get better. They loved following the game and were familiar with most of the current and former players. They were not unlike students anywhere else in the world, in that when they discovered that someone cared about them, they opened their hearts to them. Working with them over the last thirteen years has only made me love them more.

Johnny Miller, the former professional golfer and lead golf analyst for NBC Sports, has dedicated a great deal of his time every year to holding golf tournament fund-raisers for American Indian Services. He holds tournaments in Utah, Arizona, New Mexico, California, Nevada, and Idaho. He has been a valuable mentor to me and has inspired me to continue to serve the Native American people.

Working with Dale Tingey over the years taught me what a life without guile is all about. He has carried the American Indian Services on his back and has been the principal fund-raiser and the heartbeat of the whole organization. He has a bond with the Native Americans that is contagious. It would be impossible to spend five minutes of time with Dale without wanting to give part of your life to help these wonderful people. Dale served as mission president for a couple of years to Native American people. He has given his whole life to serving them. Whenever I am around Dale, I have a greater sense of giving that makes me feel good.

The second way I have chosen to "give back" is to use whatever notoriety I have to raise money for the Cystic Fibrosis Foundation. When I was playing with the Eagles, we had an annual gala that raised money for CF. I became aware then of the dreadful disease, and I have always wanted to do something about it. The drugs that have been developed over the last ten years have added ten years to the life expectancy of a carrier. That is major progress. One of the best ways that I thought I could help was to hold a celebrity golf tournament. Over the last two years, we have helped raise over $200,000 for the CF organization. It has been fun and inspiring to see the support from good people as we rally to help find a cure.

I put together a board for my tournament that consists of members of the local CF chapter and people who either have the disease, have kids with the disease, or care about someone who has the disease. Since everyone who is on the board has that kind of connection, it is not hard for every person to give of himself to make the golf tournament special and a success. As a board, we do not receive one dollar for our efforts, but we do receive great satisfaction from trying to help find a cure for CF. I can't wait until there is a cure for the disease. It will be a beautiful moment. I will smile and think of all the hours that have been put in by so many around the world, and I will be glad to have been a small part of the effort to eradicate the disease from the earth. I'm confident that our small efforts here in Utah are contributing to the great effort to find a cure.

Paul Shoemaker, the same guy who threw me a touchdown pass during my first spring game at BYU, helped me establish a relationship with CF. After I retired from football, we called their foundation and asked them if we could organize a golf tournament to help them raise money for a cure. Their response was immediate in the affirmative. They were thrilled to join forces. Nancy Bill, the executive director of the Utah and Idaho Chapter of the Cystic Fibrosis Foundation, threw down the welcome mat and told us that she was willing to work together to make our vision a success. She did just that. She was at every board meeting and gave freely of her time and energy.

Even though we were organizing a first-class event for the state of Utah, I didn't initially know how much impact it would have on people. I became much more aware of how important our efforts were when a mother of children afflicted with CF showed up at the golf tournament just to see the people who were making the sacrifice to help. As soon as she saw the number of people and celebrities who were involved, including Johnny Miller, LaVell Edwards, Bronco Mendenhall, Kyle Whitingham, Ty Detmer,

Elder Robert D. Hales, Elder Craig Zwick, Shawn Bradley, Vai Sikahema, Jeff Thomason, Dave Akers, Ryan Denney, Tom Holmoe, and many others, she started weeping right there at the clubhouse.

When I went over to say hello, she could not hold back her tears. She stood with her son and just thanked me for doing something so nice for her family. She kept staring at all the people as they loaded onto their golf carts to start the tournament. It was an impressive sight, but not as impressive as the gratitude that welled up in her tears. Her raw emotion caught me off guard. I felt, maybe for the first time, what it really meant to people who have to deal with the disease on a daily basis. I was so grateful to be a part of something so great, not only to be a part of it, but to be surrounded by it.

Our tournament has been supported by companies such as the Cleaning Services Group led by Dennis O'Brien, who has been our title sponsor. Other corporate sponsors, who have all put their money where their mouths are, include Big-D Construction, Delta Airlines, Polaroid, Xango, Coca Cola, Jacobsen Construction, Great American Minerals, and many others. Through their support, each is demonstrating a desire and willingness to make the world a better place.

I know there are a million worthy causes to put money toward, and I was absolutely blown away by the number of individuals and companies who stepped forward to lend a helping hand to this particular cause. In a world where there is so much news about selfishness and bad behavior, it was inspiring to find so much goodwill, generosity, and willingness to help. I am very hopeful that the effort we are making will eventually help put an end to this cruel disease and lift forever the burdens carried by those who are its victims.

Though it takes dozens of volunteers to stage the tournament, Brandon Ross, Matt Meese, and David Parkinson are three of the heavy lifters on the golf-tournament board. They have all dealt with the disease. Matt Meese has the disease. Brandon is married to Matt's sister. David has two children with the disease. I love meeting and working with them because their motivation is so pure. They are not looking to make a buck off anyone. They are committed to raising money to find a cure. Period. It is that simple. The unselfish way they give of their time, energy, and hearts is an inspiration to me.

CHAPTER 26

COACHES, TEAMMATES, AND TRAINERS

I was a very average football player growing up. I loved playing flag football in elementary school because it was a perfect way for me to learn the game without worrying about getting hit. My friends and I had all played football in our backyards, and flag football seemed like a natural extension of those backyard battles. I didn't start playing tackle football until the seventh grade. I was always a good athlete and I felt like I had better-than-average co-ordination, which was probably a result of jumping on a trampo-line every day growing up. I learned to control my body and gained a spatial awareness of where my limbs were while tumbling in the air. But I was super lean and not too mean. That combina-tion doesn't usually make a tough football player.

My ninth-grade football coach was a legend in Orem, Utah. His name was Lee Salmans. He was the toughest person I had ever met. His diminutive size belied his grit. He was short, probably no taller than 5'6", but he was a warrior. A real warrior. He was raised in Kansas and was taught by his parents that toughness was a virtue. He told us that he was the fastest person in the whole state. I wasn't going to argue with him because he was way too tough for that.

He fought in the Korean War and had harrowing experiences that he would share with us every so often when he thought we needed to hear them. He told of going on night patrols every night for several weeks. He never knew if he would return to his camp. He knew that he could be killed at any second. He said that he didn't like the thought of getting killed but that he was there to do his duty and serve our country and dying might have been part of the sacrifice. He told us that he was not a hero. He let us know that the heroes were his buddies who didn't come home from the war. They were the ones who paid the ultimate price for our freedom. That sure made me think. Some of the people whom he loved and fought alongside hadn't come home.

Coach Salmans walked with a noticeable limp. He had lost about four inches from one of his legs after an explosion of shrapnel tore through his hip and almost killed him. He always showed up to practice in his painter pants and an Orem High School football shirt.

When we were not playing with passion, and practice was dragging, he would let us know that we were not playing like Orem Tigers. He would take off his glasses, take out his false teeth, pull up his pants so that he could get in a three-point stance, and scream at us to try and knock him over. That was a scary sight. We didn't want to hurt him with our hard helmets and the first time he did it we protested. We told him that he was going to get hurt. That only made him madder. We had no choice but to face his wrath. That was scary for a ninth grader to look into the eyes of a grown man who had lived through war. I would never forget it. He cared about us so much that he wanted us to get tough.

His offensive and defensive schemes were just as simple and straightforward as they could be, but he worked us into winners because he got after us every day. We had only about four offensive plays: the cross-buck, scissors, quick pitch, down and out, and if there was another one, I forget what it was.

He loved to challenge us. He didn't care who we were, what our names were, who our parents were, how much money we had, how big we were, how fast we were, how popular we were, or how smart we were. He only cared how determined we were to compete and win. He made sure through the way he talked to us that every person on the team felt he was a part of the team. He loved us, but he was tough. No player who had a starting job could sit back and get fat and lazy. He offered what he called "challenges" to the whole team. If someone, anyone, no matter what their size or skill level, wanted to challenge one of the starters for a starting job, he would have the chance to do it every week.

His challenges consisted of the whole team standing shoulder to shoulder in a tight circle. He would ask if anyone wanted to challenge anyone else for his position and a chance to start. If anyone raised his hand, Coach invited him and the person who was being challenged into the ring. He had both players get into a three-point stance and face each other with their helmets about six inches apart. When he yelled, "Hit!" that meant it was go time. It was a small war.

There were no real rules; we just beat up on each other until only one of us was left standing. The challenges looked more like two little bears brawling than anything else. I was a wide receiver and I remember being challenged by Tom Skousen. We got in the ring and went at it for about thirty seconds but felt more like ten minutes. I can't remember the outcome of the challenge, but I remember the battle and the feeling of fighting for what I wanted. I also came away from that contest with more respect for Tom because he was a challenger.

If the person issuing the challenge won, he was able to start that week's game, no questions asked. It didn't matter if he couldn't play a lick; he was still given the start. Coach Salmans made the decision on how long he played, but he got his chance.

The reason we knew that Lee loved us was because he told us. He never got mushy about it; he said it in a tough way, a way that a warrior would tell his buddy that he loved him. Since I was too young to have had any experience with any other warriors, Lee was my warrior role model.

Every couple of weeks he would show up at practice driving his old black truck with a yellow garbage can in the back of it. We knew that the yellow garbage can would be full of ice and sodas. Lee would have a few of us lift that garbage can out of the truck and carry it across the field. It would sit there until practice was over and then he would let us "have at 'em!" He always had the real sodas, too. Never any of those cheap, imitation sodas for us.

We eventually came to appreciate what it meant that we always got the real thing, because Lee was a painter. He painted signs on buildings, buses, trucks, and billboards as his profession. It was a humble, hard way to make a living, and we knew that he did not have an abundance of money. Yet every once in awhile, he would pull up at practice with that special garbage can.

The look in his eyes as he offered us those cans was part of the honor of playing for him. Could I have described that look at the time? Impossible. It was just a look that a young ninth-grade kid could understand but wouldn't be able to define. Now I see it for what it was: love, pride, and dedication.

At the end of that year, Lee invited the whole team to the city park for a party. He reminded us all year that if we gave everything we had he was going to treat us to a real steak dinner, and now he was going to deliver on his promise. He asked us to walk across the street to Safeway and get the meat that he had bought for the dinner. We did so. We found a grocery cart weighed down with over sixty pounds of steaks. He had bought a one-pound T-bone steak for every single one of us.

Two legendary coaches in my life, Lee Salmans (left) and Tom Rabb (right) at the BYU Athletic Hall of Fame in 2007.

We pushed that grocery cart across the street to the park, and Coach cooked them up on three or four charcoal grills. He had baked potatoes, salad, and soda pop for the whole team. We were young, but we ate like kings. We all wondered how Lee was able to pay for such a meal. We would never dare ask him; we respected him too much. But we loved him for going to such a length for us.

Many years later, Lee sat on the front row at Lincoln Financial Field in Philadelphia and witnessed his first NFL football game. I was his first player to play in the pros. We had a great weekend together reminiscing about old times. We enjoyed a real Philly cheesesteak at Pat's and sat at one of their picnic tables in the cold with grease dripping off our chins. Try as I might, I would never be able to thank Lee enough for teaching me about toughness and love.

As I have already written, Tom Rabb was my coach at Orem

High School. My junior year, the varsity team was stacked with speed, size, and talent. That team won the state championship and several of the guys went on to play college football. But my senior year, there was only one returning starter from that team and that was Bryan Rowley. He was the running back on the championship team and would be our quarterback the next year.

As juniors playing on the junior varsity team, we had only won one game, and that was against the worst team in the league. The score at the end of regulation was 0–0. We were a fumbling group of futility. We won the game in overtime when Clark Childs ran it in from a few yards out. We rejoiced when we finally won a game. But what would Coach Rabb be able do with us the next season? We were the worst. All of the teachers at school worried about what would happen the next year when we were seniors.

We started our senior year with a flat performance at home against our neighbor-city rivals, Provo High. The next game was against our conference rival, the American Fork Cavemen, and that game was to be played in Cougar Stadium at BYU. The night before we played the game, Coach Rabb taught us a lesson that would inspire us to victory the following night. We practiced at a local park that had lights so we would be better prepared to play a night game.

After we finished our walk-through, Coach Rabb showed us a glass jar. He told us a story about a bunch of grasshoppers that were captured and thrown into the jar. The lid was secured on the top to prevent them from jumping out. The grasshoppers were wild and tried as hard as they could to jump out of their enclosure to freedom. He said they sounded like popcorn jumping into the lid and crashing against its hard surface. After a few minutes of popcorn frenzy, the grasshoppers started to realize that their heads were taking wicked blows that hurt. Once they were aware of the pain they stopped jumping.

Then he made his point. He said that after the grasshoppers had been conditioned to fail, the lid of the jar could be removed without one of the grasshoppers trying to escape.

He told us that we were that bunch of grasshoppers. We had been conditioned by our losses to stop trying. After trying and failing, we decided that the pain of giving our all wasn't worth it. We were content to jump around with little or no effort and pretend that we were jumping as high as we could. We were not even aware that the lid of our bottle had been removed. We were a bunch of trained cowards and we didn't even know it.

He held up the bottle for the whole embarrassed team to see. We all knew that he was speaking the truth. We had been gutless in our efforts even though we acted like martyrs, suffering through training camp, trying to win, and feeling sorry for ourselves when we lost. He said that all it took for the grasshoppers to get themselves out of their sorry situation was for *one* grasshopper to have the courage to jump out of the jar. As soon as one did it, the others would clue in that the lid was off and all they had to do was jump. He said that as soon as they started to jump like they meant it, they would all be out of the bottle on the spot.

Coach Rabb told us that in order for us to get ourselves out of our jar, someone, anyone, even if it were just one, had to jump out of the jar. As soon as one player started playing with the emotion necessary to win, that feeling would spread like wildfire through the team and we would all then start doing the same. We sat there in silence listening to his cold, hard, proverbial wisdom. He was right and we knew it.

The next night we played with all of our hearts. All throughout the game we would yell to each other to "get out of the bottle!" All four quarters we encouraged each other to be the one to jump out. We went into double overtime and eventually beat the Cavemen. Thanks to one unbelievable play from Bryan Rowley after another, the rest of us were able to support him enough that we won. That was the beginning of an up-and-down year that ended with our team fighting like crazy to get into the state championship game. There were some games that we played nearly as poorly as when we were juniors. But Coach Rabb's determination, genius, and leadership lit enough of a fire in our hearts that we were able to jump out of the jar.

He was one of the most influential people in my life because of his willingness to teach me the truth about myself and inspire me to try harder than I thought possible. When the Eagles beat the Packers in the play-offs in 2003 with the famous Donovan to Freddie Mitchell fourth and twenty-six pass, Coach Rabb was sitting in the front row of the south end zone supporting my efforts to help our team jump out of the jar. He spent the night before the game in Coach Andy Reid's hotel room in the Airport Marriott talking about football. I told Andy that Coach Rabb would be there for the game, and he made sure that I brought him up to his room. We watched the end of the Panthers versus Rams play-off game and we knew that if we beat the Packers, we would be playing the Panthers in a home NFC Championship game. I will never forget watching those two coaches, who each had such an impact on my life, talking to each other about football, building young men, and life. I felt like the luckiest fly on the wall in that room. How could I have been blessed with such great coaches?

In high school, Paul Clark was our defensive coordinator. He was the animation for Coach Rabbs's reserved personality. As we were getting ready to head to the state play-offs my senior year, he used Coach Rabb's exercise of each one of us visualizing playing perfect football. We were getting ready to play a team that had killed us earlier in the year, and he had us all concentrate on playing football with superhuman strength. As I sat in that meeting room with my eyes closed, I could feel the emotion that would be

*Orem High School State Champions! This was one of the best feelings of my life.
I am #28, second from left, on my knee.*

required to play with that kind of strength. It was such a great feeling that I wanted to play that night.

Fortunately, the emotion carried over to the next day when we beat that team to propel us into the state championship game. In that game, every player seemed to play with the superhuman strength that Coach Clark had talked about. Regular guys were making spectacular plays. We were physical, tough, and superhuman. Coach Clark was responsible for that. Coach Rabb retired after my senior year, and Coach Clark went on to lead Orem High to a few more state championships. As a school, Orem High was jumping out of the jar.

I played defensive end and tight end in high school. My defensive end coach was Bus Gillespie. He was also one of the wrestling coaches at Orem High and he taught me some great moves. Since I was light in the legs he knew it would be a chore to get low enough to take on the fullback's block and stuff the hole. So one of the wrestling moves he taught me was to quickly crouch down underneath the fullback, which would send him flying over the top of me, and immediately pop up to make the tackle on the running back. It worked many times for me that year. Bus got the most he possibly could out of my skinny frame. He was creative as a coach and was able to adapt my skills with some new moves that were nontraditional. It would be a great thing if more coaches at every level were as creative as Bus Gillespie.

Robert Steele was my tight-end coach in a long line of great coaches. He became the head coach at Orem High, where he continues to coach today. His tough, hard-nosed but fun-loving style was just what we needed at Orem.

One of my teammates from BYU, Dustin Johnson, was playing football for the Seattle Seahawks. He had been a fullback and tight end at BYU, where he had a very nice career. He was a great blocker and an excellent receiver. He was a guy who played with all his heart every time he stepped onto the field. He earned the respect of every player because he played the game the way it was meant to be played. He was drafted by the New York Jets, got injured that first year with a severe wrist dislocation, and was released. He got picked up by the Seahawks when he was healthy enough to play and made their team. During the first game of the year, he got hit really hard on a kickoff. He was sick all week and by Thursday he said that he felt as though he was going to die.

He was taken to the hospital and diagnosed with swelling of the brain. He was rushed into surgery and had just enough time to say good-bye to his wife before they put him under. He was told that there was a chance that he would not survive the surgery, and if he did, there was a good chance that he would go blind. He and his wife, Dawn, had just a few moments to process how serious his condition was and how bad it could get. He said that was one of the most difficult times of his life.

During surgery, they drilled six holes in his skull to relieve the pressure that the swelling had caused on his brain. He did not lose any of his eyesight and started to recover from the lifesaving and life-altering surgery. A few days after his surgery, he started to feel some of the same wicked headache pains that he had felt previously. His condition was carefully monitored by the doctors and they finally decided that the swelling had returned and would kill him unless a shunt was inserted into his brain to drain the fluid. A cerebral shunt was a one-way valve used to drain the excess cerebrospinal fluid from the brain to another part of the body. It was usually placed outside of the skull, but under the skin, somewhere behind the ear.

Dustin had a second surgery and a shunt was permanently placed in his body. It went from his brain, with the tube connected to the valve that ran down his neck just under the skin, and ended up in his abdomen. The fluid would continually drain from his brain and be absorbed in his abdomen for the rest of his life.

Football was out of the question. He would never be able to play again. His skull would not be strong enough to handle the impact of even the lightest contact. His wife, who had previously coached gymnastics, resumed her career to help support their family. Dustin and Dawn kept such a positive outlook through their whole ordeal. If you didn't know their history, you would never know that they were going through such a traumatic situation. They were never ones to complain about anything. They were strong and tough. They were great examples to me.

Dustin had some residual effects from his two brain surgeries. His short-term memory was shot. He could not remember a phone number or an errand he needed to run unless he wrote it down on a pad of paper that he kept with him at all times. He had a difficult time sleeping. He also developed severe headaches that limited his ability to function normally. He was not able to have a job because of the many issues that he had to deal with. And yet he continued to remain positive and happy. His life was flipped upside down and turned over again, but he still stayed strong and refused to turn into a complainer.

He became my off-season partner for the rest of my career. If he was feeling well enough, he would lift weights with me. If he was not feeling well enough to lift weights, he would assist me in my running workouts by finding out what kind of training people were doing around the world. He helped me stay at the top of my game by using a combination of old-school workout programs and the latest and most innovative things other people were doing.

Another teammate from BYU who played at the same time as Dustin and I was Ben Cahoon. He became one of the Canadian Football League's greatest receivers. He also trained with Dustin and me. We pushed each other each day to run faster, lift more weights, catch more balls, and get better. A couple of years later I tried to get Ben signed with the Eagles by introducing him to Andy Reid one day when Andy was in town to receive an award. Andy didn't show much interest in Ben. At 5'9", Ben didn't look like a world-beater. If only there was a better way to determine the size of a guy's heart combined with his ability to make plays, there would be a lot more Ben Cahoons in the NFL.

Ben's highlight reel is so chock-full of the craziest and most miraculous catches I have ever seen that I couldn't figure out why the NFL didn't scoop him up. I knew that he could have helped us win the Super Bowl if he were only given a chance. Instead, he helped his team, the Montreal Alouettes, go to the Grey Cup year after year. I felt as though we lost out big-time by not bringing him in to put his fly-paper hands and acrobatic body in front of Donovan McNabb, the Pro Bowl quarterback for the Philadelphia Eagles. The off-season workouts were productive for me because I was surrounded by great guys who were positive and had a desire to work harder than anyone in the business. That was one of the keys to the success that I had—I was surrounded by greatness every day in the off-season.

I've already written about George Curtis, who was the head trainer at BYU. He was also one of the guys who was instrumental in helping me have a successful college career and make it in the NFL. He took his job home with him. If any player ever needed his time or attention, he would make himself available. He even used to invite us over to his house for treatment if it were too late to get together at the school facilities.

In addition to being our trainer, he had extensive expertise in weightlifting. He made himself available as a weightlifting mentor to the players on two conditions. Number one, we had to meet him at 6:00 A.M. and not a minute later. Number two, we had to work with him in the old gym at BYU, which did not have any nice equipment. There were a number of people who chose to work with George. He would put us through the paces for two hours before school. I remember him pushing me so hard that I would want to throw up from exhaustion. He was relentless as a coach.

He pushed us on and on and on, to doing additional reps that we thought we couldn't do. With his help, we did them. It was the first time in my life that I experienced major strength gains. An example of why I started to get stronger was that we started every workout by doing fifty pull-ups. We had to do them as fast as we could. It would be almost impossible to do them all at one time without a break, so he would encourage us to keep at them until we had all fifty. It would take a couple of minutes to do, and that was just the beginning. Those who worked with him in the morning were also invited to an annual chili and scones night at his home. It was not just for the group, but was available to any player who wanted to join us.

After working at BYU for many years as the head trainer, he

was forced to retire when his body got sick. His mind was still as strong as ever, but he developed progressive supranuclear palsy and was not able to continue with the demands of the job. He is dealing with that disease with all the toughness and determination that typified the rest of his life.

Steve Pincock was another trainer at BYU. He was a power-lifter and would lift with our early morning group. He taught me the importance of having a good spotter when lifting weights. We were bench pressing together one morning, and I was spotting him. He had about 225 pounds on the bar and he was cranking through a number of reps. His lifting grip did not utilize his thumb over the top of the bar. It looked a little different than the grip I was used to seeing guys use. He had all of his fingers and his thumbs on the underneath side of the bar.

While I was staring at his grip, the bar inexplicably slipped off of Steve's hands. I reached for the bar as it fell but was not quick enough to catch it. I should have been more diligent as a spotter. Sure enough, gravity directed the bar straight down onto Steve's throat and pinned his neck against the bench that he was lying on.

I had the bar off his throat almost as fast as it landed on it, but the damage had been done. The bar crushed his windpipe, and he gasped for several minutes trying to get air in his lungs. He could not talk. We didn't know exactly what kind of damage he had sustained to his throat, but he was in serious pain. It was totally my fault. I should have been there as his spotter to catch the bar when it slipped. That was my job and I had failed.

Steve could not speak louder than a whisper for two weeks. I was worried that his voice might not ever come back. I was so relieved when it did, but I still felt guilty for not doing my duty. That was an important lesson to me that if I was called upon to spot, I needed to spot. The greater lesson I learned from Steve was forgiveness. He would have liked for me to catch the bar before it fell on his neck, but he knew it was an accident. He did not hold any ill will towards me. He forgave me without hesitation. The fact that we were friends meant more than being angry and holding a grudge. When I hear Steve's voice, which is back to normal, it reminds me of his class.

Ollie Julkinen was another trainer at BYU. He was from Finland but spoke excellent English with a nice little accent. He was a very short guy who wore glasses and had a bald head. He may be the funniest person I've ever met. He was famous at BYU for two things. Number one, he had the most incredible hands of any trainer alive. His hands were magical. They were fine-tuned divining rods that could feel or find any knot or muscle tear under the skin. If any player ever had a muscle pull or a cramp, Ollie would grab a bottle of lotion and run his fingers and hands over the affected area until he had a prognosis. As players, we were more confident in what Ollie had to say than what any X-ray, MRI, or any other person thought. He was the standard.

He spent his whole life helping athletes. He even traveled to the Olympics as a personal trainer for some of the best athletes in the world. One of his close friends was the world-famous Namibian sprinter, Frankie Fredericks, who attended BYU. Ollie helped Frankie win numerous medals by keeping him in top shape.

The second thing that Ollie was famous for was that he would take care of any athlete regardless of his standing. It didn't matter if he was the newest walk-on or if he were competing in the Olympics. Ollie would take care of everyone.

He took the same care of me when I walked on to the football team as he did when I was a senior. When I would return to BYU in the off-season to work out, he was still there for me. When he worked on your muscles he could inflict pain that could not be quantified, but athletes would put up with it because they had total trust that Ollie could make it better. He was the best.

During preparation for the first game of my senior year, I

pulled my groin in a blocking drill. It was Ollie who worked on my leg. It hurt so bad that I thought for sure I would miss the first few games of that season. Ollie assured me that I would be back for the first game. We opened up the year in the Pigskin Classic against Texas A&M. They were nationally ranked and we wanted to pay them back for the whooping they handed BYU several years before in the Holiday Bowl. It was a huge game, and I did not want to miss it. Ollie reassured me each time my faith wavered that I would not miss the game.

He worked on my leg every day and would stretch it and put me through muscle strengthening exercises that wore me out. But Ollie was right. He not only had me ready to play, but made it possible for me to catch the first touchdown of that game, a diving, one-handed grab that would not have happened if it weren't for Ollie's skill and determination to get me back to health. I thought Ollie was personally responsible for a couple wins each season for BYU because he was able to get guys onto the field who, without his genius, would not have been able to play. Ollie passed away in April of 2000, and with his passing the world lost one of its most gifted trainers. I miss Ollie's friendship, humor, and miraculous touch.

Gaye Merrill was another trainer at BYU who had several gifts. She could tape an ankle with perfection. Players would line up at Gaye's taping bench to get her to tape their ankles before practice. The line was always too long and people had to jump into another line or be late for practice. Not only was her tape job a thing of beauty but when she tore each piece of tape, she tore it so perfectly that there were no lose strands. Gaye would create heel locks and figure eights that did not have a single wrinkle. When she was finished with a tape job, it was almost as if an artist had painted it on your ankle. It did not seem humanly possible to produce an ankle wrap that looked and felt so good. It was almost a shame to cover her tape with socks and shoes. Gaye was made the

Courtesy of Mark A. Philbrick/BYU

Playing football at BYU for Coach LaVell Edwards
was one of the great honors of my life.

head athletic trainer at BYU when George Curtis retired. She was deserving of the promotion and had the respect and admiration of every person she ever worked with. Every one.

Kevin Morris was hired by BYU to take over as the head football trainer. He had many of the same attributes as his predecessor, George Curtis. Kevin loved to work with the athletes and do whatever he could to help them recover from injuries and get healthy.

He really helped me when I suffered my serious Lis Franc injury in 2005. He knew how painful the injury was because he had treated other athletes with the same malady. He also knew the kind of rehab that it would take to return to health. Even though I was far removed from my playing days at BYU, he still helped me walk again. BYU was family.

Since Ollie had passed away, Kevin called the next best person to work on my foot. He had me work with a Hopi Indian woman named Vivian. She took over where Ollie left off. She nursed many of the athletes back to health because she was blessed with some of the same gifts as Ollie. She could use her hands to travel through the layers of tissue and muscle to find a knot or a strain or a tear. She worked on my foot day after day helping flush the fluid that was trapped inside. She also helped break up the scar tissue that caused so much pain when I started walking and running again.

Just the thought of how much the trainers sacrificed for the athletes made me feel so lucky to be was surrounded by such talented and skilled professionals. This book could be filled with hundreds of stories of how the trainers helped me on and off the field.

Without their skill and hard work, my career would not have been possible.

CHAPTER 27

NEIGHBORS

Do you remember the kinds of things that you prayed for when you were a little kid? I have a vivid memory of asking God to make me Superman. I wanted to be able to fly. How sweet would that be? I wanted to be more powerful than a locomotive and run faster than a speeding bullet. I think part of that prayer was answered when I went to Taiwan to serve as a Mormon missionary for two years.

The people there called me *Superman!* But not because I could fly or run faster than their trains. It was because I looked more like Clark Kent than I did Superman. As I have noted, I wore big glasses that portrayed the special nerdiness of Clark Kent. At 6' 6'' and weighing 200 pounds, I completed the image of Clark.

The Chinese people would use English and point at me and say, "Superman!" It sounded more like Soo-puh-man. If I could not understand what they were saying for some reason, they would say, "You, Clark Kent!" (or Claw-kuh Ken-tuh), and point to my glasses. It was funny each time someone said it. It turned out to be a term of endearment for me, and I enjoyed them smiling and having fun with me.

As a five year old, everything would have been better if I were Superman. That is what I thought anyway as I tried to fly a kite out in front of my house one morning with no wind. That posed a problem. If I could only run as fast as the Man of Steel, my problem would be solved. Wind is essential to good kite flying; good legs can help only temporarily.

The string was let out just long enough to get the kite started with a good run. I put the kite on the ground in just the right way, with the nose forward and tilting up a little bit. The first effort resulted in the kite being dragged across the blacktop. With no wind, there was no lift. A kite dragging across the street is not ideal; it produces a sound as if the road were a giant cheese grater with an appetite for plastic. Another try produced minor success and a little lift, enough to get the kite in the air, but not enough to keep it flying.

Try after try was made with similar results. Up and down the street I ran trying to get the kite in the air. My mind was telling me to run faster. So faster I ran.

I must have run myself dizzy because I lost all sense of my surroundings. Did I forget that streets are made for cars and trucks and not for little boys? I started another attempt with blazing speed, but in the exact direction of the back of an old, faded blue-green pickup truck parked on the side of the road!

I know from personal experience what it feels like to be tackled by Ray Lewis, who is one of the most intense and fierce tacklers in the NFL. There is an animosity in his tackling that makes you wonder how he could want to kill you without even knowing you. I know what it sounds like to have your helmet smashed against your own face and skull with the one million pounds per square inch of force that comes with a hit from Jeremiah Trotter. I know the discombobulating feeling that comes after a nice pop from Pat Tillman. And I also know that John Lynch is a one-man wrecking crew. But the power of those NFL football players pales in comparison to the density, strength, and cold-steel rigidity of an old Ford fender and tailgate. I was simply no match.

How long did it take before my wits came back to me? I can't remember. How long was I screaming on the ground before someone came to help? I can't remember. I do know that little Superman discovered a new Kryptonite and that it was the rear end of a parked truck.

The next thing I do remember was being scooped up into the arms of a neighbor, Jim MacArthur. I've already introduced him as a great friend of our family. He was a BYU professor who lived three doors down from us. I had crash-landed right out in front of his house. The thought of not helping me probably never crossed his mind. Jim had ten kids of his own and has always been known for his gigantic heart. Two years before, when our family moved into the neighborhood, Jim had done a front handspring on our driveway as a way of throwing down the welcome mat. I wasn't thinking about any of that. My threshold of pain had just been tested by a tsunami, and I cried all the way home. As he carried me, he assured me that I was going to be all right.

I grew up surrounded by great neighbors. All the families on my street were my friends; the Holdaways, Johnsons, Heaps, and on down the line were just wonderful. I didn't fully realize it at the time, but I was the luckiest kid in the world growing up with them. I have many more great stories about each one of them that I will hopefully be able to share at some point. Although I may not have had any choice as to who my neighbors were, it is easy to recognize the greatness of their character.

Mike and Kari Geddes are my neighbors here in Cedar Hills, Utah. Theirs is an awesome story of goodness and determination. During the heat of the summer of 2003, a Church group of young men and some of their parents from my neighborhood headed to Lake Powell for a week of fun in the sun and water. Lake Powell is one of the greatest vacation destinations on this planet; just ask anyone who has been there.

Lake Powell lies on the Utah-Arizona border and was formed when the Glen Canyon Dam was constructed on the Colorado River. With more shoreline up and down its many canyons than all the West Coast, it is a waverunner's paradise. Its deep blue clean waters lie in stunning contrast to the deep red canyon walls that form its boundaries.

One of the boys on this trip was Andrew Geddes, and he was accompanied by his brother Dustin and his dad, Mike. We have been neighbors for about three years, and I have always been impressed by the cheerful personalities of the kids and their parents. Every one of them has an infectious smile that makes you wonder if they know something great about life that you don't. They seem to be as happy a family as there is anywhere.

Andrew was just turning sixteen the week they were at Lake Powell. He was a small guy who loved to ride his skateboard with his friends through the neighborhood. The group was camping in tents on the sandy beach of the Rincon, which is part of the lake between the most popular boat marinas of Bullfrog and Wahweep.

The guys were having fun running down a gentle slope and diving into the shallow water, which only gradually got deeper and deeper. Andrew ran down the slope into the shallow water and jumped headfirst with the intention of doing a front somersault or a roll. He did not make it all the way over to his back but ended up going into the water on his head, which hit the sandy bottom of the knee-deep water and immediately broke his neck. When fine sand like that at Lake Powell is wet, it has a density that resembles concrete more than fluffy sand castles.

Andrew failed to get out of the water. He floated face down because he could not move. The other guys were laughing, thinking he was just kidding around by not coming right out of the water. His dad quickly saw that something was seriously wrong.

He ran into the water and carefully turned Andrew out of the water and into the air. After taking in a gasp of air, the first thing he said to his dad was that he had broken his neck. Mike asked if he was sure, to which Andrew responded that he felt his neck snap and that he knew he was paralyzed.

As any good father would do, Mike held Andrew very carefully until help could arrive. It just so happened that only a few yards down the beach was a boat that held a man and a woman from Colorado who were trained in emergency care. They quickly responded to cries for help and were critical in helping stabilize Andrew so that no further damage would take place. They were an enormous comfort to Mike and the rest of the guys, who were all in shock. It took about an hour for a rescue helicopter from Grand Junction, Colorado, to arrive and fly Andrew to the hospital.

Back home, news of Andrew's horrific accident instantly spread through the neighborhood. Early reports were that Andrew's neck was broken and he was totally paralyzed.

Andrew's mom, Kari, made the four-hour trip to the hospital to be with him. As neighbors, we waited with heavy hearts for each new piece of information about his condition. I remember the first time I saw Mike Geddes when he reported Andrew's status to our church congregation. His eyes were full of tears, but his heart was full of gratitude for the prayers and concern of others, and his smile, though heavy with grief, was a flash of hope and faith that things would be okay.

Andrew remained in Grand Junction for several weeks. He was given the option of surgery to fuse his neck to give it stability. Mike asked the doctor what he thought about the surgery. The doctor told him that if Andrew were his son, that he would encourage him to do it. Andrew thought that things couldn't get any worse and so he chose to have it done. The fusion would give him more hope of walking again and it enhanced his ability to breathe.

He also had a "halo" attached to his head to provide stability while his neck was healing. The halo looks a lot like the word sounds. It is a circular brace made of titanium rod that was attached to his skull with four screws. Andrew was not able to lie in a regular bed but was suspended in a special traction device that periodically rolled his body over so that he would not develop blood clots or bed sores.

Andrew was able to breathe in only one-quarter breaths. He could only speak in half sentences. He had a feeding tube in his nose, and he couldn't feel anything from his shoulders down to his feet. He said that lying in that contraption was the worst part of his whole ordeal. He said that looking back on that experience, all seemed dark. The room was dark, the situation was dark, and the memories all seemed like shadows.

After surgery, the doctor handed him his prognosis. He thought that Andrew would eventually be able to sit up and even move his shoulders. Andrew asked him the question that every one who was in that situation would have asked. Would he able to walk again? The doctor told him that it might be possible. That was welcome news to Andrew and his family.

One good thing was that he was not feeling any residual pain from the accident or the surgery. He said he was also greatly inspired and comforted by the many visitors who traveled to Grand Junction. He loved to see his cousins, the Boyers from the neighborhood, the priests quorum (the guys who were in his age group at church), and Bill Markham, who was a neighbor.

He eventually took a five-hour ambulance ride from Grand Junction to Salt Lake City, Utah. He was given some Valium for the long ride that helped mellow him out, but also made him sick. When he arrived, he was nauseous and throwing up. Even though he didn't feel well, he was glad to be closer to home.

He was admitted to Primary Children's Hospital in Salt Lake City, which allowed his friends to visit him. He seemed happier

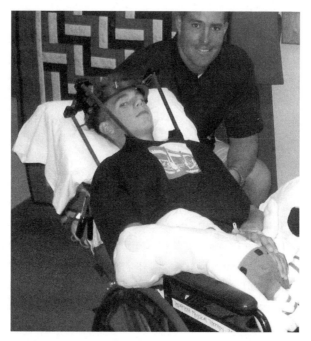

Visiting Andrew Geddes in the hospital. He showed courage wearing the halo and his sense of humor with his yellow SpongeBob pillow.

than I thought he would be. He wore his favorite DC shoes given to him by Bill Markham, who also arranged for Tony Hawk and other professional skateboarders to visit him in his hospital room. Andrew kept a huge yellow SpongeBob SquarePants pillow by his side. It was hilarious, and it gave a measure of comic relief to the awful situation.

In time, he graduated to a sweet new wheelchair that had everything but shocks and pegs. Although he could barely move a muscle, he always had a big smile on his face, complete with his big dimples and braces. It was inspiring to see this little guy who was going through so much smile and express his appreciation to his friends for caring about him.

One of the first things that his physical therapist asked him when he got to Primary Children's was what he wanted to do. Andrew told him that he wanted to *walk* out of the hospital when he was done. The only thing Andrew could move at the time was his thumb. But that didn't deter the physical therapist. He told Andrew that they would work on first things first and get started.

Andrew stayed at Primary Children's Hospital for two months. On September 10, at the end of his stay, he was able to accomplish his dream of walking out of the hospital. He was wheeled to the main entrance and then he got out of his wheelchair and walked from the entrance to his car. He said that it felt awesome to walk out of there. He felt as though he had accomplished a lot, but he knew he still had a long, long way to go. He loved all the visitors that he had at the hospital. He felt like they helped him recover. He enjoyed the outpouring of support and was excited to get back to his life.

He got home and loved being back with his family. It was exciting at first just to be there, but he said he quickly got bored with being at home and wanted to get back to school. He waited only one week before he was back at Lone Peak High School. He took a half schedule from then until the Christmas break. He was assigned an aide who would write his notes for him. The aide was one of his friends and that was nice companionship for him.

After Christmas, he took a full load of school classes and never looked back. By Christmas he had worked hard enough in rehab that he had built up his strength to be able to walk. He put away his wheelchair and rejoined the world of walkers. He had grown up left-handed, but his left hand was slow to progress, so he retrained himself to write with his right hand.

Andrew said that most of the students at school were very understanding of what he had been through. They helped him whenever they could in the halls or in class. He said that occasionally some people would use slow, babylike speech when they talked to him, as though he were retarded in some way. That was a little frustrating because mentally he was fine. But he never got bitter or developed a victim's mentality. Instead, he responded with the same smile that he always had. He could have become discouraged when progress was slow. But he didn't. He was a warrior.

He had many friends before his accident with whom he liked to skateboard. Many of them stuck around for a while during his rehab process, but most of them slowly faded away. His best friend was his neighbor Jake Castle. Andrew was grateful for Jake because Jake was not afraid of Andrew's injury or afraid of any changes in his life. He cared about Andrew and was a solid friend. With his family and his best friend, Jake, Andrew was surrounded by greatness.

In April of that year, Andrew had a dream to get back in the mountains on his snowboard. His family drove an hour up to Snowbird Ski Resort in Little Cottonwood Canyon to the east of Salt Lake City. Snowbird offered the Wasatch Adaptive Sports Program, run by Peter Mandlar for individuals who had special needs.

Steve Young holds a benefit fund-raiser every year called the Steve Young Ski Classic to help keep the program going. Steve brings in sports and entertainment celebrities from all over the world, and they race against the participants in the Adaptive Ski Program. Participants include people with brain injuries, Down syndrome, Hunter's syndrome, or visual impairments; quad-riplegics, paraplegics, those missing legs or arms, and other dis-abled persons. Andrew's younger brother Derek, who is autistic, had been a participant in the Adaptive Ski Program and so Andrew was familiar with Snowbird.

As excited as he was to be back on the mountain, Andrew was just as frustrated because it was so difficult for him to board. He went down the Chickadee, the most basic lift and run, with his dad and cousins. He said his dad was awesome because he was so patient with him, but Andrew was still frustrated because he thought he would have been better than he was. But he was there.

He was on the mountain. He was trying. He was giving his all to live the way he wanted to live. He was not content sitting at home eating applesauce. He was battling.

When summer rolled around again, Andrew wanted to go back to Lake Powell and visit the spot where he broke his neck. His dad suggested it and Andrew jumped on the idea. They went back to the same place in the Rincon where the accident had happened. The water level changes each year due to variations in spring runoff, and when they got there, the water level was much lower. The whole scenery looked different. Andrew said it was a little eerie being there again.

His dad encouraged him to get out of the boat and walk up the hill to the spot where the accident happened. Andrew walked on the sand and rock that had been underwater when he broke his neck. When he arrived at the spot, he said that the visual image of the whole ordeal came back to him. He could see it and he could feel it. He thought how different his life would be if he hadn't broken his neck. If he had just landed in the water differently. If he hadn't jumped in headfirst . . .

By the end of that summer, he tried wakeboarding again. Wakeboarding is a difficult sport for a healthy and strong individual. But for Andrew, it required every ounce of strength, balance, coordination, determination, and focus just to attempt it. He could not get up the first few times. He said that he was ready to give up, but that he just kept trying, one time after another. He tried for several weeks with no success.

He was working with Leighton Weber to gain strength. Leighton ran a rehab program called Sit Tall Stand Tall. He had worked with hundreds of patients to help them recover from strokes, injuries, and accidents, including my dad in the two years after Dad's stroke. Andrew was working with Leighton to get more strength in his hands and arms so that he could hold on to the ski rope tight enough to allow him to wakeboard.

At the end of the summer, after endless futile attempts and working hard to strengthen his hands and arms, Andrew finally did it. He was able to stand up on his wakeboard again. He was very wobbly and shaky, but he was up. What used to be so natural for Andrew was now a major triumph.

When school started for his senior year, he was excited to be back. He said that it was a break-out year for him. He felt normal again even though his body still had serious paralysis from the accident. He got his driver's license. That was huge. He put a spinner knob on his steering wheel and a blinker adaption for his arms. That was freedom for him to be able to drive. He also took an art class, using his right hand to paint and draw. He painted a sweet picture of me in my Philadelphia Eagles uniform running with the ball. He brought it over to my house and showed me. It was incredible. And I told him I couldn't do that with my two hands that were strong, healthy, and coordinated. Andrew was incredible. He was not afraid of anything.

At his high school graduation, he *walked* with his class. That took on a whole new meaning for him after having to learn how to do it all over again. It was the class of 2004. He was able to catch up on any classes that he missed when he was taking only half a load. He had all the credits that he needed and did not have to take summer school to graduate. He graduated in the top portion of his class.

Andrew spent the summer wakeboarding and getting ready for his first year of college. He was nervous to leave his parents' house and move into an apartment. He wondered if he could live on his own. He chose to attend BYU and was accepted. He roomed with his cousin Brad and took the challenge of moving forward with his life. He said it was a big test and that he had some trepidation. But he did it. He went to school. He didn't stay at home cocooned in his fears. He went to school and took on any barrier that was in front of him. He chose life.

As a member of The Church of Jesus Christ of Latter-day Saints, Andrew had prepared his whole life to serve a mission when he turned nineteen years old. There was some question whether he would be able to serve or not due to his limited ability to get around. He filled out his missionary application papers and sent them to Church headquarters in Salt Lake City.

If he was to be allowed to serve, he was hoping for two things: to be called to a mission in a warm weather location since his body would function better in warm weather and to serve in a mission where he would have a car instead of a commonly used bicycle for transportation. Andrew did receive his mission call, but it was not to sunny Florida or pleasant California. It was to Detroit, Michigan, where the winters are so cold that missionaries use a hockey puck to knock on doors instead of cracking their frozen knuckles on hard metal or cold wood. He was also told to be ready to ride a bike as part of his service.

Ordinary kids might grumble about such news. They might wonder if the Lord really wanted them to serve in cold weather on a bike. Andrew did not waste any time wondering if the Lord was really aware of his particular needs. Instead, he got to work purchasing cold weather suits and overcoats that would prevent him from freezing, and that was not all. My favorite part came next.

He asked his little brother Braden if he could borrow his bike so that he could learn how to ride! I saw Andrew practicing riding up and down the street on this bike. He had some scuffs on his arms and legs from crashing into parked cars and falling on the ground, but what he didn't have was a lack of determination. Not only did he persist in his efforts to balance his semi-paralyzed body on a bike, but he did it with his signature dimpled smile and tremendous positive attitude.

What a great lesson in facing challenges the right way. Andrew faced them head-on. He could have grumbled loud enough for everyone around him to hear. He probably could have found an audience that thought he was a victim and that he should not have been called to a cold-weather and bike-riding mission. But he did not grumble. He did not complain. He prepared.

After Andrew had been in the Detroit area for a couple months, I got a letter from him informing me that he could now tie a tie—no small feat for someone who could barely use his fingers. He had left home with a whole bunch of new zipper ties. They were quite an invention, especially for someone with limited use of his hands. Here is a part of his letter to me.

> I recently had another sweet recovery experience. My first companion, Elder King, had some sweet ties I wanted to wear. All of mine were *zip* ties because I'm unable to tie my own tie. At first I had him tie one for me then put it on, but I said I want to be able to tie it myself because those zip ties are expensive and I want a lot of ties. I tried to tie it myself a couple of times but had to have him bail me out because I just couldn't quite get it. Rather than just give up, I said I will be able to tie my own tie! I finally found one I could tie. It took me probably 25 minutes to tie it. Still persistent I started wearing regular ties every day and tying them myself. It was very frustrating at first and not easy for me. After a few weeks of daily practice I can tie *any* tie and now have 17 sweet, non-zip, normal ties, and I can tie them in under five minutes. So I was proud to accomplish my goal and not just give up.

Super Bowl XL was in Detroit that year, February 2006. I was asked by NFL Commissioner Paul Tagliabue to join him at the international press conference because of my efforts in China to help the League build its brand there. I was given enough time off on Saturday before the press conference that I could drive up to Fenton, Michigan, and see Andrew. Normally, friends and family

*Andrew Geddes: another walking miracle. I hiked Mount Mahogany
with him on Memorial Day, 2009. It is a difficult hike for anyone,
and an exceptional effort for Andrew.*

are discouraged from visiting missionaries who are serving because
it disrupts their work and could perhaps make them homesick. In
Andrew's case, the mission president, Bill Winegar, who was responsible for the nearly two hundred missionaries in that particular area, gave me permission to work alongside Andrew and his
companion for the afternoon.

I had the NFL car and driver take me to Fenton, where I
worked with Andrew for four hours that cold and wet February
afternoon. I paid the driver for his time and asked him to pick me
up four hours later.

We spent our time knocking on doors and sharing the message of Christ with anyone willing to listen. We visited some faithful Christians in the area and finished by going to lunch and eating burritos the size of our heads. It was such a great day.

I saw that Andrew's optimistic personality was infectious with all the people with whom he worked. It was my honor to spend the day sharing our testimonies of Christ together. I will not soon forget the image of Andrew struggling to walk in the penetrating cold, up and down the streets, in an effort to share his faith in the Savior. He did it all with his beautiful smile. I spent that afternoon surrounded by greatness. The ride home in that brand-new Cadillac Escalade was something special. I felt like a VIP, not because of my NFL status, but because I had just spent the day with one of the greatest guys ever.

Andrew finished his mission and returned home to his wonderful family. They couldn't wait to see him and be with him again. He wasted no time getting back into school at BYU. He has been diligent in his studies and continued to work hard, the same as he did when he was a missionary. His life has been full of hard work. He is not afraid of anything. Having a neighbor such as Andrew Geddes and the whole Geddes family is a reminder of how lucky I have been to be surrounded by greatness.

CHAPTER 28

FAMILY

My parents have been and continue to be the guiding stars of my life. I have been able to depend on them for direction just as mariners through the ages have been able to navigate through the open sea to ports of safety by following the stars. Mom and Dad have always given me safe and clear answers through the challenging times and decisions of life. Even though they haven't always known all of the answers for my life, just as the North Star they have always pointed me in the right direction. My parents rely on faith and prayer to get through adversity, and they continue to work together the same way they did all those years ago in the hospital during Dad's illness.

My dad can still walk and he can drive. He has never recovered to the point where he can run a marathon like he once did, but he still has the same toughness and resolve to set and accomplish difficult goals. He ties his shoes with one hand. He ties his ties with one hand. When the weather is nice, he hikes the steep, one-mile trail up to the huge Y on the mountain just east of the BYU campus in Provo, Utah. On my best days, I am lucky to be his hiking companion.

My dad helped me build this giant face made out of snow in 2004;
our own version of an Easter Island statue.

On September 11, 2008, we hiked to the Y together. I carried the American flag that was presented to me when I earned my Eagle Scout award. It is a special flag because it was flown over the nation's capitol in my honor in recognition of the completion of years of work to receive the Eagle rank. I will always treasure it.

I fixed the flag on top of an extra long pole so that my mom could see us hiking if she looked up on the mountain through her binoculars. We hiked to the top of the Y and fixed the flag in the ground. The breeze was blowing gently and the flag flew for the whole world to see.

While we were resting and talking, my mom called and asked where we were. We told her that we were sitting on the top of the Y. She drove her car to a spot where she could get a better view. After not being able to see us for a minute, she shouted into the phone, "I see you! I can see the flag waving!"

Sitting with my dad on top of the Y overlooking
Utah Valley on September 11, 2008.

Mom was not able to hike with us because of the pain in her knees but she was there with us. What a moment. She's spent her whole life looking for me and for my brothers as we played football and other sports. She looked for our names to appear on the honor roll, she looked for us to pull into the driveway after being out with friends or dates, she looked with great anticipation for our letters when we were missionaries, she looks forward to our phone calls all the time, and she looks forward to loving her grandchildren the same way she loved us.

There I sat on the top of the Y next to my dad, talking to my mom on the phone, and she was still looking for me! The gratitude for my parents swelled. I was surrounded by greatness.

The walk down the mountain was even greater than the hike up because Dad needed to use my shoulder for a support since the trail was steep and composed of loose dirt and gravel. My mom watched us hike down the twelve switchbacks. I held the flag high in the air so she could follow our progress when the oak bushes and other shrubbery blocked her view of us. She could see the flag flying above the green foliage and she knew we were there.

My parents are the best people I know. I only hope to honor them. They are my North Star.

Growing up in Orem, Utah, as one of five Lewis boys created an active environment full of sports, laughing, fighting, hiking, camping, Scouting, reading, and praying. Besides getting together for family dinners and important events, we have implemented a program called "Brothers Trips" and we have been doing it for a decade. We travel somewhere, usually within four-hours driving distance, and we camp, hike, or bike for a day or two. It allows us time to reconnect with each other on a deep level.

We usually pick a location that will allow our dad to fully participate in what we are doing. Except for a bike ride, he has been able to do it all. One year we drove to Mann Gulch in northern Montana. It was the sight of a famous fire that took the lives of thirteen smokejumper firefighters in 1949. Norman Maclean, the author of *A River Runs Through It,* immortalized the tragedy in a book published posthumously by his son, titled *Young Men and Fire.* Mann Gulch rises away from the Missouri River for a couple of rugged miles. Our father was not going to miss out on walking in the footsteps of those courageous firefighters with the rest of us. He required some help getting up the mountain and traversing the hillside where markers hallow the ground at the spots where each of the thirteen men lost his life.

We used Dad's walking staff as a handle for him to hold on to. If two of us held the stick parallel to the ground, he could walk in between the two and hold on to the staff like a railing. Our guide, a guy named Tim, commented that my dad was the toughest guy that he had ever taken on the mountain. He is not just tough; he is great.

One of our "brothers' trips" to Lightning Ridge in the famous Uinta mountains in northeast Utah. Left to right: Dad, Mike, me, Dave, Todd, Jason.

Michele's parents recently taught me another lesson in love and service. Doug had both of his knees replaced. Geneva took care of him with the kindness and love she is known for. He told us how much he appreciated her and loved her for the service rendered. She said the same thing, even though she was on the work end of the service. She said that her love for Doug grew while she fixed his meals, took care of his clothing and bedding, and provided anything he needed while recovering. That is greatness.

Michele is the joy of my life. She is my best friend. We have seven beautiful children: Emily, Sarah, Jacob, Jefferson, Maxwell, and baby twins, Tanner and Todd. I would be nothing without Michele. If surrounding myself with greatness means anything to me, it means that Michele is at the center of my life. She is the foundation that makes it all worth it.

She is selfless in her care for me and for each of our children.

During my rookie year with the Eagles, she was pregnant with Sarah. Emily was only a year old. While carrying Emily downstairs one evening, Michele slipped on the carpeted stairs and landed directly on her tailbone, breaking it. With the instincts of a mother, instead of reaching down with her arms to save herself from the fall, she held tight to Emily, cradling her safely in her arms. That selfless act is representative of Michele's love for our family. She willingly sacrifices herself for me and for each of our children. She is the brightest light in my life. Without her I would be blind.

The book *The Man without a Country*, by Edward Everett Hale, portrays love of family, country, and God in a way that defines my feelings and love for my family.

The story takes place in the early 1800s. A young man by the name of Phillip Nolan gets entangled with the wrong crowd and a skunk by the name of Aaron Burr and makes a grave mistake. Phillip is caught in a treasonous activity and upon receiving the guilty sentence from a Revolutionary War veteran, Colonel Morgan, Nolan responds, "I wish I may never hear of the United States again!"

Edward Everett Hale details the tragic life of Phillip Nolan. He is banished by Colonel Morgan from the United States and is held as a perpetual prisoner aboard a US naval ship where he stays for the rest of his life. He is never allowed to see his country again. Moreover, he is not allowed to hear or speak the words *The United States*. He is not allowed to read a paper or a book containing the words *The United States*. He became known as "the man without a country."

At the end of his homesick life, the naval ship Phillip is sailing on comes upon a ship transporting slaves, after the treaty condemning the slave trade in the Atlantic Ocean has been signed. The US Navy seizes the slave ship and captures its crew. The human cargo of the ship is set free but chaos erupts as the liberated Africans try to communicate with the men who have freed them. No one can understand their language, and the situation begins to spiral out of control. The captain of the US ship then asks if anyone onboard his own ship can speak Portuguese. Phillip Nolan says he can and is taken by a small boat accompanied by a few sailors to interpret the cries of the occupants.

The US naval captain instructs Nolan to tell the freed prisoners that they are to be taken back to Cape Palmas. The problem is, Cape Palmas is as far from their homes in Africa as New Orleans or Rio de Janeiro in Brazil would be. The liberated men were very distressed at being told that. The captain could see they were angry but wanted Phillip to translate their complaint.

Phillip Nolan, the man without a country, the man who had not even seen or heard about his family or his home or his country for the whole of his adult life, interpreted the words of the spokesman.

"'Not Palmas.' He says, 'Take us home, take us to our own country, take us to our own house, take us to . . . our own women.' He says he has an old father and mother who will die if they do not see him. And this one says he left his people all sick, and paddled down to Fernando to beg the white doctor to come and help them, and that these devils caught him in the bay just in sight of home and that he has never seen anybody from home since then. And this one says,' choked out Nolan, 'that he has not heard a word from his home in six months, while he has been locked up in an infernal barracoon."

The captain of the US ship knew all too well why Phillip Nolan was choked up translating those words of *home, family,* and *country.* Then, with a message that transcended the liberated men's ability to understand, the captain declared, "Tell them yes, yes, yes; tell them they shall go to the mountains of the Moon, if they will. If I sail the schooner through the Great White Desert, they shall go home!"

As the sailors rowed the small boat back to their own ship,

Phillip Nolan says to one of the young seamen who is escorting him: "Youngster, let that show you what it is to be without a family, without a home, and without a country. And if you are ever tempted to say a word or to do a thing that shall put a bar between you and your family, your home, and your country, pray God in his mercy to take you that instant home to his own heaven. Stick by your family, boy; forget you have a self, while you do everything for them. Think of your home, boy; write and send and talk about it. Let it be nearer and nearer to your thought, the farther you have to travel from it; and rush back to it when you are free, . . . O, if anybody had said so to me when I was of your age!"[8]

That love, that emotion, that deep concern for family is exactly what I felt when I stood on the sideline of the Super Bowl with my broken foot and looked back at my family in the stands. As a child throwing the football to myself I had dreamed of making the game-winning catch in the Super Bowl. I am grateful for the revelation that came to me that my *family* was my Super Bowl. They had been with me my entire life. I looked away from them, toward a game, for my greatest dream, but then I realized *they* were my greatest dream.

My friends Kent Watson and Larry Harmer have recently stood at their fathers' bedsides as their dads passed from the pain of mortality into the peaceful arms of eternity. At the time of a parent's passing, the importance of family relationships is perhaps more clear than at any other time. In that trying and emotional moment, it is not the glitter and glitz of stuff that is most important. Family is what it's all about. And God's love assures and sustains us in such losses.

My religion teaches that families are eternal in nature and that it's possible for these relationships to continue beyond the grave. The knowledge that parents and their children share more than a temporary association and are an eternal unit has been the basis of my greatest happiness. Now, I see clearly: my parents are the ones who cradled me through infancy, shepherded me through the trials of adolescence, and continue to guide and love me today. They have always been with me. And they will always be with me. That is greatness.

I have been surrounded by greatness . . . and so have you!

ACKNOWLEDGMENTS

This book is the result of being raised in a wonderful family. My parents, Roger and Jan Lewis, are the inspiration of my life. So are my brothers and their wives: Dave and Jonna, Mike and Julie, Jason and Angie, and Todd and Megan. Mike especially encouraged me to write this book. He stayed after me for years until I finished it. I married into the world's coolest family, and I love Michele's family as much as I love my own: Doug and Geneva Fellows, Kent and Christine Gunnell, Steve and Jenny Fellows, Mark and Becky Fellows.

I would like to extend special thanks to the following people:

President Kent and Connie Watson changed my life in Taiwan. Without them, there is no book. Tim and Robin Stratford and John and Shirley Carmack made serving in Taiwan a joy.

My friends and mission companions who helped me collect my thoughts, especially Rob Lamb, Larry Harmer, Andy Hogan, and an endless list of great guys.

Donovan McNabb, the best quarterback in the NFL. He made playing football so much fun. He is a class act and lifelong friend.

All my teammates, from the quarterbacks who threw me the

ball—Shawn Bandley, Bryan Rowley, John Walsh, Steve Sarkisian, Ty Detmer, Rodney Pete, Bobby Hoying, Kurt Warner, Koy Detmer, and AJ Feeley—to the tight ends who made life fun—Greg Kennedy, Itula Mili, Luther Broughton, Jeff Thomason, Mike Bartrum, L. J. Smith—and the greatest kicker in the NFL, Dave Akers. There are so many incredible teammates whose stories could fill a whole series of books: Morris Unatoa, Justin Ena, Reno Mahe, Tom Young, Bryce Doman, Hema Heimuli, Greg Pitts, Dustin Johnson, and Ben Cahoon.

Steve Young and Lee Johnson, for taking me under their wings early in my career. Their guidance and friendship made a huge difference.

My coaches, who taught me how to play the game and make the most out of life—Lee Salmans, Tom Rabb, Ray Rhodes, Jon Gruden, LaVell and Patti Edwards, Norm Chow, Lance and Leslie Reynolds, Robbie Bosco, Chris Pella, Dick Vermeil, Lynn Stiles, Andy and Tammy Reid, Pat Shurmur, Tom Melvin, Rod Dowhower, Ted Williams, Brad Childress, John Harbaugh, David Culley, the late Jim Johnson, and Leo Carlin.

Vai and Keala Sikahema, who opened their hearts and home to us in Philly.

To the owner of the Philadelphia Eagles, Jeffrey Lurie, and President Joe Banner. Thank you for giving me a shot.

To the best agents in pro football—Don Yee, Steve Dubin, and Carter Chow.

To Paul Tagliabue, Roger Goodell, Pete Abitante, Gordon Smeaton, and Michael Stokes of the NFL, who have made working in China so much fun.

Derek Boyko, Bob Lange, and Rich Burg of the Philadelphia Eagles Media Services Department.

The BYU football family and the athletic department, with Tom Holmoe and Brian Santiago, and Duff Tittle of the BYU sports information department.

Dr. Lyman Moody and Dr. Karl Douglas Nielsen, for spending

three hours at my parent's house reliving the stroke, surgery, and recovery. Don Norton transcribed the whole conversation for posterity. Dr. Rod Peterson took the time to educate me on the radiology and the miracle of the whole event.

Johnny Miller and Keith Clearwater, for setting a standard of excellence in their friendship.

Andrew Geddes and his family for being such an inspiration.

Elder Craig Zwick and Jan Zwick and their boundless enthusiasm.

Brandon Ross, Matt Meese, and Paul Shoemaker, who have made my involvement with the Cystic Fibrosis Foundation possible. Matt, you are worth all the effort.

Stephen M. R. Covey, who has been like an older brother with his helpfulness, and Jim Ferrell, who walked me through the process at a critical time.

Phyllis Bestor, my high-school English teacher, who has been a mentor and friend for years.

Zane Taylor, for his sacrifice for our country and for his eyes and heart that are filled with light and love.

Cory Maxwell (the man without guile), Chris Schoebinger, and Sheri Dew at Shadow Mountain. They have been a dream to work with.

My editor and friend, Richard Peterson.

Todd Leany, of Pacific Coast Steel, for giving me a great opportunity to join the builders of our nation.

Dale Tingey and everyone associated with American Indian Services.

My neighbor and friend Howard Bingham who helped me with many rough drafts.

President Gordon B. Hinckley and President Thomas S. Monson, who have given such steady and strong leadership and inspiration.

Of course, I have failed to mention some of you, but I will give the rest of my life making it up to you.

NOTES

1. George M. Cohan, "The Yankee Doodle Boy," also known as "(I'm a) Yankee Doodle Dandy," from *Little Johnny Jones,* 1904.

2. Henry Clay Work, "Grandfather's Clock" (New York: C. M. Cady, 1876).

3. Johnson Oatman, Jr., "Count Your Blessings," in *Hymns of The Church of Jesus Christ of Latter-day Saints* (Salt Lake City: The Church of Jesus Christ of Latter-day Saints, 1985), no. 241.

4. Theodore Roosevelt, "Citizenship in a Republic: The Man in the Arena," speech given at the Sorbonne, Paris, France, April 23, 1910.

5. Douglas Malloch, "Good Timber," as quoted in Sterling W. Sill, *Making the Most of Yourself* (Salt Lake City: Bookcraft, 1971), 23.

6. http://www.philadelphiaeagles.com/fanzone/index.html.

7. Howard E. Ferguson, *The Edge: The Guide to Fulfilling Dreams, Maximizing Success and Enjoying a Lifetime of Achievement* (Cleveland, Ohio: Getting the Edge Co., 1991), 1–1.

8. Edward Everett Hale, *The Man without a Country,* in Harvard Classics Shelf of Fiction, sel. by Charles W. Eliot (New York: P. F. Collier & Son, 1917), 10:446, 460–61.

INDEX